Barry F. Anderson is professor of Psychology at Portland State University.

THE COMPLETE THINKER

A HANDBOOK OF TECHNIQUES FOR CREATIVE AND CRITICAL PROBLEM SOLVING

Barry F. Anderson

A SPECTRUM BOOK

Prentice-Hall, Inc., Englewood Cliffs, New Jersey 07632

Library of Congress Cataloging in Publication Data

ANDERSON, BARRY F
   The complete thinker.

   A (Spectrum Book)
   Bibliography: p.
   Includes index.
   1. Problem solving.   I. Title.
BF441.A52   153.4′3   80-12199
ISBN 0-13-164590-0
ISBN 0-13-164582-X (pbk.)

To DELIA and ERIK

10   9   8   7   6   5   4   3   2   1

For permission to use material, grateful acknowledgement is extended to the following: John Wiley & Sons, Inc. for permission to quote from *Studies in Cognitive Growth* by J.S. Bruner, R.R. Olver, P.M. Greenfield, et al. (New York: John Wiley & Sons, 1966); International Universities Press, Inc. and Delachaux & Niestlé, S.A., for permission to quote from *The Origins of Intelligence in Children* by Jean Piaget (New York: International Universities Press, Inc., 1952); Consulting Psychologists Press, Inc. for the Welsh Figure Preference Test, reproduced from *The Welsh Figure Preference Test* by George S. Welsh, Ph.D. © 1949; Charles Scribner's Sons for permission to reproduce Osborn's Checklist from *Applied Imagination*, 3rd edition, by Alex F. Osborn, Copyright 1953, 1957, 1963 by Charles Scribner's Sons; Opera Mundi for permission to quote from *Minute Mysteries* by Austin Ripley (copyright 1949 by Press Alliance, Inc., and published by Pocket Books, Inc.); Harper & Row, Publishers, Inc., for permission to reproduce the synectics dialogue from pages 38–39 in *Synectics* by William J.J. Gordon, copyright 1961 by William J.J. Gordon; McGraw-Hill Book Company for permission to reproduce the structure of intellect cube from *The Nature of Human Intelligence* by J.P. Guilford (New York: McGraw-Hill, 1967).

PRENTICE-HALL INTERNATIONAL, INC., *London*
PRENTICE-HALL OF AUSTRALIA, PTY., LIMITED, *Sydney*
PRENTICE-HALL OF CANADA, LTD., *Toronto*
PRENTICE-HALL OF INDIA PRIVATE LIMITED, *New Delhi*
PRENTICE-HALL OF JAPAN, INC., *Tokyo*
PRENTICE-HALL OF SOUTHEAST ASIA PTE., LTD., *Singapore*
WHITEHALL BOOKS LIMITED, *Wellington, New Zealand*

Contents

Preface

The unassisted hand and the understanding left to itself possess but little power. Effects are produced by the means of instruments and helps, which the understanding requires no less than the hand. . . .

Sir Francis Bacon, Novum Organum, *1620*
First Book, Aphorism 2

We move, perceive, and think in a fashion that depends on techniques rather than on wired-in arrangements in our nervous system.

Jerome S. Bruner, et al., Studies in Cognitive Growth, *1966*

Who of us wouldn't like to be able to think better? We all forget, make errors in reasoning, find it hard to come up with ideas, and make decisions we later regret. We all could cope more effectively than we do with the problems with which this difficult world so frequently confronts us.

Happily, thinking can be improved. This is currently being demonstrated in a number of programs around the country. (See Whimbey and Whimbey, 1975.) By learning and practicing appropriate attitudes and techniques, we can come to deal with problems more and more effectively. (If you would like a quick demonstration that reading this book can improve your thinking, turn to the beginning of Chapter 2.)

The reason thinking can be improved is that intelligence is as much a matter of what we do as of what we have. It is true that we are born with different brains, just as computers are built with different speeds and capacities, and that we can't trade our old brains in for new ones. Yet the effectiveness of both brains and computers depends to a great extent on how they are programmed. Intelligence, whether of humans or computers, is largely a matter of methods, techniques, or procedures. It is a matter of what we do. Because we can learn to do different things, we can learn to think more intelligently.

This book tells how to deal with different kinds of problems. It is a "program library" and, as such, is uniquely complete. It contains procedures for dealing with all the major kinds of problems: memory, reasoning, creative thinking, and decision making.

In addition to methods, attitudes are also important. Good problem solvers differ from poor problem solvers both in their attitudes towards problems and in their attitudes towards themselves as solvers. Moreover, it appears that adopting the attitudes of good problem solvers can make one a better problem solver.

Chapter 1, "The Nature of Problems and Problem Solving," defines "problem," identifies types of problems and steps in solving problems, considers why techniques are needed and how they work, and presents some general suggestions about attitudes and methods helpful in solving problems.

Chapters 2, 3, and 4 present techniques for getting ideas. In easy problems, ideas are merely retrieved from memory (Chapter 2). In more difficult problems, ideas have to be arrived at by reasoning (Chapter 3) on the basis of information retrieved from memory. In still more difficult problems, creative restructuring (Chapter 4) is required to provide a fresh start for remembering and reasoning.

Chapters 5, 6, and 7 present techniques for getting rid of ideas. This involves evaluating ideas and making decisions in order to narrow down the ideas to one that has the highest probability of success (however we may define success). Chapter 5 deals with problems that are so complex that educated guesses are necessary in order to simplify them to the point where they are manageable. Chapter 6 deals with the problem of the uncertainty of the future. The alternative that would be best in one possible future is often not the one that would be best in another. Some way is needed to take simultaneous account of the probabilities of various possible futures. Chapter 7 deals with the problem of the multi-faceted nature of the goals we seek. The best alternative for one goal is often not the best one for other goals, and we need some way to take account of many goals simultaneously.

Some of the techniques involve estimating numbers and performing simple arithmetic operations on these numbers. Some readers will feel comfortable with this; but for those who do not, let it be clearly said at the outset that by far the greatest value in this book is to be derived from its qualitative aspects. Skip over the quantitative techniques, if you wish. Or, better, read about them and keep them in mind as ideals toward which to strive when using the intuitive approximations suggested along with them.

Procedures, such as those presented in this book, can be best taught by (a) stating them clearly, (b) illustrating their application with a number of examples, and (c) providing ample opportunity to practice using them. I have tried to state each technique as explicitly as possible, in terms that refer to what you actually do. I have summarized the techniques in a set of tables, which should make it easier for you to get, and keep them in mind. Examples, I think you will find, are abundant.

Practice, however, is up to you. It should be stressed that practice is of great importance for improving any skill, athletic, musical, intellectual, or whatever. The person who wants to become a better thinker, no less than the person who wants to become a better soccer player or a better guitarist, must practice, practice, practice. If you hope to improve your thinking by simply reading through this book, you will almost surely be disappointed. Reading about the techniques is just the first step. Once you have read the book or a part of it that you are particularly interested in, you should attempt to apply the techniques to real problems, continuing to refer back to the book until you have mastered the techniques and made them habitual. It is probably best to begin with a small number of techniques and master these before going on to others. You might prefer to begin with the general suggestions in the first chapter or you might prefer to begin with the more specific techniques in some later chapter. In any case, treat the book as a handbook and plan to live with it for a while.

This book has certain limitations which should be made clear at the outset. First, of course, it cannot produce changes beyond the limits imposed by heredity. Certainly, no amount of training could transform a mentally retarded adult into an Einstein, a Bismarck, or a Picasso, and there are very definite limits to what this book—or any book—can do for even an above average adult. While the techniques can enable you to think better than you could without them, they, of course, cannot guarantee that you will be able to think better than any other person could without them. For example, while the memory techniques can greatly improve your memory, they cannot give you the kind of photographic memory that some people seem to possess with little or no training. This does not mean that the techniques are not important. It simply means that they are not all-important.

Second, this book cannot make thinking effortless. Indeed, one of the most important things you might learn from this book is that thinking is, by its very nature, an effortful process. As Henry Ford once said, "Thinking is the hardest work there is, which is the probable reason why so few engage in it." Almost all of the techniques require effort. In some cases, they reduce effort by enabling you to expend effort more efficiently; yet, even in these cases, they require effort. In other cases, they actually increase effort by giving you more toward solving your problem. What they do, in such cases, is enable you to do more justice to the full complexity of the problem before you, and thus come up with a better, if not easier, solution. Fortunately, the techniques will require less and less effort as you become more practiced. Also, the book will show how to distribute effort so as to put less into less important problems and more into more important problems.

Third, this book provides only general methods for thinking, not methods specific to particular subject areas and certainly not facts specific to particular subject areas; and yet such specific knowledge is essential to thinking about real problems. You can't play chess well without knowing the rules of chess and some chess plays, and you can't think well about repairing a car without knowing something about how motors work and about what instruments and tools are available for diagnosis and repair. The person who wins the chess game or who performs the more insightful repair job is not always the person with the better general problem-solving skills; sometimes it is the person with the more extensive knowledge in the particular area. Again, though general problem-solving skills are important, they are not all-important.

And, fourth, while this book can lead you to water, it cannot make you drink. As Sir Winston Churchill once said, "Men occasionally stumble on the truth, but most of them pick themselves up and hurry off as if nothing had happened." You might very well read the entire book, understand the techniques, be convinced of their value, and intend to apply them—and yet never actually do so! Or you might apply them for a time, but then eventually drift back to your old ways. This is a problem in what is called "self control," getting yourself to do what you want yourself to do. If you find yourself with this very common problem, there are some excellent books available that can help you deal with it: for example, M. J. Mahoney & C. E. Thoresen's *Behavioral Self-Control* or Robert L. Williams' *Toward a Self-Managed Life Style*. While the present book provides the basic "programs" of general intelligence, these books tell how to "program yourself."

Intelligent behavior is thus composed of a number of ingredients. It requires certain inherited givens; it requires knowledge of facts and methods, and it requires motivation. There is little that any of us can do about the inherited givens, other than to accept them with grace. Motivation is an important factor and one about which something can be done, but one that is beyond the scope of this book. Knowledge of facts and specific methods can be acquired from experience or formal study in the various areas in which you are trying to solve problems, but such knowledge is beyond the scope of any single book. Knowledge of general methods of problem solving, however, can be acquired and can, ideally, at least, be done justice in a single book. It is this important ingredient of intelligence that will be our concern in the following pages.

I would suggest reading Chapter 1 first, but beyond that I'm not sure that any one order of reading the chapters is much better than any other. My suggestion would be to sample a little from each and then begin your in-depth reading with whatever interests you most.

I would like to thank Bill Boore, Rupert Buchanan, Don Moor, Walt and Judy Perdue, Charles Schwenk, Tom Strange, Bill and Thelma Wiest, and especially Kostas Dervitsiotis and Jim Paulson for helping me accumulate good ideas and divest myself of bad ones as I put this book together. I would also like to thank those with whom I have done decision consulting and decision counselling for the many opportunities they have provided for working through the application of general techniques to practical problems. I would also like to thank my family, Aliki, Delia, and Erik for putting up with another book.

1

The Nature of Problems and Problem Solving

A problem exists when there is a discrepancy between where you are and where you would like to be and you do not know how to get from one place to the other. In the following true story, the person was in her apartment; she would have liked to have been outside, but she didn't know how to get out. She had a problem.

> Returning home at an unusual hour one morning to get some papers that I had forgotten, I rushed into my living room and found myself confronted by a husky stranger. The man, who had obviously been ransacking drawers, moved without a word to block my escape through the hall door. There was no one at home at that hour, I knew, in the other apartments. Since I didn't want to make a dash for the door and risk violence, I had to figure out some way to outwit the man. What would you have done? (Reprinted from *The Saturday Evening Post,* © 1951, The Curtis Publishing Company.)

In solving the problem she must have begun by quickly generating ideas. Undoubtedly, she rejected some of these, including the idea of making a dash for the door. Finally, she hit upon a promising one: Her solution was to look around the apartment, rather than at the man, and say in a bewildered tone, "Oh, excuse me, I must be in the wrong apartment"; then walk past him and out the door. It worked!

Problems come at us from many directions and appear in many forms. There are the "mind benders," and there are the "mind bogglers." The first kind presents us with a lack of ideas and requires us to think creatively in order to come up with ideas; the second kind presents us with a profusion of ideas and requires us to think critically in order to get rid of the less valuable ones.

The kind of problem we just considered requires creative thinking. It was a problem to come up with a satisfactory course of action. Other examples of such problems are to find a way to get into a car that you have locked yourself out of, to find a way to use up some extra egg whites, or to find a way to keep your expenses from exceeding your income. These are problems in invention.

Another kind of problem that requires creative thinking is the problem of anticipating possible consequences of some course of action. What could be some of the more important consequences of changing jobs, of vacationing in Alaska, of developing nuclear power plants? These we might call problems in anticipation.

Other kinds of problems require essentially critical, rather than creative, thinking. One is deciding which of several possible consequences are probable and which are not. It could rain or shine this weekend, but which is more likely? The coming recession could last one year, two years, or longer, but which of these possibilities is most likely, and which is least likely. These are problems in prediction.

Problems in explanation are closely related to problems

in prediction. Does changing the engine speed (by revving the engine in neutral) change the likelihood of getting the noise you keep hearing? If so, the cause of the noise is probably somewhere in the engine. Does stopping jogging reduce the frequency with which you get backaches? If so, jogging is probably at least one cause of your backaches.

Another kind of problem that requires critical thinking is choosing from among alternative courses of action that are already before you. This is the problem of a person trying to decide between two suitors, or a family trying to decide whether to accept or reject an offer for their house, or a person trying to choose from among the enormously large number of stereos that are on the market. These are problems in choice.

We should also add "hidden problems," or problems in awareness, in which you are either not aware of any difficulty or not aware that your chosen course of action will not resolve the difficulty. The person who has a lump that he does not know is cancer has a hidden problem, as does the person who is taking a quack treatment for cancer. Personality problems often fit into this category, because defense mechanisms make it difficult for us to become aware of such problems. "It's not that I am not warm enough toward others; it's that they don't like my political beliefs." Organizational problems also frequently fit into this category, since it is often difficult for employees to bring problems to the attention of management.

In addition to simple problems, in which one type of difficulty, awareness, invention, anticipation, prediction, explanation, or choice, is paramount, there are also complex problems, those in which more than one type of difficulty is important. Life's most important problems seem to be of this type. In finding a lifestyle, a mate, or a vocation, for example, awareness, invention, anticipation, prediction, explanation, and choice all seem to be involved. Morever, these are not problems that we solve at a single sitting, but ones that we work on for months or, more probably, many years.

GENERAL CHARACTERISTICS OF PROBLEMS

Despite the variety of problems, it seems possible to discern a common structure that underlies them all. In all problems, as we have said, there is a discrepancy between an initial state and a final state; moreover, it is not immediately apparent how to get from one state to the other. This structure seems to be common to all of those situations that we consider problematical and may be taken as a definition of "problem." The existence of an initial state and a goal state and the selection of responses to reduce differences between the two characterizes goal-directed behavior in general. Traveling a familiar route or preparing a favorite meal are examples of goal-directed behavior. What a problem is is an interruption in the normally smooth flow of goal-directed behavior. It is when a portion of the route you are traveling is blocked or you are out of a key ingredient for your recipe that you engage in problem-solving behavior. It's necessity that is the mother of invention.

Problems are alike in other respects, besides having an initial state, a goal state, and the lack of a clear path from one to the other. We can begin to appreciate these similarities if we represent problems in terms of trees. The kind of tree we shall consider now is called a decision tree. Later, probability trees, idea trees, and relevance trees will be introduced, and it will be shown how they relate to decision trees.

To take a simple example, let us say that you are thinking of not watering your lawn because it looks like rain. This is a problem in choice: water your lawn or not water your lawn. This choice would be represented in a decision tree as follows:

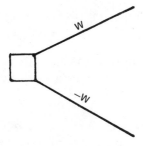

The square is called an act node. It represents the question, "What can I do?" The lines radiating from it represent the various possible courses of action that are being considered: water the lawn (W) and not water the lawn (−W). Note that the lines point in a general left-to-right direction; decision trees are conventionally "grown" from left to right.

Now consider the possible events that could follow each of these courses of action: It could rain, or it could not rain. This is a problem in anticipation or, if we begin to consider which event is more likely, one in prediction. This problem would be represented in a decision tree as follows:

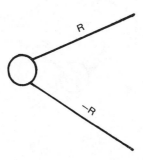

The circle is called an event node. It represents the question, "What could happen?" The lines radiating from it represent alternative possible states of nature: rain (R) and no rain (−R).

The distinction between acts and events is the one made so nicely in the Prayer of St. Francis:

> Lord, grant me the courage to change what can be changed, the serenity to accept what cannot be changed, and the wisdom to know the difference.

Act nodes represent what we can change, while event nodes represent what we cannot change but can only predict. We shall see later that, with all due respect to St. Francis, more than courage is needed at act nodes and more than serenity is needed at event nodes.

The problem of considering not watering the lawn because it looks like rain is, as simple as it may seem, an example of what we earlier called a complex problem, for it involves both prediction and choice. The entire problem can be represented in a single tree, as follows:

What this tree says is: (a) if you water, it could rain or not rain, and (b) if you do not water, it could rain or not rain. Pluses and minuses have been placed at the ends of the paths to indicate the value of each end result. If you water, it will be better if it doesn't rain; if you don't water, it will be better if it does rain.

In decisions of this complexity—and they are more common than most people realize—you must take into account an uncertain future in making your decision. Otherwise, you might be unpleasantly surprised by an event that you had not anticipated—like Harry: "Harry was looking for the perfect girl, and he found her. The trouble was she was looking for the perfect man!"

Now that we have acquired some familiarity with the tree representation, let us see how the various kinds of problems—awareness, invention, anticipation, prediction, explanation, and choice—might be represented in terms of trees.

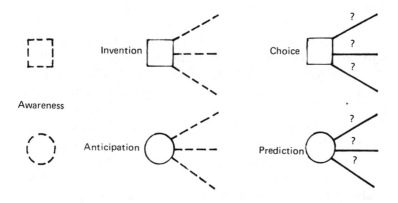

In the first column, the dashed act node indicates that the person is not aware that he has a choice, and the dashed event node indicates that the person is not aware that there is some uncertainty about what might happen. These are problems in awareness.

In the second column, the solid act node with the dashed lines indicates that, while the person is aware that he must make a choice, he doesn't yet know what he might do to accomplish his goal or goals. And the solid event node with the dashed lines indicates that, while the person is aware that there is some uncertainty about what might occur, he does not yet have any idea as to what the alternative possibilities might be. These are problems in invention and anticipation, respectively.

In the third column, the solid act node with solid lines and question marks indicates that the person knows he has a choice and knows of some possible courses of action but has not yet evaluated these courses of action to determine which is best. The solid event node with solid lines and question marks indicates that the person knows that there is some uncertainty as to what might happen and has conceived of some alternative possible states of nature, but has not yet determined the probability of each. These, of course, are problems in choice and prediction.

As will become increasingly clear, the decision tree is able to provide a very helpful framework for representing many of the characteristics of problems and problem solving. It helps us to see the underlying structure that is common to problems and thus to see how to apply the general techniques to whatever particular problem is before us.

There are two good reasons why certain techniques tend to be helpful for solving problems in general. One is that problems, as we have begun to see, have a common underlying structure. The other is that the human mind itself—which, of course, is what we use to represent and work on problems—also has a definite structure, with its own characteristic strengths and weaknesses.

BASIC LIMITATIONS
OF THE HUMAN INTELLECT

Human thought processes seem to be of two kinds (see Posner, 1973; Anderson, 1975), one automatic, effortless, and unconscious; the other voluntary, effortful, and conscious. Each kind of thought process has its own weaknesses, and each weakness calls for special techniques. (We shall see on p. 131 that yet another important distinction cuts across this one. Both automatic and effortful processes are sub-divided into those that engage in abstract, analytic, verbal thought and those that engage in concrete, global, spatial thought.)

One way to show the difference between automatic and effortful processes is to set one against the other. The figure on the left below can be found in the larger figure on the right, yet it is difficult to do so.

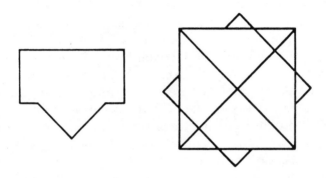

The reason for the difficulty is that the effortful processes you use to arrange and rearrange mentally various parts of the larger figure, in your search for the smaller figure within it, tend to be opposed by automatic perceptual processes that arrange these parts differently.

As a second example, when you're trying to learn a new response, such as "chairperson," to replace an old one, like "chairman," the effortful processes you use to produce the new response are opposed by automatic associative processes that tend to produce the old response. This is, of course, one reason why it's harder to teach an old dog new tricks.

Automatic processes have two major weaknesses: They tend to make thought stimulus-bound, and they tend to make it habit-bound. Our thought tends to be stimulus-bound in that we tend to take as real only what can be repre-sented by the automatic processes of perception. (A "stimulus" is simply something that we see, hear, feel, or sense in some other way.) Out of sight is often out of mind. It is much easier, for example, to get people concerned about pollutants that they can sense than about those that are colorless, odorless, and tasteless. Differences in beauty or in skin color are easily treated as more real than such less tangible variables as kindness or moral courage. Social ills are more often blamed on individuals whom we can see and point to, than on abstract properties of systems. And, to bring the point home, differences in problem-solving ability seem more often to be seen as characteristics of the individuals themselves than of the methods they are using!

Our thought tends to be habit-bound in that we tend to interpret and respond to events only in accustomed ways. Stairs never move; boats never go under water; libraries never come to people; blacks never perform brain surgery. Creative problem solving requires breaking the bonds of perception or habit—"bending" our minds—and for this, effortful processes must be employed.

Effortful processes have one major weakness: an extremely limited capacity. They can deal with, at most, some half dozen items at a time. This is, presumably, why there are only seven wonders of the ancient world, seven deadly sins, seven days of the week, and seven digits in our telephone numbers (see Miller, 1956). It is also presumably why we tend to think in terms of simple category systems (see Anderson, 1975, pp. 230–264). And it is why we so often complain that the problems of life are "mind boggling" in their complexity. The problems of life usually involve a large number of possible courses of action, states of nature, or both. Such complexity can easily overwhelm our limited capacity for the effortful processing of information.

A third weakness of the human intellect should also be mentioned: Our minds tend to seek immediate pleasure (Mather & Stana, 1978). It is not the pursuit of pleasure itself that is the problem but the emphasis on immediacy. Too often we pay for a small amount of immediate pleasure with the loss of a great amount of pleasure later on; the emphasis on immediate pleasure reduces total pleasure.

One way our minds seek immediate pleasure is in preferring pleasant thoughts to unpleasant ones, even though giving more attention to the unpleasant thoughts could well enable us to avoid the even less pleasant realities they foreshadow. The ancient Trojans, we are told, refused to heed Cassandra's warnings of the destruction of Troy. Jews who had made a decision to "sit tight" and hope for the best, following the German occupation of Hungary, refused to believe eyewitness accounts from respected community members of the slaughter and mass deportation of Jews in neighboring communities. And, today, we give too little thought to such things as the consequences of consuming resources recklessly or of not limiting population growth.

Another way our minds seek immediate pleasure is in preferring effortless thought processes to effortful ones. We are more inclined to jump to conclusions on the basis of automatic processes than to check them by means of effortful processes, and we are more inclined to look up the answer to a problem than to struggle with the process of arriving at it, ourselves. Serious thinking is difficult and time consuming, and we tend to avoid it.

GENERAL SUGGESTIONS
FOR PROBLEM SOLVING

What can be done to enable our imperfect intellect to cope more effectively with the problems of reality? Techniques are available, methods of thought that have been evolving slowly over generations and that now, with the emergence of the information sciences (managerial science, cognitive psychology, computer science, and related branches of mathematics), have begun to be elaborated at an increasingly rapid pace.

The basic technique for dealing with the limited capacity of effortful processes is decomposition. Complex problems are broken down into simpler problems, the simpler problems are solved, and then the results are combined to yield a solution to the original complex problem. The general idea is to "divide and conquer." Since we shall be concerned with effortful processes throughout the book, we shall make frequent use of decomposition, in memory, reasoning, creative thinking, and decision making. In decision making, to take just one example, we shall see how to deal one at a time with a number of possible futures and one at a time with a number of relevant goals.

There are two general ways to deal with the stimulus- and habit-bound nature of automatic processes. One is to employ stimulus control to make these characteristics work for, rather than against, us. Thus, we can repeat stimuli to reproduce thoughts in remembering, and we can vary stimuli to produce new thoughts in creative thinking. We arrange for the repetition of stimuli when we think ahead to the context in which we will have to recall something that we are now learning or when we think back to the context in which we last recalled something we are now trying to recall. We arrange for the variation of stimuli when we go through a checklist or talk with others to get ideas.

The other way to deal with the stimulus- and habit-bound nature of automatic processes is to employ stimulus substitution, substituting new stimuli (which we call "symbols") for old ones, so that effortful processes will not have to fight against processes that would be automatically activated by the old stimuli. Using the word "person," instead of "man" or "woman," can help to free us from sexist associations; using the metaphor of the brain as a computer can help to free us from old ways of thinking about how the brain works; and using trees to represent problems can help to free us from old habits for dealing with problems.

It is in the chapters on memory and creative thinking that we shall be most concerned with probing the automatic processes of associative memory, and so it is in these chapters that we shall make the greatest use of stimulus control and stimulus substitution.

Stimulus substitution can also be used to deal with the immediate-pleasure-seeking nature of the human mind (which is probably just a special case of effortless responding to current stimuli). Replacing positive and negative stimuli with neutral ones should lead to a more evenhanded treatment of all aspects of a problem. For example, representing success and failure as two branches on an event node should make it easier to treat those two vastly different possibilities symmetrically.

Finally, there are several things that could be done to get people to use effortful processes more. Instruction, simply describing effortful processes and pointing out their importance, might lead us to use these processes more frequently. Models in the form of descriptions of outstanding problem solvers and the methods they use might also be helpful. More helpful than these, no doubt, would be providing opportunities actually to solve problems successfully, so that the experience of deferring immediate pleasure and engaging in hard intellectual effort will be followed by the experience of an even greater reward. Instructions, descriptions of the methods of outstanding thinkers, and example problems will occur frequently throughout the book.

As a preview of the rest of the book, let us look now at some general suggestions for problem solving. The general suggestions (summarized in Table 1) fall into two categories: those having to do with attitudes and those having to do with specific actions you can take.

Attitudes

You will be more likely to solve problems if you think positively and if you think systematically. Three suggestions can be made.

One. Think positively about problems. Poor problem solvers tend to find problems unpleasant, often threatening, and tend to avoid thinking about them. They either tell themselves that there is no problem, put off working on it, or shift the responsibility for solving it to someone else. It is important to recognize that problems are a normal part of life. The world is complex, and the understanding of even the brightest of us is, by comparison, quite humble. Consequently, the world is able to present us frequently with gaps that we cannot see immediately how to cross. This is not something to be ashamed of, avoided, and denied, but an indelible part of the human condition, a fact that must be accepted and faced up to by all of us. Having problems does not mean that there is something wrong with you; it means that you are human and living in a very real world.

It is also important to remind yourself that awareness of problems is necessary for their solution. There is a joke about a kid who said, "I want to be an inventor, but I don't know what to invent." His difficulty was in finding problems. One characteristic of good problem solvers is that they are good at finding problems. They are sensitive to problems and, moreover, actively seek them out. Outstandingly creative people differ from less creative people (see Barron, 1965) in tending to agree with statements like, "The unfinished and the imperfect often have greater appeal for me than the completed and the polished," and tending to disagree with statements like, "A person should not probe too deeply into his own or other people's feelings but take things as they are."

The first suggestion, then, is to be a problem seeker. Look for imperfections. Look for trouble. Think about your desires and discomforts and the desires and discomforts of others, and ask what it is that is causing them. Looking for problems will not only help you to recognize problems in time to do something about them, it will also help you to consider more aspects of whatever problem you are working

TABLE 1.
General Suggestions for Problem Solving

A. Attitudes
   1. Think positively about problems.
      Be a problem seeker. Think about your discomforts and the discomforts of others, and ask what it is that is causing the discomfort. Think of risks associated with your present course of action and with alternative courses of action. Look for trouble.
   2. Think positively about your ability to solve problems.
      See yourself as a problem solver. Know the sources of your strength. Be aware of external resources that can help you to solve problems. Allow sufficient time for problem solving. Set subgoals.
   3. Think systematically.
      Stop and think. Don't jump to conclusions. Plan for a step-by-step attack on the problem.
B. Actions
   1. State the problem.
      State clearly where you are and where you would like to be. State the problem broadly.
   2. Get the facts.
      Think carefully about each of the facts in turn. Look for implied facts.
   3. Focus on the important facts.
      Think most about those facts that most constrain search; in particular, think about important characteristics of the givens and of the goal.
   4. Generate ideas.
      Generate many ideas, especially unusual ones. Defer negative evaluation of ideas. Think of general possibilities first, then of particular ideas for each general possibility. Vary stimuli to vary your thoughts.
   5. Choose the best idea.
      Take into account all the important criteria for evaluating the ideas and all the important events that might affect the value of the ideas.

on and thus to do a better job of solving problems. Looking for problems will help you with both problem finding and problem solving.

If you know of no way at all of getting from where you are to where you want to be, it is relatively easy to recognize that you have a problem. Yet, even if you think you know of a good way to work towards your goal, you may have a hidden problem; your preferred course of action may entail risks that you are not yet aware of. The low ability pre-med student has such a hidden problem. It is not that he knows of no way at all of achieving his vocational goals. He knows of a way: He is going to be a doctor. The problem is that, with his level of ability and current study habits, he is simply not going to get into medical school. Similarly, the regular smoker has a hidden problem, which may not reveal itself until heart or lung trouble develops.

To become aware of hidden problems, you should spend some time thinking about risks associated with your present or planned course of action (Janis and Mann, 1977). Because we tend to avoid thinking about unpleasant things, we often adopt a course of action without being sufficiently aware of the risks involved and, hence, without sufficient deliberation. You should also spend some time thinking about risks associated with alternative courses of action, otherwise you might simply switch to some other course of action that also contains a hidden problem (Janis and Mann, 1977.) Switching from pre-med to pre-law may not actually solve the first problem, and simply swearing off smoking may not work as a permanent solution for the second problem. It is important to be aware that there is some question about what the best course of action is. As Erich Fromm has said, "Thinking man is necessarily uncertain."

Look for problems that are due to lack of change, as well as those that are the result of change. It is easy to spot a problem when it is associated with a change from the past (a new person in the office, new behaviors in a child). Often, however, problems are associated with a lack of change, frequently with insufficient movement towards a distant goal. Thinking about your goals should help you to identify such problems.

The message of this section is to look for trouble and to regard finding it as a positive thing. Trouble is bad, alright, but finding it is good. Finding trouble doesn't create it; it just gives you a chance to do something about it. A former chairman of the board of General Motors was clearly looking for trouble when he once said to the board, "None of you seems to see anything wrong with the plan, and I don't see anything wrong with it, myself—so I suggest we delay our decision for a month until we've had time to do some real thinking about it!"

Two. Think positively about your ability to solve problems. It's important to have confidence in your ability to solve the problem you are working on (Janis and Mann, 1977). Good problem solvers have confidence in their ability (MacKinnon, 1962); and, more to the point, increasing a person's confidence in his ability to solve problems, by having him imagine that he is a good problem solver, seems to increase his ability to solve problems (Stein, 1974, pp. 65–66). One thing increased confidence may do is keep a person from giving up too soon. It has been found (Hyman, 1964) that many people stop working on a problem before they have come up with the best ideas of which they are capable; if people are encouraged to continue working beyond the point at which they feel they have done the best they can, they often come up with even better ideas. We are capable of more creative ideas than we realize; we just have to try harder.

The story of the naming of the schooner *Lizard King* illustrates the fierce confidence that good problem solvers tend to have. A few years ago, two men from Oregon decided to build a Boston clipper to the specifications of a design from the early eighteenth century, using as much as possible the materials and methods of that time. They worked for many months, encountering one problem after another. Repeatedly, people told them that they would never finish, that they should give up.

One day, while engaged in recreational reading, one of them ran across a character called the Lizard King, a great power behind the scenes in the Holy Land at the time of the

Crusades. At one point, a crusader who had been having no success with his crusade went to the Lizard King and asked, "Can you help me?"

"Can I help you?" came the astonished reply. "I am the Lizard King!"

The Lizard King's assuredness rang true. Afterwards, when the shipbuilders ran into a difficult problem, they would say defiantly, "I am the Lizard King!"—and persist until they had solved it. Five years after they had laid the keel, they completed the boat, christened it the *Lizard King,* and sailed it triumphantly across the Pacific.

There are a number of ways in which you can realistically increase your confidence in your ability to solve problems—and thus come to see yourself as a Lizard King.

1. Be more aware of your existing strengths. Perhaps you have a good memory, or a logical mind, or an abundant imagination, or great persistence.
2. Be aware of external resources (people, books, etc.) that can help you to solve problems.
3. Allow sufficient time for problem solving. Settle down, make yourself comfortable, and plan to spend more time than you think you will need on your problem. If you take less time than this (which is not too likely, since we all tend to underestimate the amount of time it will take to get something done), you will just feel that much better about yourself as a problem solver. If it does take the full time, then you at least won't feel that it took you overly long to solve the problem, and you can feel good about yourself as a planner. You can make more time available for problem solving by getting an early start on the problem, by making efficient use of the time you have, and, if necessary, by trying to extend deadlines.
4. Read this book, practice solving problems, and thus actually increase your ability to solve problems.
5. Set subgoals, breaking difficult problems down into steps and attempting to accomplish just one step at a time. Subgoals are less overwhelming than goals.

This last way to see yourself as an effective problem solver is closely related to the next general suggestion, to think systematically.

Three. Think systematically.   Don't act impulsively. Don't jump to conclusions.

Problem solving is a sequential process, as the decision tree suggests. It proceeds step by step towards a solution. Poor problem solvers don't seem to understand this and tend to take a "one-shot" approach to problems—if they cannot solve a problem immediately, they either make a wild guess or give up (Bloom and Broder, 1950). They don't "stop and think"; they avoid effortful thought. Good problem solvers, on the other hand, approach problems in a planful, step-by-step fashion. (The good problem solver that whips out solutions immediately and unerringly is a myth and one that all too many people compare themselves unfavorably with.) Artists whose work is eventually judged to be more original take more time to select their subjects and to decide on their approach (Getzels and Csikszentmihalyi, 1976). And the role of the management consultant is often to slow the group down in its problem-solving activities (Schein, pp. 48, 51).

The following example will illustrate the importance of step-by-step thinking:

> What day follows the day before yesterday if two days from now will be Sunday?

Poor problem solvers frequently try to go from Sunday (the only day named in the problem) directly to an estimated answer without taking the necessary intermediate steps (Whimbey, 1977). Actually, this problem consists of a sequence of very simple problems:

What day is two days before Sunday? (Friday)

If today is Friday, what day was the day before yesterday? (Wednesday)

If today is Wednesday, what day is tomorrow? (Thursday)

Once the problem has been analyzed into its component subproblems, it is really quite simple—divide and conquer!

The following problem is another example of the same kind:

> If the word "sentence" contains fewer than nine letters and more than three vowels, circle the first vowel. Otherwise, circle the consonant that is farthest to the right in the word.

Later, we shall see how trees can be used to help keep track of complex sequences such as these when more involved thinking must be done about them.

Actions

More specific than attitudes are actions, thing you can do. Here, we shall discuss the major kinds of actions, or steps, in problem solving in a very general way. Later, in the rest of the book, we shall present more specific and powerful techniques for accomplishing these steps.

One. State the problem.   The first step in actually solving any problem is to state the problem clearly. As a golfer once said, "I have two problems with my game: direction and distance!"

"A problem well stated," it is said, "is a problem half-solved." To state a problem well, describe as clearly and completely as you can where you are and where you would like to be. The ideal is to specify all the constraints on the solution, yet not to assume any constraints that do not exist. The following problem illustrates the importance of a clear statement of initial and final states:

The two volumes of Gibbons' *Decline and Fall of the Roman Empire* stand side by side in order on a bookshelf. A bookworm commences at page one of volume one and bores its way in a straight line to the last page of volume two. If each cover is ⅛ inch thick, and each book without the covers is two inches thick, how far does the bookworm travel?

The reason most people fail to solve this problem is that they do not take sufficient care in describing the initial and final states of the worm. The initial and final states of the worm are not two book thicknesses away from each other. If the worm begins at page one of volume one, it is beginning at the right-hand side of volume one in the picture below; and, if it ends at the last page of volume two, it ends at the left-hand side of Volume two. Thus, the worm has to bore through only the two covers!

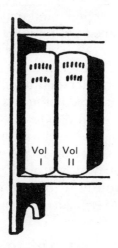

Personal and behavioral problems provide an example of a kind of problem for which careful definition is especially important. In many cases when people see their problem as one of defending themselves against or retreating from the attacks of others, the problem would be better defined as one of dealing with the feeling that others are opposing them. This latter definition of the problem leads one to seek facts to determine whether or not the feeling reflects the reality of the situation.

When we are told that Johnny is "misbehaving" in class, we should ask exactly what he is doing and exactly what it is desired that he do. This is a matter of specifying responses. Let us say that what he is doing is talking to the children around him and taking things from them during work periods and that what we would like him to be doing is working and letting others do their work. His "misbehavior" does not include lying or cheating or stealing or bullying. This provides us with a much more precise statement of the problem. We can now proceed to get some facts about what is causing the changeworthy behavior and what might produce the desired behavior.

It is important to keep in mind that a common difficulty in defining many problems is defining them too narrowly. Instead of asking, "How can I build a better mousetrap?" it is usually better to ask a broader question, such as, "How can I get rid of mice?" A broader definition opens up a greater range of possible solutions. Another way to say this is: Don't confuse means with ends. Building a better mousetrap is not an end in itself but simply one of a variety of possible means to the end of getting rid of mice. So, once you have stated your goal, ask yourself why you want to achieve that goal. Often, this will make you aware of your real goal—and, at the same time, of alternative means to achieve it.

Two. Get the facts.   The next step, though this step is often intertwined with the preceding one, is to get the facts of the problem clearly in mind. Getting the facts straight seems to be the main difficulty with the hotel problem:

> Three men checked into a hotel. The manager told them that the price of the room was $30. Each man paid $10, and they

went up to their room. Later, the manager discovered that the price of their room was really $25, so he sent the bellboy up to return $5 to them. The bellboy, who was nobody's fool, realized that the $5 could not be split three ways evenly, so he kept $2 and gave the men back $3. Thus, each of the three men got back $1 of his $10 and hence paid out $9.

Now, three times $9 equals $27, and this plus the bellboy's $2 equals $29. What happened to the other dollar?

This problem is solved simply by a more careful accounting of the facts. Adding $27 to $2 is adding apples and oranges; the $27 is what the three men don't have, and the $2 is what the bellboy does have. Instead, let's see what everybody does have out of the $30. The manager has $25; the bellboy has the $2 that he took; the three men have the $3 that the bellboy returned them; and $25 + $2 + $3 = $30.

In many problems the important facts have to do with causes and effects. In behavioral problems these are stimuli, responses, and reinforcers. What events precede the behavior? What events follow the behavior and reinforce, or reward, it? We have already seen that Johnny's "misbehavior" tends to occur during work periods. Let us say that we make some observations and find that the only event that reliably follows his "misbehavior" is the teacher's scolding him. Perhaps this attention is reinforcing the behavior that we would like to change—and perhaps we can use the same reinforcer to increase the probability of the desired behavior. We would then suggest to the teacher that he or she pay attention to Johnny when he is working well and ignore him when he is "misbehaving." (This suggestion, incidentally, has solved innumerable problems of this kind.)

It is especially important in many problems to think about the stated facts so as to become aware of implied facts. Think about each of the stated facts in turn, and ask yourself whether you can infer anything additional from it. The following cartoon illustrates the difference between facts that are given directly and facts that must be inferred:

Drawing by O. Soglow; © 1941, 1969
The New Yorker Magazine, Inc.

One fact that is given directly is that the boat is tipped toward the basket in the first picture and toward the man in the second. Another is that the cover is on the basket in the first picture and off in the second. And still another is that the man's stomach is flat in the first picture and distended in the second. What must be inferred is that the man ate the lunch that was in the basket.

Seeing all that is contained by implication in the stated facts is what is involved in insight problems, and it is the kind of ability that Sherlock Holmes, Hercule Poirot, and Ellery Queen are said to possess to such an extraordinary degree. The following "minute mystery" (Ripley, 1949) illustrates the process:

> Fordney glanced curiously at the interior of the sedan with its blood-soaked rear seat and followed the stretcher into the morgue of the small northern town.
>
> As the corpse, blasted by a shotgun charge, was lifted to a table, McHugh said, "I found this man on the old logging road about fifteen miles north of Oakdale. I was driving from my cottage on Black Ghost Lake to town when my headlights picked him out. I examined him, saw he was dead, and brought him here."
>
> "Don't you know that you are not supposed to move a dead body?" roared Police Chief Swanson.
>
> "Certainly!" snapped McHugh, "But the nearest phone is twelve miles. Did you expect me to leave him to the animals?"
>
> "You're lying," Fordney said.
>
> How did Fordney know that McHugh's statement was false?

One of the givens was that McHugh said that the victim was dead when he put him into the car. Another was that the seat was soaked with blood. Knowing that a person will not bleed profusely enough to soak a seat with blood unless his heart is beating, Fordney inferred that McHugh's statement was false.

In real-life problems it may take days, or even years, to get the facts straight. This is certainly true for problems in scientific research, and it is also true in many trouble-shooting problems, such as trying to find out why an individual feels tired most of the time, or why a company's profits are slipping, or why the nation's economy is sluggish. Getting the facts straight is the major step in solving many problems and an important step in solving most problems. We shall take up the problem of getting the facts straight in chapter 3.

Three. Focus on the important facts.   As was said earlier, there are usually a large number of possible states of nature, courses of action, or both. Problems can get enormously complicated, and we have to take care lest we lose ourselves in a mass of details.

The St. Ives problem provides a very simple illustration of the way in which focusing on the important facts can facilitate the solution of a problem:

> As I was going to St. Ives,
> I met a man with seven wives.
> Each wife had seven sacks;
> Each sack had seven cats;
> Each cat had seven kits.
> Kits, cats, sacks, and wives,
> How many were going to St. Ives?

There is, of course, only one important fact here: I was going to St. Ives.

Choosing a stereo is a good practical example of a problem where the principal difficulty is overwhelming complexity. If you are considering buying a component system, you will probably be thinking about at least a cartridge, a turntable, a receiver, and speakers. And, for each of these components, there are a number of characteristics with which salespeople and sales literature will bombard you: wow, flutter, and rumble; power output, power bandwidth, and frequency response; efficiency and crossover, to name just a few. On top of all this, the number of available brands and models is staggering. You need some way of simplifying all this.

The most general way to simplify complex problems is to focus on the important aspects of the problem and, for the time being at least, to let the details go. The "20–80 rule" states, as a rule of thumb, that 20% of the facts account for 80% of what is going on. These are the "vital few" among the "trivial many" (MacKenzie, 1972, pp. 51ff). The most important factors in choosing a stereo, for most people, would seem to be sound quality and cost. Other factors include durability, versatility, attractiveness, and resale value. Furthermore, the only importance of most of the characteristics of the various components, such as wow, frequency response, and crossover, is in the effect they have on sound quality. A very simple way of reducing these many characteristics to a single measure in which each is weighted in exact proportion to its contribution to sound quality is to listen! If one set of speakers, for example, sounds better to you than another, then it must be better in terms of the factors that count for you. You needn't bother yourself with what these factors are; that's a problem for the engineers.

Another way to simplify the problem of choosing a stereo by focusing on important aspects is to devote most of your attention to selecting the speakers and the cartridge. It is generally agreed (and you can demonstrate for yourself by listening tests) that these components make the greatest contribution to sound quality.

In chapter 5, we shall consider a number of more

specific techniques for simplifying problems than simply the suggestion to focus on the important aspects of the problem.

Four. Generate ideas.   The next step once you have the important facts clearly in mind, is to generate ideas for solving the problem. Again, while all of these steps must occur and while they tend to occur in the indicated order, there is often much overlapping and moving back and forth between them (Patrick, 1935, 1937; Janis and Mann, 1977). Ideas can be generated at any point in problem solving, from before you have defined the problem carefully until after you believe that you have solved it.

It is important to generate many ideas, for those who generate more ideas are more likely to generate good ideas. Photographers take a large number of exposures to get just one outstanding photograph, and a writer commits far more of his efforts to the wastebasket than he will ever send on to the public. You have to be prepared to do the same when you are generating ideas.

Before deciding to do anything of importance, generate alternatives so that, instead of making a yes/no decision on a single alternative, you will be choosing from among a number of alternatives. The person who is debating with himself about whether to stay in school or drop out, for example, should really be comparing being in school with working at any of the jobs that are available to a person with his level of education. It's not simply a school/no school decision, but a school/job decision.

Get in the habit of asking yourself, before you make a decision, whether there isn't some alternative that you are not considering. Also, ask yourself whether there isn't some possible event that could affect your decision that you are not taking into account. And, in evaluating the alternatives, generate as many favorable and unfavorable arguments for each as you can.

114407

In addition to generating many ideas, it is also important to try to generate ideas that are unusual—if the usual ideas worked, you wouldn't have a problem. Among the silly ideas in the following cartoon, there are some genuinely promising ones:

TEN WAYS TO IMPROVE A COFFEE CUP
(A CREATIVE EXERCISE)

Drawing by C. Barsotti; © 1977
The New Yorker Magazine, Inc.

It is important not be negatively evaluative during the stage of idea generation. When you come up with an idea or hear an idea that someone else has proposed, don't think of why it won't work—think instead of how you can *make* it work. A good exercise would be to think about each of the ways to improve a coffee cup, and ask yourself how you could turn each idea into a really good one. For example, wheels on a coffee cup, while ridiculous in itself, suggests something that would enable a coffee cup to slide smoothly across a surface without scratching it. Perhaps some washable material could be permanently attached to the bottom of coffee cups that would keep them from scratching delicate surfaces and, while we're at it, from burning them. A cap suggests a cover to keep the coffee warm in the cup (and why not make it look like a cap?) And so on. . . .

In generating ideas, it is helpful to think first of general possibilities for a solution and then of particular ideas for each general possibility (Covington, Crutchfield, Davies, and Olton, 1974). The following problem is one in which the chief difficulty is not one of getting the facts nor one of choosing among ideas once they have been generated but simply one of generating ideas:

> The worst worry of my new job as a grocery store cashier proved to be a customer who wouldn't believe the cash register. The total always far exceeded her expectations, and she would insist on having me recheck the order, item by item against the sales slip. All this took time and infuriated the customers behind her. It wore my patience thin, and I began to fear I might get blazing mad at the woman and lose my job for it. Luckily, I worked out a way to cope with her. Can you guess what I did?

One general possibility would be to try, in some way, to help the woman achieve her goal of being convinced that the total is accurate. Most solution attempts fall in this category: Have her call off the items as they are rung up, have her check the result on a hand calculator, etc. Another general possibility, however, would be to get her to change her goal, to get her to hope for an inaccurate total. This was the approach that the cashier actually took.

> The next time the woman came through my stand, I purposely failed to ring up a dozen eggs. When she had me recheck the list item by item, I "found" the eggs and added them to the total. On her next visit, I "overlooked" a large jar of mayonnaise which I subsequently "found." The third time, the store was the loser by a pound of butter, for she didn't give me a chance to correct my "oversight" there. But it was worth it—though she comes in as regularly as ever, we haven't had to recheck another order for her. (Reprinted from *The Saturday Evening Post*, © 1949, The Curtis Publishing Company.)

In addition to starting by thinking of general possibilities for a solution, vary stimuli in order to vary your thoughts. Observe directly—if possible, manipulate—the elements of your problem. Read related material. And talk with different people about your problem.

In chapter 4, we shall consider a variety of techniques for getting ideas.

Five. Choose the best idea.   The final step is the decision-making step. The problem now is to choose the very best of the remaining ideas.

It's important to think ahead to the probable long-term consequences of any course of action that you are considering. People who smoke or drink heavily tend not to take long-term consequences as seriously as they will later. Similarly, those who contribute to population growth or to the needless consumption of nonrenewable resources tend not to give sufficient weight to long-term consequences. It takes a "gas crunch" to make a possible future that is very real to a few, real to many.

There are two ways of dealing with the uncertainty of the future. One is to attempt to predict which of several possible alternative futures will in fact occur and to plan for that future. Another, safer thought requiring more creativity, is to conceive of a course of action that will lead to desirable results in any of several possible futures. Plans that keep your "options open" are examples of the latter. Instead of taking a three-year pre-med program that will leave you with little if you fail to make it into medical school, get a four-year degree in something like biology, so you will have something whether or not you get into medical school. Instead of zoning land for residential use, zone it, if possible, for agricultural use—it's easier to rezone agricultural land later, if need be, than to rezone residential land once it has been built on.

Also, in making decisions, several criteria and their relative importance must usually be taken into account. A problem that will illustrates the difficulty of choosing on the basis of multiple criteria is choosing among jobs. Vocational choice is very difficult and takes most people many years. Consider, for example, how difficult it. could be to choose between even just two jobs where they differed on income, interest level of the work, chances for advancement, security, kind of environment for family, and extent to which parents and friends regard the work favorably. It can help in making such decisions to make a separate list of the arguments for each alternative course of action and then to cross out comparable items on the different lists, continuing until you have narrowed the considerations to a small number.

As in the case of multiple futures, there are two ways to deal with multiple goals, one a decision-making approach, the other a creative-thinking approach. You can choose the course of action that sacrifices the least for what it achieves, or you can try to conceive of a course of action that sacrifices nothing for what it achieves. You could serve pie, which might please the adults but not the kids, ice cream, which might please the kids but not be very interesting for the adults, or pie à la mode, which would suit both.

In dealing with multiple futures and multiple goals, make an effort to see their mutual relevance. At the very least, jot them all down in a single list. As Schein (1969, p. 40) has noted: "One common problem which I have observed in committees, task forces, and executive teams is that they tend to work sequentially and process one idea at a time, never gaining any perspective on the totality of their discussion." Chapters 6 and 7 will present special techniques for taking multiple futures and multiple goals into account.

Let's close this chapter with a mnemonic which, by telling you just what it means to be SMART, can help you to remember the general suggestions for problem solving given in this chapter and, at the same time, of course, the outline of the book.

SENSITIVITY. Identification of problems.

MATTERS of FACT. Clarification of facts and their implications.

ACTS. Exploration of a variety of alternative courses of action.

RISKS. Anticipation of the consequences of possible events.

TRADE-OFFS. Evaluation of end states in terms of all relevant goals.

And mnemonics leads right in to the topic of the next chapter, which is memory.

RECOMMENDED READING

COVINGTON, M. V., R. S. CRUTCHFIELD, L. DAVIES, and R. M. OLTON, JR., *The Productive Thinking Program.* Columbus, Ohio: Ch. E. Merrill, 1974.

2

Memory

This chapter will open with a demonstration that is designed to amaze, to delight, and to convince. Two lists of words will follow shortly. If you wish to play the game, you should read the first list, close the book, and attempt to recall this list; then read the second list, close the book, and attempt to recall this list. Read each list at about the same rate, one word every few seconds, and read each list just once before trying to recall it. Are you ready for-the first list?

The first list is: PEACH, HAMMER, CHURCH, APPLE, HAT, SAW, BANK, COAT, CHERRY, STORE, DRILL, ORANGE, BELT, SCREWDRIVER, WAREHOUSE, STOCKING. Now, test yourself immediately.

The words on this list fall into four categories: fruits, tools, buildings, and articles of clothing. The trouble was that these categories were all scrambled up—like some people's notes.

One of the techniques for improving memory is to organize the material you have to learn into categories. Organized material can be much easier to learn and remember than unorganized material. The words on the second list also fall into four categories, but, this time, all the words from each category will be presented together. This should make the list easier to read and easier to remember. Are you ready for the second list?

The second list is: CARROT, BROCCOLI, CORN, PEAS; KNIFE, PISTOL, SPEAR, BLACKJACK; TRUCK, CAR, BOAT, PLANE; DOCTOR, LAWYER, PLUMBER, SAILOR. Now, test yourself immediately.

You should have remembered more items from the second list. Of course, since this is a demonstration and not a carefully controlled experiment, we cannot say how much of the improvement can be attributed to the difference in organization and how much to other factors. However, there is abundant research evidence (e.g., Bousfield, 1953; Kintsch, 1970) to show that this organizational difference alone can produce large differences in recall.

We shall have much more to say about organization shortly. Yet even this simple demonstration should be sufficient to show that how much you can remember depends, not just on the brain you are blessed or cursed with, but also on what you do with it. You can remember more by doing different things. Your thinking *can* be improved!

One more demonstration and then we'll get on with the chapter. Again, you will be shown two lists of words and asked to read each through once and then attempt to recall it. Are you ready for the first list?

The first list is: LION, ICE CREAM, CLOCK, TREE, HOSPITAL, HAND, MAGICIAN, DRUM, HELICOPTER, BOOK, LAMP. Now, test yourself immediately.

The technique for improving memory that will be demonstrated this time is the use of imagery. In reading the next list, (a) imagine yourself walking along a familiar route, say, through your house or around the block, and (b) mentally place an image of each item on the list in some prominent place along the route. For example, if you had applied this technique to the first list, you might have imagined a lion on your front porch, a mountain of ice cream on your living room floor, a loudly ticking clock in the dining room, and so forth. In recalling the list, you would have simply gone back over your walk and "seen" the items on the list as you came to them. This is the kind of thing you should do for the second list. (Be sure to make the images vivid.) Are you ready for the second list?

The second list is: FOOTBALL, BANANA, INDIAN, STAMP, BUS, GOAT, CAKE, MILK, RIVER, ROPE, BABY. Now, test yourself immediately.

You should have remembered more items from the second list. Again, because this is a demonstration and not an experiment, we cannot be sure how much of the improvement was due to the use of imagery. Again, however, there is abundant evidence (e.g., Wallace, Turner, and Perkins, 1957; Bower, 1970, 1972) to show that imagery alone can produce large differences.

Memory is important. Getting ideas always involves memory in an important way. Indeed, the reliance on memory is so pervasive in thinking—both the directed thinking of problem solving and the undirected thinking of dreaming and daydreaming—that it is difficult to become aware of. Because it is always there, it, like water for the fish, is difficult to discover.

Let us say that there was a freezing rain last night and that the streets are as slick as an icicle. You are deliberating about how to get to work this morning, or even whether to go to work. In doing so, you are using your memory continuously. In the first place, it is only because you remember what has happened to you or what you have heard has happened to others in icy weather that you are aware that there is some risk associated with your usual course of action, driving to work, and also with various alternative courses of action—in other words, that you have a problem.

In the second place, you use your memory in generating ideas for solving the problem and in choosing among the ideas. You begin by remembering that tire chains are helpful under such conditions, and you remember that you have chains in your car. But you also remember that putting chains on is an unpleasant job. You search your memory for someone in the neighborhood with chains who might be going your way, but you come up with nothing. You remember that there is a bus line near your house and that the buses continue to run in all kinds of weather. You remember also that it is unpleasant to wait in cold weather for buses that are running off-schedule and that it is uncomfortable to ride standing up on a crowded, steamy bus. But you compare this memory with the memory of fitting tire chains on with cold, numb fingers and of the anxiety of driving on icy roads even with chains, and you decide that the bus is the lesser of the evils. So you take the bus.

The solving of any problem could be described in such terms. Memory is involved at every step. In all thinking, memory is important. Indeed, the essential difference between thinking and acting is that in thinking we manipulate representations of things, rather than things themselves. In thinking, we operate, not on the world, but on what we remember about the world. This is what gives thinking its power to escape the bonds of time, space, and particularity. Yet it is also a source of its weakness, for memory can fail. The demand placed on memory in the icy morning problem was trivial, but, in other cases, it can be considerable. To solve some other problem, you might have to remember a measurement, a telephone number, a name, or a procedure, and whether you succeed or fail in your attempt to solve the problem may depend crucially on whether you are able to retrieve this piece of information from memory.

Indeed, it seems that we "solve" many, if not most, problems by recalling solutions to similar problems, rather than by constructing solutions anew. The person who is more likely to solve a problem is often the person with the more extensive fund of relevant ideas, rather than the person who is better at manipulating ideas. To obtain a large fund of ideas, you must expose yourself to information and you must store it in a manner that permits ready access. The techniques in this chapter will help you to store information in a manner that permits ready access, but it is up to you to expose yourself to information. This you can do, of course, by means of reading, conversation, or direct experience.

Memory involves three phases: information storage, information retention, and information retrieval. People frequently talk about their "poor memories" as if the problem had to do with loss during retention—they say their memory is "like a sieve"—yet most memory psychologists (see, for example, Hilgard and Bower, 1975, pp. 298–305; Hulse, Deese, and Egeth, 1975, pp. 336ff.) believe that, as long as there is no injury to the brain, retention is perfect for everyone. Retention does not seem to be where the problem lies. Memory failure is believed, instead, to be virtually always a failure in information retrieval; the "forgotten" material is still in memory but, like a misplaced book in the library, cannot be found. The fact that we are often able to retrieve the material on a later occasion—the classic case is remembering the answer to an exam question after having left the exam—is evidence that the material was in memory, all along. Most memory psychologists also seem to agree that the time to do something about failures in retrieval is not during retrieval itself but during storage. What we call a "poor memory" is thus more accurately characterized as poor habits of learning; to be able to retrieve information better, you must store it better. Storing information is an activity. You have to attend to the information, and you have to do things with it.

The view that a "poor memory" is more a matter of what we do than what we have is encouraging in one respect, but limiting in another. It is encouraging in that it means that we can remember better simply by doing different things. It is limiting, however, in that it means that, if we are to continue to remember better, we must continue to do these things. Even stage memory experts, who can perform amazing feats with the techniques to be discussed in this chapter, forget many things to which they do not apply the techniques (Lorayne, 1957, p. 168). The mind is not so much like a muscle that becomes stronger with use as it is like a computer that can be given more and more powerful programs. Take away the programs, and the computer is no better than it was before. So reading about the techniques, understanding them, and practicing them is not enough. If you wish your memory to remain improved, you must continue to use the techniques. Using them will become easier with practice, but you must, nevertheless, continue to make some effort to apply them.

It is worth observing that the memory techniques are useful not only for remembering facts and procedures and thus for thinking creatively and critically in solving problems, but also for remembering the plans you have come up with as solutions to problems, remembering to carry out these plans, and remembering where you are in their execution. This is important, for, while a person who forgets a telephone number is said only to have an unreliable memory, a person who forgets to make a telephone call is said to be an unreliable person. Many of the techniques for being better organized, or managing one's life better, are simply memory techniques applied to the execution of plans. We shall consider the application of memory techniques to both the formulation and the execution of plans.

This chapter has been written as a "self-memorizing" chapter in that it is organized in terms of the very techniques it presents. You should be able to recall the main parts of the chapter from memory once you have finished reading it.

Thus, the entire chapter should provide a demonstration of its own effectiveness.

The overall organization of the chapter is represented by the mnemonic:

The ABC ROAD to a Better Memory.

The letters A, B, C, and R, O, A, D stand for Analyze, Bind, Cue, Repeat, Overlearn, Actively recall, and Distribute practice, the main parts of the chapter. (See Table 2.) Let us turn to the first of these, Analyze.

ANALYZE

Analyzing means, first, looking over the material you have to learn and breaking it down into units of manageable size, units small enough to be handled by the limited capacity of effortful processes. In doing this, you essentially produce an

TABLE 2.
Techniques for Remembering

A. Organize
  1. Analyze the material into units of manageable size, subclassifying or cross-classifying if the number of units exceeds five.
  2. Bind the material together with images, word associations, and/or rules.
  3. Cue the material by associating it with especially arranged or naturally occurring stimuli.
B. Repeat
  1. Repeat the material until new associations are well established.
  2. Overlearn the material, continuing repetition well beyond the point at which errors are no longer made.
  3. Actively recall the material to strengthen and test the information retrieval plan itself.
  4. Distribute practice, taking short breaks between practice sessions.

abstract or summary of the material. This chapter, for example, taken as a whole, represents a fair amount of material to learn. If you begin, however, by looking through it to get an overview, you will see that it can be broken down into just two major parts: organization, the ABC part, and repetition, the ROAD part. The first thing we do in learning material is to organize it, or make it more meaningful (using the ABC techniques), in such a fashion that it can be learned with as little repetition as possible, and then we do what repeating is necessary (using the ROAD techniques) until it is firmly implanted in memory.

It is generally advantageous to analyze large amounts of material into parts, rather than to attempt to learn them as wholes, because the time it takes to learn material increases at a faster rate than does the amount of the material (Lyon, 1917). For example, if you double the amount of material, it takes more than twice as long to learn it. Conversely, if you divide the material into halves, it takes less than half the time to learn each half. Of course, it does take some time to put the pieces back together, so you do not want to divide the material too finely.

Analysis involves classification. Classification was the first of the techniques demonstrated at the beginning of this chapter. And here we have just classified the techniques for improving memory into techniques for improving the efficiency of organization and techniques for improving the efficiency of repetition. One rule is that analysis should be into no more than about five classes at any one level (Broadbent, 1975; Mandler, 1975). The reason has to do with the reassembly problem mentioned in the previous paragraph: It is difficult to put more than five pieces together into a single pattern. If we had begun by analyzing the chapter into the classes: analyze, bind, cue, repeat, overlearn, actively recall, and distribute practice, we would have violated this rule, for there are seven classes here. So we started with two classes, a number well within the limit of five. (The number five is actually not a precise figure and varies from person to person. The general point is that analysis should be into no more than a small number of classes.)

Yet we must eventually learn these seven classes—and in more complex cases must learn many more than seven. How can we do this without violating the restriction to five classes? The answer is by subclassifying or cross-classifying. For the material in this chapter, subclassifying seems more appropriate. Just as we classified all the techniques into two, those having to do with organization and those having to do with repetition, so we can in turn subclassify the techniques having to do with organization into three, those having to do with analysis, binding, and cueing, and the techniques having to do with repetition into four, those having to do with repetition, overlearning, active recall, and distribution of practice. Other names for subclassification are hierarchical organization and outline form. In terms of the familiar outline form, for example, our subclassification would look like this:

I. Organization
   A. analyze
   B. bind
   C. cue

II. Repetition
   A. repeat
   B. overlearn
   C. actively recall
   D. distribute practice

Cross-classification cannot always be used, but when it can it is a powerful technique. For example, this is undoubtedly the way we think about the standard playing deck of 52 cards. Instead of remembering 52 separate items, we cross 4 suits (hearts, clubs, diamonds, and spades) with 13 values (ace, 2, 3, 4, 5, 6, 7, 8, 9, 10, jack, queen, and king) and thus have to remember only 17 items, a saving of 67%.

But certainly we cannot remember 17 items straight off,

for even this is much larger than the limit of 5. Something more must be going on here. Actually, the number sequence 1–10 is a well-learned unit, and king-queen is also a well-learned unit. It seems that we use both subclassification and cross-classification here, subclassification to generate the suits and values and cross-classification to generate the individual cards from there. The subclassification we use to generate the suits and values probably looks something like this:

    I. Suits
       A. hearts
       B. clubs
       C. diamonds
       D. spades

   II. Values
       A. 1–10
          1. ace
          2. 2
          3. 3
           ·
           ·
           ·
         10. 10
       B. Jack
       C. King-Queen
          1. Queen
          2. King

Even here, the breakdown under IIA exceeds five classes, and we should probably represent the numbers 1–5 as one class and the numbers 6–10 as another. It seems that, even in well-learned sequences, the rule still applies that the number of classes at any one level cannot exceed five. In learning the alphabet as a child, for example, you probably used the following singsong grouping to learn the alphabet.

          ABCD, EFG;
          HIJK, LMNOP;
          QRS, TUV;
          WX, Y-and-Z.

Note that, in this scheme, no class consists of more than five letters. If you believe that this is a thing of the past and that you now know the alphabet as a single, unbroken string, try saying the alphabet backwards, and you will notice that the points at which you have the greatest trouble coincide fairly well with the breaks in this "childhood" grouping.

Our memory for the 52 cards thus seems to involve both subclassification and cross-classification. In cross-classification, each class on one basis of classification, for example, king, applies to every class on the other basis of classification, for example, hearts, clubs, diamonds, and spades. Thus, there is a king of hearts, a king of clubs, a king of diamonds, and a king of spades. Similarly, cultural institutions (government, religion, family, etc.) can be crossed with cultures (Hopi, Winnebago, Roman, modern English, etc.) In subclassification, this is not the case. For example, the distinction among hearts, clubs, diamonds, and spades applies to suits but not to values, just as the characteristics flowering-nonflowering apply to plants but not to animals, and the techniques of analysis and binding apply to organization but not to repetition. You will find, when you have more than five classes to learn, that subclassification will more frequently be the technique you can use to extend your classification system beyond five. However, when cross-classification is possible, it is a very powerful technique.

BIND

The second ABC rule for organizing material is to bind the pieces together. Whereas analysis reduces the amount of material to be taken in in each mental glance, binding puts the pieces together by means of images, word associations, or rules. Images, word associations, and rules seem to involve different mechanisms, and we shall take them up separately.

Imaging was the second of the techniques demonstrated

at the beginning of this chapter. Virtually all memory experts seem to make extensive use of imagery. Harry Lorayne says, "If I can't form an image of it, I can't remember it." The effectiveness of imagery as a mnemonic technique seems to have been first noted by the Greek poet Simonides (Yates, 1966). He discovered the technique when he was asked, as the only person to escape death when the roof fell in at a banquet, to identify the bodies of the others. Though the bodies had been crushed beyond recognition, he found that he was able to identify them on the basis of their positions around the table. He generalized the technique and suggested that one could remember items by forming images of them and mentally placing the images in different locations. The technique was adopted by Greek, and later Roman, orators, who remembered the major points in their speeches by generating images for them and mentally locating the images around the room. It may have been this practice that gave rise to the term "topics" for the major points in a presentation (*topos* being the Greek word for place) and to the phrases, "in the first place," "in the second place," etc. This method is now called the loci system, because it deals with locations. One variation is known as Galton's walk: Galton's suggestion was to take an imaginary walk down a familiar path and mentally locate the items to be remembered along the walk. This was the specific imagery technique demonstrated at the beginning of the chapter. It helps to have a "walk" worked out in advance with definite places in which to put the images.

Another system that makes use of images to aid recall is the peg-word system. To use this system, you must first have learned a list of peg-words, words that are in themselves easy to remember and that are easy to generate images for. Perhaps the best known such list is the following:

> One is a bun.
> Two is a shoe.

Three is a tree.
Four is a door.
Five is a hive.
Six is sticks.
Seven is heaven.
Eight is a gate.
Nine is a line.
Ten is a hen.

Learning this scheme is made easy by the fact that the paired terms rhyme and by the fact that you probably already know half of the paired terms from the nursery rhyme that begins, "One, two, buckle my shoe; three, four, open the door. . . ."

With this scheme in mind, you can now easily commit to memory a list of ten items. Let us consider the words "moon" and "eyeglasses" as though they were the first two items on such a list. "Moon" is the first item, so an image of a moon has to be integrated into the same image with an image of a bun. You could imagine a full moon sandwiched between two halves of a bun, perhaps with an astronaut cracking his teeth on it.

The next item is "eyeglasses," and the next position in the plan is, "Two is a shoe." A pair of eyeglasses and a shoe must be integrated into the same image. Perhaps a wise-looking old wrinkled shoe with gold-rimmed spectacles will do the job, or a high-heeled shoe with curvaceous glasses, or a tennis shoe with sunglasses, or a military boot with a mona-cle. Coding the same thing in many ways increases the prob-ability that at least one of the retrieval mechanisms will suc-ceed.

Once you have coded a list in this fashion—and it is surprisingly easy to do—you can then read off all the items backward or forward, or, if you really want to impress your friends, you can read off the odd-numbered items in for-ward order and the even-numbered items in reverse order. Both Galton's walk and the peg-word system enable you to learn items in a specified order, but only the peg-word system enables you to enter the sequence easily at a specified, numbered place.

It is important that the images be interacting, active, and vivid. Making the two terms interact with one another will strengthen the link (Asch, Ceraso, and Heimer, 1960; Bower, 1970; Neisser and Kerr, 1973.) For example, rather than simply placing an axe next to a door, have it sticking in the door. You should also put movement into the image if you can—even better than an axe sticking in the door would be an axe actively chopping a hole in the door. Finally, you should make the image vivid, imagining that it is right before you in detail (Bower, 1972; Anderson and Hiddle, 1971)— hear the sound of the axe as it thunks into the wood, see the wood split and the chips fly. Added detail will keep you from confusing the image with images of other objects. Avoid the error of the fellow described by Mark Twain who used the image of a Franklin stove to remember the name of a Mrs. Franklin and then greeted her, the next time he saw her, with, "What a nice surprise to see you again so soon, Mrs. Potbelly!"

To apply imagery to the contents of this chapter, you could think of the image of a book. On the outside, you can see the title, which represents the cue, to be discussed shortly. Inside, you can see the table of contents, which analyzes the contents of the book into classes and which is usually in out-line form, though sometimes in the form of a cross-classification. And, in the body of the book, you can see the material that binds the classes together: pictures, words, and rules. Because there is no conventional image for rules, we will have to make one up. Perhaps we could let equations stand for rules.

Though the one-is-a-bun kind of application of imagery makes a good stage demonstration and is useful for remem-bering shopping lists and other relatively arbitrary lists, it would not seem to be very useful for, for example, studying for an examination or committing a sales pitch or a talk to memory. A better way to apply the power of imagery to the task of learning meaningful materials would seem to be to organize the materials as much as possible around images that relate to the meaning of the material, such as graphs, diagrams, demonstrations, and even metaphors. For example, in studying for a psychology exam, you might relate the material to an information-flow diagram or a diagram of the brain. In learning the sales pitch for a product, you can often associate the various parts of the sales pitch with different visual features of the product itself. In learning history, you can mentally locate events on a map or a time line. And much of the material in this book, as we shall see, can be related to the decision-tree representation. Images are powerful, but for meaningful material there are more appropriate images than buns and shoes.

There are many devices for binding items together with familiar word associations. Acronyms use key letters to make up familiar words. For example, the letters in FACE represent the notes in the spaces on the musical scale, and similarly, SMART, ABC, and ROAD use familiar letter sequences to represent parts of this book and this chapter. Acrostics use key letters to make up the initial letters of words in phrases or sentences. For example, Every Good Boy Does Fine represents the notes on the lines in the musical scale. Rhymes make use of rhythmic structure and similarity of sound, as in, "A pint's a pound the world around," "Thirty days hath September, April, June, and November . . . ," and "One is a bun." Also, in the above mnemonics for the notes of the musical scale, "face" rhymes with "space," and "fine" rhymes with "line."

A word association technique that is particularly easy to use is the link or story system. In the link system you find associations to link successive items in a sequence, and in the story system you do this in a manner that generates a story. For example, you could remember the first list in this chapter with a story that begins, "There was a PEACH on the tree.

I knocked it off with a HAMMER, took it to CHURCH, and dropped it in the collection plate in exchange for an AP-PLE. . . ." The story will be even more effective if you develop imagery to go along with it, thus using associations and images redundantly. The link or story system can also be used in connection with either Galton's walk or the peg-word system.

Many other variations of the word association technique are also possible. For example, "Spring forward in the spring; fall back in the fall," reminds us to set our clocks ahead to daylight savings time in the spring and back to standard time in the fall. And, an example that we shall have occasion to return to, "Friday is the 9-to-5 drag in College, but I've got only 32 minutes to go," reminds us how to convert degrees Celsius to degrees Fahrenheit($F = 9/5 \; C + 32$).

The most sophisticated system for using word associations to aid memory is the phonetic system. The phonetic system can be used to remember numbers, words, or images. The basis of the phonetic system is the following table, which associates a consonant sound with each of the ten digits (Loisette, 1896). Note that what is associated with each digit is a sound or group of similar sounds, not a letter or group of visually similar letters.

1	t, d, th	"t" and "d" each have one downstroke
2	n	"n" has two downstrokes
3	m	"m" has three downstrokes
4	r	"r" is the last letter in "four"
5	l	"L" is the Roman numeral for 50; the hand with its thumb and fingers forms an "L"
6	j, sh, ch, soft g	reversed "j" resembles "6"
7	k, q, hard c, hard g	"k" is made up of two "7"s (⅄)
8	f, v, ph	script "f" resembles "8" (ƒ)

| 9 | b, p, | inverted "b" and backwards "p" resemble "9" |
| 0 | z, s, soft c | "z" is the first letter in "zero" |

One way to use the phonetic system is to remember numbers by coding them into sounds and then making up words from the sounds. For example, 233-3511, the telephone number for bus scheduling information in Portland, Oregon, can be coded as NUMB-MAMMAL-DIED. These words must then be held together in some way. An obvious way, in this case, would be to use the sentence, "The numb mammal died," which suggests the image of a fuzzy creature, lying all frozen, feet (and mammary glands) up, in the snow by a bus stop—"If only the poor creature had known the schedule!"

Another example is the "rule of 73": The number of years it takes an investment to double at X% interest compounded annually is equal to 73 divided by X. The difficulty is in remembering what number to divide by X. Using the phonetic system, we can code 73 as CoMpond, which is easy to remember, since the rule applies to compound interest.

It is not always so easy to make up sentences, however. Fortunately, the peg-word and loci systems provide alternatives that demand less creativity. To use the peg-word system, you would associate the first word with "bun," the second word with "shoe," and so forth. In the telephone number example, you might find it difficult to associate the adjective "numb" and the verb "died" in this manner and might want to change them to, perhaps, "name" or "gnome" and "toad," "tattoo," or "teeth." To use the loci system, of course, you would simply take Galton's walk and mentally place images of the words along the way.

The phonetic system can also be helpful for remembering items other than numbers. You can use it to code each of the numbers from 1 to 100 or beyond into words and then use these words as peg-words in an extended version of the one-is-a-bun scheme. In preparing such a list of peg-words, it would help to consult Higbee (1977, pp. 172–176), who has compiled a dictionary of words made up from two-digit numbers using the phonetic system.

(Just for the fun of it, there is a very impressive memory trick you can perform with the phonetic system. On one occasion, you assign a four-digit number to each of as many people as you want; then, on a later occasion—even years later—you tell each person what his or her number is. The trick (and it is a trick) is to use the phonetic system to make the numbers up from the first four consonant sounds in each person's name. Thus, Bob Jones would be given the number, 9962, and Mary Smith would be given the number, 3403. Of course, you have to know the people's names or arrange to be told their names, but that is usually not difficult.)

A convenient alternative to the phonetic system for remembering telephone numbers is the digit-to-letter code on the telephone dial. It has the advantage that you don't have to commit the code to memory, since it will be in external memory whenever you have to dial a number. You will have to make up a code for "Q" and "Z", however, since these aren't on the dial. If you used "0" and "1", which don't have any letters associated with them, you could let "Q" = "0" and "Z" = "1".

One final point should be made about coding numbers. It is a good idea to look at the number as a number before rushing to code it into speech sounds or letters. If the number is as meaningful as 445-1776 or 771-4321, it may be easy enough to remember it as is without going to any additional effort to add meaning to it.

Though applications of the word-association technique such as we have been discussing are useful for many purposes, they do not seem to be especially appropriate for meaningful material. It would seem more appropriate to recode meaningful material only into more familiar words and word sequences that retain the meaning of the material. This is what is meant by the phrase, "putting the material into your own words." Consider the following passage:

> It is not enough that a sensorial image be recognized when it reappears for it to constitute by itself an external object. Any subjective state can be recognized without being attributed to the action of objects independent of the ego. The newborn child who nurses recognizes the nipple by the combination of sucking and swallowing reflexes without making the nipple a thing. So also a month-old child can recognize certain visual images without, however, really exteriorizing them. What is the next condition necessary for the solidification of such images? It seems to us essential that the visual schemata be coordinated with other schemata of assimilation such as those of prehension, hearing, or sucking. They must, in other words, be organized in a universe (Piaget, 1952, pp. 74–75).

Putting this in your own words, you might come up with something like:

> Psychologically, an object is something that we know by more than one sense, for example, by sight and touch, by sight and hearing, or by hearing and touch.

The second version is easier to remember, not only because it is shorter, but also because it is more nearly in "plain English." Both the words and the grammatical constructions are more frequently encountered in everyday discourse. It is thus easier to form associations among the words and to understand and remember the sentences. Putting material in your own words, while it has less theatrical appeal than the other techniques, may be the most generally useful way to employ familiar word associations to bind ideas together.

Items can be bound together, not only by means of images and word associations, but also by means of rules. For example, you can remember the sequence 1–4–9–16–25–36– by noting that it consists of successive squares. And the phonetic system makes use, in addition to the digit-sound associations, of the rule "make each sound a sound in a word" or the rule "make each sound the sound at the beginning of a word." As another example, you can remember the driving times to a great many places simply by remembering certain key distances, inferring other distances by the rules of addition and subtraction and inferring driving times by employing the distance = rate × time rule.

Learning rules for constructing words from Greek, Latin, and Anglo-Saxon roots is an efficient way to add to your vocabulary (Grummel, 1961). The Greek root for "good" gives us "euphony," "euthanasia," and "eulogy," while the Latin root for "good" gives us "benefit," "benevolent," and "benediction." The Greek, Latin, and Anglo-Saxon words for "bad" give us, respectively, "dysfunction," "dyslexia," and "dispepsia"; "malaise," "malady," and "malapropism"; "miscreant," "misanthrope," and "misconstrue."

Relating classes by rules seems to be what we mean by understanding. When you understand material, you store just a portion of it and use the rules to infer the rest. It is a curious fact that, while material that is understood is better remembered than material that is not, virtually all memory books fail to stress its importance sufficiently.

Recall the formula for converting degrees Celsius to degrees Fahrenheit: $F = 9/5\ C + 32$. We could, as we saw earlier, remember this formula by means of the mnemonic, "Friday is the same 9-to-5 drag in College, but I've got only 32 minutes to go." Such mnemonics are what most memory books tend to suggest for any kind of material—meaningful, as well as meaningless. Certainly, when the material to be committed to memory is not amenable to understanding, such mnemonics are the techniques of choice. Yet much of what we have to learn can, fortunately, be understood. And, when understanding is possible, learning with understanding is almost always preferable to learning without it. Material that is understood is better remembered than material that is memorized, and material that is understood is also more readily applied creatively to new situations (Katona, 1940; Mayer and Greeno, 1972). (Material that is memorized can usually be retrieved more quickly, however; so, if speed is an important factor, memorization will generally be desirable instead of, or in addition to, learning by understanding.)

What understanding seems to involve is classification on the basis of substance, rather than appearance, and the relating of classes to one another by means of rules, rather than simply images or associations. You can understand the formula for converting degrees Celsius to degrees Fahrenheit by relating it, by means of rules, to some facts you probably already know. One very elementary fact is that scales like the Celsius and Fahrenheit scales consist essentially of just a zero point and a unit (which is repeated along the scale). Another fact, or set of facts, is that water freezes at 9 degrees Celsius and 32 degrees Fahrenheit and boils at 100 degrees Celsius and 212 degrees Fahrenheit.

(If you don't know the freezing and boiling points of water on the Fahrenheit scale, you will, of course, have to memorize them. Using the phonetic system, you could, for example, remember that the scale extends from the cold of a MiNe to the heat of a suNny DuNe. The "s" in "sunny" is a zero that does not affect the answer.)

To make a conversion from one such scale to another, then, you must: (a) change the location of the zero point and (b) change the size of the unit. Let us begin with the size of the unit. While there are only 100 degrees Celsius between freezing and boiling ($100 - 0 = 100$), there are 180 degrees Fahrenheit between these same two points ($212 - 32 = 180$). There are more Fahrenheit degrees than Celsius degrees between any two points; so, in going from Celsius to Fahrenheit you have to increase the number of degrees. This you do by multiplying the temperature in Celsius by 180/100, or 9/5. (Now you *understand* where the 9/5 comes from!)

Next, you have to change the zero point. While the zero point for the Celsius scale is at the freezing point of water, the zero point for the Fahrenheit scale is 32 degrees below this. The Fahrenheit scale has already gotten up to 32 degrees by this point and is thus 32 Fahrenheit degrees "ahead" of the Celsius scale. So, in going from Celsius to Fahrenheit, you have to add 32 degrees to the result of the first calculation. (Now you understand where the 32 comes from.)

(Note that these 32 degrees you add are Fahrenheit degrees. Because Fahrenheit degrees can be added only to Fahrenheit degrees, and not to Celsius degrees, you must perform step one before step two in going from Celsius to Fahrenheit. For the same reason, in going from Fahrenheit to Celsius, you must reverse the order, subtracting the 32 degrees and then multiplying, though by 5/9 this time, instead of 9/5.)

Thus, if you know that all there is to such scales is zero points and units, and if you know what the freezing and boiling points of water are in each system, you already know, in a sense, how to convert from one system to another. All you have to do is connect these pieces of information by rules, such as: If you are going to a scale with a lower zero point, you add the difference between the zero points (being careful to add like units).

Though the "9-to-5 drag" mnemonic is undoubtedly easier to remember than the equation, you do not actually have to remember either the equation or the mnemonic. Moreover, once you understand how to get from Celsius to Fahrenheit, you can easily figure out procedures for converting between other such scales, something the "9-to-5 drag" mnemonic can give you no help with. Though understanding often takes more time initially, in the long run it gives you more for less. You will add less material to memory, but it will be better remembered and can be used creatively in a wider variety of situations. Even in learning how to improve your memory, you will be better off if you try to understand the principles involved in analysis, binding, cueing, and so forth than if you simply memorize a few mnemonic techniques. Though images and associations can add useful redundancy to rules, where you have a choice it is usually best to use rules to get you from one item in memory to another. We shall consider rules and reasoning with rules in the next chapter.

CUE

Cueing is a matter of providing yourself with prompts in the environment to help you recall material. The old string-on-the-finger technique illustrates cueing. Tying a string on your finger (or turning your wrist watch around backwards or putting your keys in a different pocket or a ring on a different finger) prepares a novel stimulus that you are sure to think about during the day and that you have associated with the material to be remembered (calling someone, buying something, etc). The basic idea is to associate the material to be remembered with a stimulus that will be present at the time of recall.

In recalling names, a stimulus that will usually be present when you have to recall a person's name is the person, himself. By associating the person's name with his or her appearance, you provide yourself with a cue for recall. A point that is generally important in cueing and particularly important here is to attend carefully to the distinguishing features of the stimulus. It is important that you clearly distinguish the cueing stimulus from other stimuli, because confusion, or interference, among cueing stimuli may well be the most common cause of forgetting (Tulving, 1974; Feigenbaum, 1959). (Remember Mrs. Potbelly!)

In remembering names, attending to the distinguishing features of the stimulus means picking out the most salient aspects of the person's appearance and associating his name with these. For example, if a person's name is Shirley and she is fat, think of how "surely" she could hold down the end of a rope in a tug-of-war. Or, if she is tall, think of how "surely" she could make stuff shots in basketball. Since many people are fat, or tall, you should also work other features into your mnemonic. If our fat Shirley also has frizzy hair, you might think of how she resembles the frayed end of the rope that she is holding down in the tug-of-war. (You might also think Shirley-curley.) Attending to the distinguishing features of the stimulus provides constraints for later memory search.

In addition to the features of the stimulus itself, you can also use features of the context in which the stimulus occurs to help distinguish it from other cueing stimuli. If you are studying two confusingly similar subjects, say, French and Spanish, study them in different places and at different times, perhaps even using posters of France and Spain to enhance the distinction.

It is also helpful during information retrieval to think about the context or contexts associated with the material you are trying to recall. In trying to recall a person's name, for example, think about where you last heard his name and what you were doing. In trying to recall the answer to an exam question, think about your place of study and what the text looks like, or about the professor's voice and manner of lecturing, or about material in related parts of the course.

You can also use context to help activate attitudes and methods conducive to effective work, such as studying, by having a special place and time for work. Establishing distinctive cues will reduce the time it takes to "warm up" to work and increase the length of time that you will be able to maintain concentration. In establishing such cues, it is advisable to start with short work sessions and lengthen them gradually, however, so that you will not fatigue and start daydreaming in the presence of these cues.

What we are talking about in this section has also been called external memory (Newell and Simon, 1972). Often our environment does much of our remembering for us. For example, a half-painted wall tells us where to take up again after an interruption, and the sound of running water reminds us that we have not turned off the faucet. Even when our environment is not disposed to do any remembering for us, we can arrange things so that it will. One way we can do this, of course, is by writing things down. Writing is a form of external memory. "Writing" can be done in many different ways, however, limited only by your imagination. Put your briefcase by the door, so you'll remember to take it with you when you leave; put all the ingredients for a recipe on the table and put them away as you use them, so their presence on the table will remind you that you have not yet added them to the recipe; leave the hood up when you are changing the oil in your car to remind yourself to add the new oil; put your alarm clock on the floor to remind yourself of something you think of while lying in bed and want to remember in the morning.

The idea is simply to make a noticeable change in your environment and to associate it with the material to be remembered. In doing this, it is important to arrange the environment so the cue is easy to see, for example, in the middle of a clear area and against a contrasting background, and so that it is in a place where you habitually look, for example, by the door or on your coat or on the mirror or basin you will use to wash up in the morning. It may be that the most helpful technique for improving your "memory" is not to use your own memory so much as to use the environment to remember things for you. The next time you have to remember something, try asking yourself, not "How can I remember this?" but, "Where can I put something that will remind me of this?"

The following words from *Through the Looking Glass* make the point in a way only Lewis Carroll could:

> "The horror of that moment," the King went on, "I shall never, *never* forget."
>
> "You will, though," the Queen said, "If you don't make a memorandum of it."

In addition to arranging cues, you can also make use of naturally occurring cues by associating what you have to remember with images of scenes in which you might have to recall it. To remember an intention, imagine the situation in which you will have to carry it out and vividly imagine yourself carrying it out or imagine something associated with the intention. If you have to buy some soap on your way to the gym, imagine yourself walking to the gym and then turning off to go to the drug store, or imagine yourself walking into the gym and seeing a huge bar of soap there. To remember where you are putting something, imagine yourself wanting to find it and then looking in the place where you are now putting it. To be able to remember the trail back to camp, look back everytime you come to a junction. To remember conceptual material, ask yourself questions that the material answers—when you are searching your memory for conceptual material, you will most likely be doing so with a question in mind, and it will help if that question has already been established as a cue for recall.

To apply the cueing principle to learning this chapter, you should take the time to think of situations when you could use this material. If you plan to test yourself at the end of the chapter, you should imagine having finished the chapter and vividly imagine yourself recalling ABC ROAD and its various parts in this context. More important cues would be the image of yourself studying for an exam, reading or hearing some material (a fact, a name, a procedure, a joke) and wanting to remember it, preparing a talk that you want to remember and make memorable to your listeners, putting an object down or parking a car and wanting to remember where you left it, or intending to do something on some later occasion. It should pay you to take the time now to imagine in a vivid, active, and interacting way such scenes and your thinking of the ABC ROAD techniques in those scenes.

ABC is the first part of the plan for efficient information storage. ROAD is the second. What we have so carefully organized must now be committed to memory by a strengthening process. Even very clever mnemonics can be forgotten if not repeated sufficiently, a point that is seldom made in discussions of memory techniques. "What you don't use you lose!"

So you should go over the ABC points we have already discussed, recalling that A means to analyze, B to bind, and C to cue. You should recall that analysis means to look over the material and to break it down into no more than five classes, subclassifying or cross-classifying if more than five are needed. You should recall that binding means to put the pieces together by having them interact in vivid, active images, by tying them together with familiar word associations, by understanding their relationships in terms of rules, or preferably, by more than one of these methods redundantly. And you should recall that cueing means associating the materials with some object in the environment, either one that you have arranged or one that occurs naturally, that will be present at the time of recall, attending carefully to its distinguishing features.

Repetition is not so much fun as organizing, but, fortunately, there are three techniques that can increase its effectiveness. These are the OAD part of ROAD: overlearn, actively recall, and distribute practice.

OVERLEARN

Overlearning means to continue repetition beyond the point at which you are no longer making any errors. What is not well known is that repetition beyond this point is not wasted but continues to strengthen associations and to increase resistance to forgetting (Ebbinghaus, 1913). When Albert Schweitzer gave medications to his natives, he had them repeat back the instructions correctly several times before letting them leave with the medicine. Of particular importance is the fact (Norman, 1976, pp. 63–65) that material that has been overlearned is less likely to be forgotten under stress, as in taking an examination or giving a presentation.

ACTIVELY RECALL

Actively recalling is to be contrasted with what seems to be the most common method of study, simply reexposing yourself to the material, by looking over your notes or rereading the text. In active recall you close your notes and your book, and you attempt to recall the material on your own. What you have done in using the ABC techniques to organize the material is to construct a plan for retrieving the information you are interested in. What you must do in repetition is to practice and strengthen the plan itself, and this you can do only by actively using it. An additional positive feature of active recall is that you get very clear feedback on your progress. You find out what parts of the material you know and what parts you don't know and, hence, where to direct your further efforts.

So we might at this point ask you again to recall the mnemonic for this chapter and to decode it into its full meaning. Go back and check your recall against what is in the chapter, and continue repetition until all the important gaps have been filled. In doing so, distribute your practice.

DISTRIBUTE PRACTICE

Distributing practice is the only memory technique that can give you something for nothing. It is one of the two techniques for improving thinking that relies entirely on automato be contrasted with massed practice. Whereas in massed practice you repeat the material again and again with each repetition following immediately upon the one before, in distributed practice you allow a period of rest between practice sessions. This period of rest presumably allows a physiological process of memory consolidation that is initiated by each practice session to run to completion before the next practice session is begun (McGaugh and Herz, 1972.) Whatever the correct explanation, distributed practice enables you to get more out of each practice session. The breaks apparently do not need to be overly long; in some cases, two to three minutes have been shown to produce maximal effects.

At this point, you might want to test yourself to see how much of the chapter you can recall. Even if you did not try to apply the techniques as you read, you will find that you will be able to recall a surprising amount of the material because, to a considerable extent, the techniques were applied for you.

In reading the next chapter, you might want to practice applying the techniques of this chapter. In fact, why not make this book the first book to which you apply your newly learned techniques? The SMART mnemonic gives you a good start. Begin by looking over the next chapter to get an overview and to analyze it into its major parts. Try to understand how the parts are meaningfully related. Supplement rules by images, particularly the image of a decision tree, and by associations, putting the material into your own words. Ask questions that the material answers. Review each section as you finish it, and review the chapter at the end.

In this chapter, we have seen how to store information in memory. In the next chapter, we will begin to see how to put this information to use in thinking.

RECOMMENDED READING

HIGBEE, K. L., *Your Memory: How It Works and How to Improve It.* Englewood Cliffs, N.J.: Prentice-Hall, 1977.

3

Reasoning

Reasoning is simply a matter of getting your facts straight. And facts are important. This is suggested by the amount of money individuals spend for education, communities spend for schools and libraries, companies spend for research, and governments spend for intelligence operations. It is also suggested by the increasing tendency for individuals to consult consumer publications before making purchases and voting records before going to the polls.

Sometimes facts solve our problems for us directly. If you learn that the brown spots on your lawn were caused by using too much fertilizer, you know immediately what to do to avoid brown spots in the future. If you know that using high-wattage bulbs in your ceiling fixtures is what caused the insulation to dry and crack, you know right away what to do to keep this from happening again. If you find that the reason you have not gotten the phone call you have been waiting for is that the phone has been off the hook, you know immediately what to do to correct the situation. These are examples of what we earlier called problems in explanation.

In other cases facts are not sufficient to solve our problems directly, but they are nevertheless vital in helping us to get ideas for solving them. If your child says he "hears voices," you might think of taking him in for a psychological examination. But the fact, which you discover on further questioning, that he hears these "voices" in only one ear suggests that the problem is audiological, not psychological. If you are thinking of opening a coffee shop, a knowledge of what areas in town have been developing most rapidly might provide a good starting point for getting ideas. For example, the fact that an area of antique shops has been developing rapidly might lead you to think of opening an early American coffee shop there. Facts, as we shall see in later chapters, also help you to get rid of ideas. For example, the facts that small shops usually operate on a narrow margin of profit and that the probability of their failing is quite high might lead you to discard any plan for a coffee shop that does not provide substantial assurance of success.

We get facts from three sources: external memory, our own memories, and reasoning. We get facts from external memory when we consult people and read books. As we saw in the last chapter, we are continually getting and using facts from our own memories. We get facts by reasoning when we think about the facts we already know. Reasoning can extend our knowledge greatly. We use it far more often than we are aware—though not nearly so often as we should.

To illustrate the way reasoning works, let us say that you remember the following facts:

Today, you congratulated Connie on her high student ratings, but she shrugged the compliment off with the reply that students tend to be generous in their ratings.

A week ago, you heard a colleague tell Connie that he thought her research was very interesting, but she commented to you, after he had left, that he didn't know the area well enough to make an informed judgment.

And, some time ago, Connie received a letter from the dean, expressing his appreciation for the fine job she had done in chairing a university committee, but she remarked that he probably sent the same letter to the chairpersons of all committees.

Up to this point, these have existed in your mind simply as isolated facts, but now you have started thinking about them, and it occurs to you that these incidents may reflect a general tendency in Connie to be suspicious of compliments. This is inductive reasoning, reasoning from a number of observations to a general statement.

You think further, and you remember from psychology that people who are suspicious of compliments tend to be low in self-esteem. From the statement that, if a person is suspicious of compliments, he is likely to be low in self-esteem and the statement that Connie seems to be suspicious of compliments, you reason that Connie is likely to be low in self-esteem. This is deductive reasoning, reasoning from statements to other statements.

By means of further deductive reasoning, you continue to elaborate the picture. You also remember from psychology that people who are low in self-esteem have a greater need to be liked and are more easily persuaded than others. So you also conclude tentatively that Connie may have these characteristics as well.

Finally, you search your memory to see whether you can recall any observations against which to test these hypotheses by further inductive reasoning. You remember that Connie rarely misses Friday beers—and, now that you think of it, is often the first to check to see whether people are going out for beers—and you remember that she tends to be very complimentary to others. These behaviors suggest a need to be liked.

However, you don't remember anything that bears on the hypothesis of susceptibility to persuasion. Since you don't recall any observations relevant to this hypothesis, you set it aside, possibly to test against direct observations in the future.

We use reason not only, as in the above example, to add to our store of facts by deriving new facts from old, but also to evaluate statements of presumed fact that we hear or read to see whether they are "reasonable," that is, whether they follow closely from the reasons given for believing them. Because facts are important in our thinking, it is important that what we take to be facts are indeed factually correct. Correct statements of fact are, of course, more likely to help us get ideas that will prove in the long run to be good and to get rid of ideas that would have proven in the long run to be bad.

Determining the truth or falsity of statements of fact requires very close thinking. It is such close thinking that we call critical thinking, or reasoning. Critical thinking is to be contrasted with creative thinking, which, as we shall see in the next chapter, is a more loose, associative process. Creative thinking is concerned with conceiving of what may be possible; critical thinking is concerned with determining which possibilities are probable and which improbable. Our present concern is with critical thinking, of both an inductive and a deductive nature.

In the next section, we shall consider attitudes that seem to be important to critical thinking. Then, in the section after that, we shall see what kinds of facts there are to think critically about. Finally, in the bulk of the chapter, we shall consider, first for inductive reasoning and then for deductive reasoning, (a) requirements for sound reasoning, (b) common errors in reasoning, and (c) techniques that can help us to overcome the errors and satisfy the requirements.

Attitudes have to do not so much with what we do as with what we want and how we feel, what we consider good and what we consider bad. Attitudes, as well as methods, seem to be important for both critical and creative thinking. Both critical thinking (Watson and Glaser, 1952, p. 9) and creative thinking (Barron, 1965, pp. 67–70) seem to require something in addition to general intelligence. This additional ingredient certainly consists in part of specific methods, but it seems likely that it is in large part also a matter of attitudes. The importance of attitudes has been well documented for creative thinking, as we shall see in the next chapter, and it seems a fair guess that attitudes are important for critical thinking as well. Just as creative thinkers want to be creative, critical thinkers, it seems, want to be critical, or at least to be certain.

Yet the critical attitude and the creative attiude seem to be poles apart. One fact that suggests this is that many people seem to develop the capacity for just one of these attitudes. On the one hand, there are those who are always telling you why ideas won't work but who never seem able to come up with alternatives of their own; and, on the other, there are those who are constantly coming up with ideas but seem unable to tell the good from the bad.

There are people in whom both attitudes are developed to a high degree (and there seems to be no reason to believe that we are not all capable of developing both attitudes), but even these people say that they assume only one of these attitudes at a time (see Wallas, 1926; Osborn, 1963; Gordon, 1961). When new ideas are needed, they put on their creative caps, and, when ideas need to be evaluated, they put on their critical caps. This fact, too, suggests that these two attitudes are different—as different, it seems, as certainty and adventure, destroying and building, stop and go.

In the next chapter, much will be said about the creative attitude, and all that will be said will be based on research evidence. The attitudes that are important in critical thinking seem to have received little if any research attention, however, and so this section will be brief, and what little it contains can be only speculative.

The central ingredient in the critical attitude seems to be doubt, a reluctance to believe. It seems to be difficult for people to doubt. This may be because doubt is a matter of effortful processes resisting automatic processes of interpretation. As Sir Francis Bacon (1620) said:

> The human understanding is of its own nature prone to suppose the existence of more order and regularity in the world than it finds (and) when it has once adopted an opinion, draws all else to support and agree with it.

More recently, and in a more down-to-earth way, Artemus Ward has said much the same thing:

> It ain't so much the things we don't know that get us into trouble. It's the things we know that ain't so.

A widespread institutionalization of doubt is the so-called "devil's advocate." When the Catholic Church is deciding whether a person should be considered a saint, it appoints a person, the Devil's Advocate, to present the case against canonization. The practice of assigning a person or group of persons specifically to argue against the prevailing opinion has been found by many organizations to be a valuable one and has been recommended (Janis, 1972) as a corrective for groupthink (see p. 90).

Doubt should express itself in at least two ways: a reluctance to believe that you have taken all the important elements of the problem into account and a reluctance to believe that you have understood correctly the way in which the elements are related to one another. The importance of taking all the essential elements of the problem into account is illustrated by the following poem (Gardner, 1969):

> There once was a horse
> That won great fame.
> What-do-you-think
> Was the horse's name.

If you are having difficulty, it is because you have not taken all the important elements into account. Reread the poem slowly, attending carefully to each element. The solution hinges on the fact that there is no question mark at the end of the second sentence and the fact that there are hyphens between "what," "do," "you," and "think." The second sentence is not a question, at all; it simply says that the horse's name was What-do-you-think!

The importance of understanding correctly the way in which the elements are related to one another is illustrated by the following problem.

> What is the area of a figure that is 100 feet on one side, 50 feet on the side opposite, and 25 feet on each of the two remaining sides?

If you think that you don't remember enough geometry to solve this problem, you are wrong. Geometrically, the problem is very simple. Though you are taking all the important elements into account—the four sides and their lengths—you are probably not understanding correctly the way in which they are related to one another. Your understanding probably agrees fairly well with this figure.

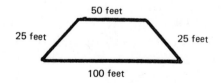

This figure is not drawn carefully enough, however. Try drawing it to scale. (Using a ruler, make the 100-foot side, say, 10 units long, the 50-foot side 5 units long, and each of the 25-foot sides 2½ units long.) If you do so, you will quickly discover that the 25, 50, and 25 add up to 100; that is, the sum of the three short sides equals the long side, and the figure is simply a line with no area, at all!

What we are talking about here is comprehension. Comprehension has been found to be important for success in many fields (Guilford and Hoepfner, 1971) and would seem to be important for success in nearly all fields. More specifically, what we are talking about is not jumping to conclusions in comprehending information, about doubting whether we have taken account, and proper account, of all the essentials.

Supposedly, Adam Smith spent more than twenty-five years preparing his monumental work on capitalism, and Albert Einstein spent some twenty years thinking about relativity before publishing his first paper on the subject. Charles Darwin (1909, p. 21), commenting on his own work on natural selection, said, "After five years' work, I allowed myself to speculate on the subject." And Montaigne said in one place (*Essays* III.13, p. 521), "I learn to suspect my steps throughout, and am careful to place them right," and in another, "Suspend judgment."

What the critical attitude seems to say is, "Stop!" It seems to tell us not to jump to conclusions without sufficient evidence. It seems to tell us to try to destroy arguments, to test their certainty by trying to tear them apart, much as manufactured products are often tested in quality control before being placed on the market.

KINDS OF FACTS

A fact is a statement about the world and, moreover, one that corresponds to the world. "Most automobiles are gasoline powered," and "Most people are Christians" are both statements about the world, but the first is a fact, and the second is not. We shall be concerned with three fundamental categories of statements about the world: statements of probability, statements of conditional probability, and statements of relationship. Furthermore, we shall distinguish between two kinds of statements of relationship: statements of predictive relationship and statements of causal relationship. Let us begin with probabilities.

Probabilities

We frequently make statements using the words "all," "some," and "no," as in, "All pomegranates have seeds," "Some M.D.'s also hold the Ph.D.," and, "No fine restaurant cooks with electric heat."

For a number of reasons that will soon become apparent, we shall find it more convenient to replace such terms with proportions or probabilities. The probability (symbolized by p) of an event is its likelihood of occurring. Probabilities are expressed in decimal fractions, ranging from 0 to 1.00, which indicate the proportion of possible occasions on which the event is in fact expected to occur. An event with a p of 0 is one that has no chance of occurring; one with a p of 1.00 is one that is certain to occur; and one with a p of .50 is one that is expected to occur half the time, that is, is as likely to occur as not. The p of getting heads in tossing a coin, for example, is $\frac{1}{2}$ or .50, and the p of a given face of a die coming up is $\frac{1}{6}$ or .17. The most direct way of determining the probability of an event occurring in the future is to determine the proportion of occasions on which it has occurred in the past. Thus, we might say, "100% of pomegranates have seeds," or "The probability that a pomegranate will have seeds is 1.00."

Statements of probability are easily represented in terms of decision trees. (When just event nodes are represented, these are usually called "logic trees" or "probability trees," but since our interest is in eventually applying probabilities to practical decisions, we shall continue to use the term "decision tree.") Let us return to the example of the early American coffee shop, and let us say that you have learned that 40% of coffee shops are successful. Taking just this information into account, you would estimate the probability that your coffee shop will be successful to be .40. In terms of a decision tree, this would be represented as:

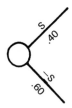

Probabilities always attach to event nodes and never to act nodes. Act nodes represent what we have control over, and event nodes represent what we can only predict. Eventually, probabilities must be attached to the branches of every event node in a decision tree. Note that the probabilities attached to the branches of the event node above add up to 1.00. This is no accident. *The probabilities attached to the various branches of any event node must add up to 1.00.* In technical language, the branches at an event node "partition" the possibilities. In plain English, this means that they divide them up like the pieces of a pie. Just as the pieces of a pie must add up to the whole pie, the probabilities attached to the various branches of an event node must add up to 1.00. (You will note that for event nodes with only two branches we always use a label for one branch and the same label with a minus sign before it for the other branch. This assures that we have a partition. The label refers to a particular part of the pie, and the same label with a minus sign before it simply refers to all the rest of the pie.)

Conditional Probabilities

A conditional probability is an "if . . . then" statement (see Wason and Johnson-Laird, 1972, pp. 89ff). (Logicians use "if . . . then" statements differently, but even they are not agreed that it is desirable to do so.) Because there are so many ways of saying "if . . . then" in English, and because the most difficult thing about using trees seems to be translating English statements into tree representations, we list below a number of English equivalents to "if . . . then":

> If A, then B.
> If not A, then not B.
> Given that A, it follows that B.
> Not A, unless B.
> As long as A, B.
> A implies B.
> A only if B.
> Whenever A, B.
> A is a sufficient condition for B.
> B is a necessary condition for A.
> All A are B.
> No A are not B.
>
> *Note:* "A if and only if B" and "A is a necessary and sufficient condition for B" each translate into two statements: "If A, then B" and "If B, then A."

The conditional probability of an event is the likelihood of its occurring given that certain conditions hold. For example, you might be told that, if a coffee shop makes it through the first year, then its p of success will be .70. This would be represented in decision tree terms as follows:

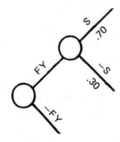

No p's have been attached to the "FY" (first year) and "$-$FY" (not first year) branches, because we do not know the probability that a coffee shop will make it through the first year. We would have to have this information, however, before we could use the conditional p to make any prediction before the first year was up. We shall return to this problem.

Predictive Relationships

Let us say that you have heard that a certain consultant will, for a fee, tell you what the chances are of your business succeeding. And let us say that you have heard further that, of those businesses for which this consultant has predicted success, 60% have turned out to be successful. Should you hire the consultant and pay for his estimate?

Well, that depends, of course, on how much the information will cost. We shall take this and related matters up in a later chapter. But it also depends on how much information you can expect to get. This is our present concern, and yet we do not even know this.

All that we have been told is that, when the consultant predicts success, the p of success is .60. This is simply a conditional probability. We need more than this. Before we can say whether the consultant is any good, we also need to know the conditional probability of success given that he has predicted failure. Let us say that this is .30. Then the information we have would be represented in decision tree terms as:

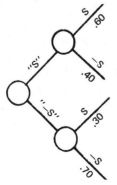

There is a difference between the p of success when the consultant predicts success ("S") and the p of success when he predicts no success ("−S"). In this case, we say that there is a relationship between what the consultant says and what happens. (Again, we have not attached p's to the "S" and "−S" branches. We shall see later how to do this.)

By way of comparison with the above, consider the following two possibilities:

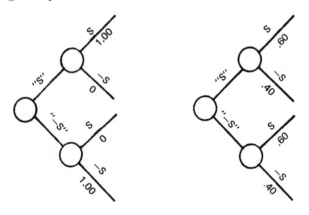

In the example on the left, when success is predicted, success occurs with a p of 1.00; and, when no success is predicted, the p of success is 0. You couldn't ask for more accurate prediction. In this case, we say that the relationship is perfect. In the example on the right, by way of contrast, the p of success is exactly the same when success is predicted and when no success is predicted. The prediction is utterly worthless, and we say that there is no relationship between the predictor and the outcome.

One of the trees below illustrates a common error in using a tree to represent a relationship. Can you tell which of these trees correctly represents the relationship between how a coin comes up on the first toss and how it comes up on the second toss?

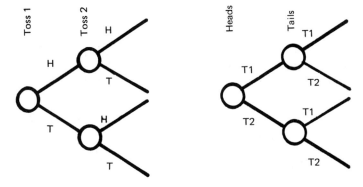

The first tree is correct, and the second is incorrect. Remember that an event node represents a question and its branches, possible answers. The questions here are how the coins will come up, and the possible answers are heads and tails. What the incorrect tree says is that the questions are whether Toss 1 or Toss 2 will yield heads and whether Toss 1 or Toss 2 will yield tails. But neither of these event nodes takes account of all the possibilities. Some of the "pie" is missing. The answer to the question as to which toss will yield heads could be Toss 1, Toss 2, or both, or neither!

Why are we interested in predictive relationships? If you are asked to estimate the probability of rain, you will look at the sky, for whether the sky is cloudy or not tells you whether it is likely or unlikely to rain. You base your estimate on the condition of the sky, because—though you may not have thought about it this way—you believe that there is a relationship between cloudiness and rain.

But let us say that you are faced with a predictor with which you have had no experience. Let us say that you are hiring for a management position and that each applicant has a score on a new Management Aptitude Test. How much weight, if any, should you give these scores in trying to predict probability of success on the job? You can't answer that

question without knowing the degree of relationship between test score and success. You won't want to put much
weight on these scores unless (a) a fairly high proportion of
people with high test scores and (b) a fairly low proportion of
people with low test scores have been successful on the job in
the past. Since you yourself have not had any experience
with this prediction, you will have to rely on the experience
of others, preferably researchers, and their experience will
be communicated to you in the form of statements of predictive relationship.

Statements of predictive relationship, in addition to
helping us to decide how much weight to place on information that we have, also help us to decide how much we should
be willing to pay, in time or effort, for information that we do
not have. If a management consulting firm tried to sell you
the Management Aptitude Test, the first thing you should
ask is what the relationship is between scores on the test and
some reasonable criterion of success on the job.

Causal Relationships

Fanning a fire to get it started provides a simple example of a
causal relationship. The probability that a fire will catch and
continue to burn is greater when you fan it than when you do
not. Let us say that the p that the fire will burn is .9 when you
fan it and .5 when you do not. This can be represented in
decision tree terms as follows:

The initial node this time is an act node, rather than an event node. Each branch of the tree for a causal relationship says that, if you make a particular event occur, a second will occur with a certain probability; whereas each branch of the tree for a predictive relationship says that, if one event occurs on its own, a second event will occur with a certain probability. If the importance of this distinction is not obvious now, it should be abundantly so by the end of the chapter.

Causal relationships tell us what changes are worth making if we are interested in altering the probability of some event. People fan fires to increase the probability that they will continue to burn, use fishing lures to increase the probability of catching fish, and stop smoking to decrease the probability that they will develop heart or lung problems. To return to our example of the early American coffee shop, if you learned that eating establishments that include contemporary foods and music are more likely to be successful than those that do not, you might consider these features in your coffee shop as a means of increasing the probability that it will be successful.

Causal analysis tells us what factors are creating our problem and what factors we can change to solve it. A high school teacher who wanted to put on a successful school dance asked himself what factors kept some students from attending the usual school dances. One possibility he thought of was that they were reluctant to ask dates. So he made the dance stag. Another was that they didn't have dressy clothes. So he made it a "come as you are" affair. Another was that they couldn't afford it. So he charged a ludicrously low admission fee. The result was that the dance turned out to be a great success.

The difference between predictive and causal relationships is important. There is a predictive relationship between car color and accident rate such that brightly colored cars are more likely to be involved in accidents. (Perhaps impulsive people prefer brightly colored cars and are also more likely

to get into accidents.) Yet the causal relationship most probably runs in the reverse direction. If a particular person paints
his car a brighter color, you would expect it to be more likely
to be seen and less likely to be involved in an accident.

Determining whether a relationship is predictive or
causal is not as simple as it might seem. The relationship
between the consultant's prediction and the success of a business, which we earlier considered as an example of a predictive relationship, could actually be causal, for example, if the
consultant is widely respected and his prediction is well pub-
licized. In such a case, it would make sense (logically, though
not ethically) to pay the consultant, not to give his honest
prediction, but specifically to predict success.

Conversely, the relationship between the inclusion of
contemporary foods and music and success, which we considered as an example of a causal relationship, could be
merely predictive. It could be, for example, that business
majors are more likely to prefer contemporary foods and
music, that those eating establishments that are run by
people with business degrees are more likely to include contemporary foods and music, and that the real cause of their
greater success is the business training their proprietors have
had. In such a case, the decision to add contemporary foods
and music to the offerings of an early American coffee shop
might not result in a greater probability of success.

We shall see how to decide whether a relationship is
predictive or causal in the next section, which will state the
rules for inductive reasoning, discuss the errors most commonly made in connection with these rules, and present
some techniques that can help you to avoid the errors and
satisfy the rules.

INDUCTIVE REASONING

Inductive reasoning moves from observations to statements.
Deductive reasoning, as we shall see later, moves from
statements to other statements. There are four basic rules for

TABLE 3-1.
Rules for Inductive Reasoning

1. Operational Definition
   To be clear in your use of words that make reference to the world, you must define them in terms of what you do to determine where they apply and where they do not.
2. Sampling
   To make an assertion about a class of objects or events, you must observe a sample of individuals from the class that is both adequate in size and unbiased.
3. Comparison
   Two make a statement of relationship, you must compare at least two classes on the predictor or causal variable.
4. Controlled Comparison
   To make a statement of causal relationship, the classes you compare on the causal variable must differ only with respect to the causal variable. Other variables must be controlled or randomized.

moving from observations to justifiable statements of fact. We shall call these: operational definition, sampling, comparison, and controlled comparison. They are summarized in Table 3-1.

The first two rules apply to all of the kinds of statements of fact that we have just considered; however, comparison applies only to statements of relationship, and controlled comparison applies only to statements of causal relationship. The applicability of each of the four rules to each of the four kinds of statement of fact is represented in the figure on page 80. We begin with these rules that apply in every case.

Operational Definition

To be clear in your use of words that make reference to the world, you define them in terms of the operations you would carry out to determine where they apply and where they do not.

A fact, as was said earlier, is a statement about the world. Because of this, it is important that the correspondence be-

	Probability	Conditional probability	Predictive relationship	Causal relationship
Operational definition	✓	✓	✓	✓
Sampling	✓	✓	✓	✓
Comparison			✓	✓
Controlled comparison				✓

tween key words in the statement and those parts of the world to which they refer be clearly established. This problem is more important with nouns, verbs, and modifiers than with other words, and it is more important with common nouns, which refer to classes of things, than with proper nouns, which refer to particular things. It is also more important with general terms, like "freedom" or "progress," than with more specific terms, like "population" or "gas mileage."

Consider the statement, "Radicals are dangerous." What is meant by a "radical"? What do you do (what observations do you make, what questions do you ask) to determine whether a particular person is or is not a radical? If you ask him simply whether he opposes our present system of government, that is one thing; if you ask him whether he advocates or employs the use of violence to overthrow our present system of government, that is quite another. And what is meant by "dangerous"? The dictionary tells us that it means "likely to cause harm," but what do we do to determine whether a particular event does or does not involve harm? Are we talking about harm to persons, harm to property, or harm to beliefs? The statement, "Radicals are dangerous," can be true or false, depending on the way in which these key terms are operationally defined.

Because it is not possible to establish the truth or falsity of a statement that has one or more terms that have not been operationally defined, such statements are called "untestable" statements. Astrologers, mind readers, and fortune tellers prefer untestable statements—for obvious reasons. Before deciding to go against the Persians, Alexander the Great, it is said, consulted the Oracle of Delphi. The Oracle told him that a great army would be defeated, and, on the basis of this statement, Alexander decided to go ahead with his plans for attack. The problem was that "great army" had not been clearly defined, and the great army that was defeated turned out to be Alexander's!

Some politicians are partial to untestable statements— and for similar reasons. When the Attorney General tells us that there were only so many wiretaps in a certain year, is he counting bugs (hidden microphones) or not? When a politician tells us that he advocates race policies that are "just and fair," what does this mean that he will do?

Some business people also frequently hide behind untestable statements. For example, automated check stands in grocery stores are claimed to be more "efficient." But, we must ask, "Efficient for whom? And over what time span?" They may be efficient for the producer, but (because of the absence of price tags) not for the consumer and (because of the loss of jobs) not for society. Similarly, the gasoline engine may be "efficient" in the short run, but not in the long run.

Only if a statement can be tested for truth or falsity can it possibly be of any aid in decision making. It is the real world that we need to know about in making decisions, not the world of words, for it is from the real world that the consequences of our decisions, favorable or unfavorable, come. It's the sticks and stones of reality that break bones, and operational definition keeps our words in touch with reality.

To return to our coffee shop example, we could define "success" in terms of profit and specify the operations involved in determining profit. But, while your operational definition of "profit" may be in terms of ready cash, the operational definition used by someone who is providing you with information about profit may include capital appreciation and even tax write-offs. You may later be disappointed to find that the "profit" correctly predicted by your consultant is not the "profit" you had in mind.

An amusing example of the kind of slippery reasoning that can occur if terms are not given consistent definitions is provided by the following argument:

> No cat has nine tails.
> My cat has one tail more than no cat.
> Therefore, my cat has ten tails!

Even the rules of deductive reasoning cannot guarantee that only true conclusions will be forthcoming from true premises, if the words are not given consistent meanings. The problem, of course, is that the meaning of "no cat" changed from the first to the second statement. This kind of change in meaning is easy to spot here, but it is more difficult to detect in a political argument, where a phrase like "public welfare" may be used one way at one time and quite another way some five minutes later.

In all the examples we have considered so far, the problem was that there was more than one operational definition for a given word. The complementary problem can also arise, that of having too many words for the same operational definition. Not only can words gloss over real differences, but they can also make distinctions where there are no real differences. What is "democracy" to one person may be "mob rule" to another; the operational definitions are the same, but the words are different. While I am "firm," you are "stubborn," and he is "pigheaded."

Having too many words for the same operational definition can give rise to circular statements. Consider the following example:

> There are ghosts in my house. You can hear them in faint rappings in the walls and swishings through the air. They appear only when the psychological conditions are favorable, however. You can tell when someone is present who creates unfavorable psychological conditions by the failure of the rappings and swishings to appear.

The statement is of the form, "If the psychological conditions are favorable, ghosts will appear." The operations you are to carry out to determine whether there are ghosts or not are to listen for rappings and swishings. If you do not hear rappings and swishings, you would ordinarily be inclined to think that there are no ghosts about, but we are told that this would be a correct conclusion only if the conditions are favorable for the appearance of the ghosts. The operations you are to carry out to determine whether the conditions are favorable are to listen for rappings and swishings. Since you do not hear rappings and swishings, you now conclude that it is not possible to tell whether there are ghosts about. The statement cannot be disproved! Whether there are, in fact, ghosts about or not, the statement stands inviolate. Because there is no conceivable world in which the statement would be false, the statement tells us nothing about the kind of world we are in. It is an unfortunate characteristic of human intelligence that it can so often be fooled into taking meaningless statements such as this as statements of fact.

To break the circularity of a statement, all you have to do is to provide different operational definitions for each of the key terms. In the example, "favorable psychological conditions" would have to be defined in terms of something other than rappings and swishings, perhaps in terms of statements of belief or skepticism on the part of the observers, who are presumed to create these conditions. If only believers are around and still no rappings and swishings occur that can be tape recorded for later observation by skeptical observers, one would presume the statement to be false.

All this can be said in terms of a decision tree. The following tree represents the statement of conditional probability that, if the conditions are favorable (F), ghosts will appear (G).

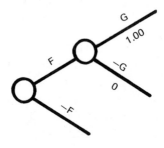

If the observations you make (listening for rappings and swishings) to determine which branch you are on at the first event node are the same as those (again, listening for rappings and swishings) to determine which branch you are on at the second event node, the statement is circular. If you go out the positive branch of the F node, you must necessarily go out the the positive branch of the G node; and, if you go out the negative branch of the F node, you must necessarily go out the negative branch of the G node. Only if the observations at these two points are different is the statement empirical, or testable.

An operational definition is a road sign. It tells us which way to branch at a node. The operational definition rule tells us to get our directions clear by asking, "What is he saying?" The remaining rules tell us to make sure the directions are correct by asking," "How does he know?"

Sampling

To make an assertion about a class of objects or events, you must observe a sample of individuals from that class that is both (a) sufficiently large and (b) unbiased.

Sample size. Once, relaxing on a rocky island beach and watching ants travel to and fro in a single line across a large rock, I began to wonder whether ants have a sense of direction and performed an informal experiment to find out. I removed an ant from the line by allowing it to crawl onto a leaf, rotated the leaf and ant 180 degrees, and then returned the ant to the line. The ant was now headed in the direction opposite to the one in which it had just been going. Would it continue in the new direction, or would it in some way sense that it was headed the wrong way and turn around?

At first, the ant seemed confused and wandered about in jerky exploratory movements. But then very quickly it headed off in the direction in which it had been originally traveling. "So," I said to myself, "ants do have a sense of direction." And I began to wonder whether it was based on the position of the sun, chemical cues laid down along the path, or tactual information gotten from the ants it was repeatedly touching feelers with.

It was not until later that I realized, with private embarrassment, that my sample consisted of only a single ant observed on a single occasion. Even if ants had no sense of direction at all, this one might have headed back in the original direction just by chance! To have done the experiment properly, I should have tested several more ants.

We all tend to be insensitive to sample size and, unless we have the sampling rule to help us, can easily fall into the trap of overgeneralizing from small samples. This is the kind of bias, for example, that would lead the public to have more confidence in a conclusion that was supported by all 3 out of a panel of 3 experts than by 10 out of a panel of 12 experts, even though the latter would be statistically more impressive (Tversky and Kahneman, 1971.) The tendency to jump to conclusions on the basis of small samples is at least one reason why first impressions are so important (Anderson and Hubert, 1963). One bad experience with a product, and we may never give it a second chance. One good first date, and we are inclined to think that this person is the person we have been waiting for. First impressions should be tempered with later impressions, for "one swallow doeth not a summer mayke."

An important way in which we often generalize from small samples is in generalizing from personal experience. When we generalize from our personal experience, as real as that may be to us, we are usually generalizing from a sample of one—ourself. The centenarian who claims that anyone who follows his diet will live longer is often making this error, as is the successful businessman who claims that anyone who adopts his philosophy of life will achieve influence and wealth.

We would not conclude from getting all heads on one or two tosses of a coin that the coin is unfair; we would insist on a larger sample. When dealing with more important matters, we should be all the more careful to insist on sufficiently large samples. The decision as to how large a sample is "large enough" is best made using statistical techniques that are, regrettably, beyond the scope of this discussion. However, although no entirely satisfactory simple answer can be given to the question "How large is large enough?" it can be said that a sample of one is never enough and, as a rule of thumb, samples of fewer than 25 are seldom sufficient. (For a more complete yet elementary, discussion of this matter, see Anderson, 1971, ch. 7.)

Related to insensitivity to sample size is insensitivity to base rate. Though the last ten days may have been sunny in both Oregon and New Mexico, you should estimate a higher probability of rain on the eleventh day in Oregon than in

New Mexico. The reason, of course, is that the base rate for rain is higher in Oregon, and your predictions should take into account, not only your current sample of data, but also the larger sample of base rate data. Usually, however, it seems that we give too little weight to base rate data—or neglect base rate data altogether (Kahneman and Tversky, 1973). When estimating probabilities, we should get in the habit of asking ourselves whether we know anything about any kind of base rate that can supplement case data and thus help us arrive at a more valid probability.

When estimating the probability that you will be successful in a particular job you are applying for, for example, don't just consider what you know about yourself, but also take into account the overall probability of success in that job. One way to take base rates into account is simply to adjust the base rate intuitively in the direction of the probability that you would estimate on the basis of the case data, adjusting it farther the more trustworthy your case data are. Though such an intuitive adjustment is certainly better than no adjustment for base rate at all, there is a better way, as we shall see later in this chapter.

Sample bias.   Having a sufficiently large sample is, by itself, no assurance that your observations can be generalized safely to the entire class. For a sample to represent the class from which it has been drawn, it must also have been drawn in an unbiased manner, that is, in a manner that gives every member of the class an equal chance of being included in the sample.

One problem is that our experience tends to be biased. The professor who deals day in and day out with people who are reasonable and of good will and the policeman who much more frequently deals with people who are irrational, self-seeking, or hateful develop different beliefs about human nature and, consequently, different beliefs about how to deal with social problems. The tourist in France encounters a sample of French people that is not only small but also highly biased, consisting largely of taxi drivers, concierges, waiters, shopkeepers, and customs officials. Similarly, the sample of a tourist's behavior experienced by such people is also very small and highly biased.

Not only do we encounter biased samples by virtue of our positions in life, but we also perceive others' behavior in a biased manner and produce biased samples of behavior in others by our behavior towards them. A story is told of a Westerner who was asked by a newcomer from the East,

"What are the people like out here?"

"What were the people like where you came from?" the Westerner replied.

"They were really fine people—warm, generous. We really hated to have to leave them behind," the newcomer answered.

"Well," said the Westerner, "You're going to find that the folks out here are pretty much the same."

Some time later, another traveler from the East came by and asked, "What are the people like out here?"

"What were the people like where you came from?" the Westerner replied.

"They were a bunch of stuffy, gossipy busybodies. That's why we left," was the answer.

"Well," said the Westerner, "You're going to find that the folks out here are pretty much the same."

Not only does our personal experience tend to be biased, but our memory also tends to be biased in representing experience. This becomes a particular problem when we estimate probabilities, rather than base them on actual counts, for estimating probabilities seems to involve memory sampling. We seem to base our judgments of probability, in large part, on the ease with which instances come to mind (Tversky and Kahneman, 1973). Because it is easy to think of men who are symphony conductors and difficult to think of women who are symphony conductors, we estimate, and correctly in this case, that the probability that a symphony conductor is a man is quite high. Since objective frequency is, in general, an important determiner of ease of recall, ease of recall is a reasonable, and sometimes adequate, basis for judging frequency or probability.

The problem is that factors other than frequency affect ease of recall. In particular, our memory seems to be biased towards recent experiences (Ebbinghaus, 1913), dramatic experiences (Von Restorff, 1935; Kleinsmith and Kaplin, 1963, 1964), and pleasant experiences (Aborn, 1953).

The tendency of our memories to oversample recent events shows up in many ways. If recent events have been going well, we tend to overgeneralize and see life as good and ourselves as effective and valued; but, if recent events have been going badly, this same tendency to overgeneralize leads us to view life and ourselves in a dimmer light and to become angry or depressed. Such mood swings are even more pronounced in children, whose sample may not extend beyond the moment, much less the day or week. Similarly, recency leads us to be more concerned about the dangers of flying shortly after learning about a terrible air accident than we will be later on, even though we should be less concerned, if anything, since safety procedures will be all the more carefully followed for a time.

In addition to recent events, our memories also tend to oversample events that are dramatic to us. If you asked four people to describe the same trip to Mexico, one might tell you about the art and architecture, one about the food, one about the beautiful women, and one about the inconveniences and dangers. We tend to remember what is salient to us. This is also why nearly everyone who was old enough at the time can remember so well what he was doing when he heard that President Kennedy had been shot. And it is why we tend to recall childhood as a series of pleasant and unpleasant events and to forget the numberless moments in between in which "nothing" happened.

Finally, it seems that we are more likely to oversample events that are pleasant and to undersample unpleasant events. Pleasantness leads us to overestimate the probabilities of events we would like to occur and to underestimate the probabilities of events we would like not to occur, a tendency which has been called "wishful thinking" (Crandall, Solomon, and Kellaway, 1955; Irwin, 1953; McGuire, 1960; Strickland, Lewicki and Katz, 1966). It was originally said of the priesthood, and is now said of many high-status occupations, that "many are called, but few are chosen." Many more people think that they will be able to succeed in an area than actually do.

In addition to personal experience and individual memory, organizational structure can also introduce sampling bias. This is essentially the problem in "groupthink" (Janis, 1972). When a leader surrounds himself with advisers who think much like he does and then uses them as his only sounding board for testing ideas, it is all too easy for him (and them) to overgeneralize and believe that this local consensus is indicative of a broader consensus.

Sample bias is a more difficult problem to detect and correct than is inadequate sample size. There are three approaches to dealing with sample bias.

1. The best way to eliminate bias in sampling is (a) to define the class carefully and then (b) to sample randomly from this class. In practice, however, this ideal is rarely possible to achieve.

2. The next best thing to do is to define the class carefully and then to try to sample from it in a way that does not produce any important bias. (In judging both probabilities and values, you should obtain estimates on different occasions and from different points of view, so that you will become aware of and be able to correct for as many sources of bias as possible, a technique called "triangulation.")

3. More often what you have to do is even less close to the ideal. Often the sample has already been drawn, and all that you can do is to define after the fact the class about which you wish to generalize, ask yourself whether any important biases exist, and attempt to take these biases into account by making appropriate adjustments.

Simply knowing that personal experience tends to be biased and that memory tends to be biased towards the recent, the dramatic, and the pleasant should make it easier to identify and correct at least these sources of bias.

Comparison

To make a statement of relationship, you must compare at least two classes on the predictor or causal variable.

If you tell people that the clouds were seeded on 100 days and that it rained on 90 of those days, many will tend to conclude that seeding was 90% effective. This conclusion is not warranted, however. Perhaps it would have rained 90% of the time if the clouds had not been seeded. The statement of relationship that we are interested in is: "The probability of rain when the clouds are seeded is greater than the probability of rain when the clouds are not seeded." In order to be able to make such a statement, you have to observe both days on which the clouds were seeded and days on which the clouds were not seeded.

The failure to consider comparison data seems to underly many superstitious beliefs. A person believes that he should fast during a particular period or dire consequences will befall him. He fasts; nothing particularly bad happens to him; and his belief is strengthened. He does not dare—or more likely does not even think—to run a comparison condition. If he tried not fasting, he might find that nothing particularly bad would happen to him then, either. A joke about a mental patient who always went around snapping his fingers makes the point. A new psychiatrist asked this patient why he was always snapping his fingers. "To keep away lions (snap, snap)," the patient replied. "See (snap, snap), it works! There aren't any lions around!"

Similarly, people who regularly read their horoscopes and feel that the stars can tell them something about their lives should compare the probability of occurrence of an event when the horoscope predicts it with its probability of occurrence when the horoscope does not predict it. (To make such a comparison, of course, the person should arrange things so that he does not know whether the horoscope has predicted the event until after he has decided whether or not it has occurred.) The way horoscopes fool people is by making very general statements that can apply to almost anyone, so that the probability of occurrence of the predicted event is high. However, the probability of the event is in all likelihood equally high when the horoscope does not predict it.

In a television discussion a few years ago, a conversation between a research psychologist and a psychotherapist went something like this.

> Research Psychologist: The evidence is that psychotherapy is ineffective. The probability of improvement is no greater for those who undergo psychotherapy than for those who do not. There is no relationship between psychotherapy and cure rate.
>
> Psychotherapist: The therapy may have been ineffective in the no-treatment group, but it was effective for those in the treatment group, because many of them showed improvement.

Notice what the psychotherapist did. He made a statement about the effectiveness of psychotherapy in the no-treatment group on the basis of a comparison, but then went on to make a statement about the effectiveness of psychotherapy in the treatment group without a comparison. (To avoid any misunderstanding, let it be clearly said that few psychotherapists would be this foolish and that there is now good evidence for the effectiveness of certain psychotherapeutic techniques.)

To avoid the error of not observing at least two classes on the predictor or causal variable, it helps to think about relationships in terms of some overall representation (Ward and Jenkins, 1965), such as the tree or cross-classification table which follows, where "S" represents seeding, "−S" represents no seeding, "R" represents rain, and "−R" represents no rain.

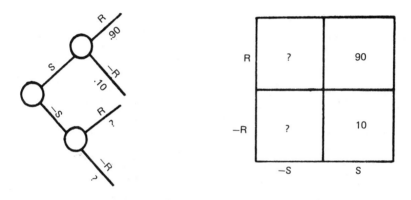

When you are having difficulty thinking about a relationship, it can help greatly to cast your data in terms of such a tree or cross-classification table.

To test yourself, consider this problem. Let us say that we went to the records and obtained data on the first 100 days of the year and classified them according to whether the clouds had been seeded ("S") or not ("−S") and whether it rained ("R") or not ("−R"). Assume that they seeded and it rained on 81 days; they seeded and it did not rain on 9 days; they did not seed and it rained on 9 days; and they did not seed and it did not rain on 1 day. On a scale of from 0% to 100%, what is the relationship between seeding and rain?

If you didn't draw a tree or a cross-classification table, go back and do so—the techniques are of no value unless you use them! The most commonly given answer is 82%, but the correct answer is 0%. There is no relationship at all, because the p of rain is the same whether the clouds are seeded ($81/90 = .90$) or not ($9/10 = .90$).

Controlled Comparison

In order to make a statement of causal relationship, the classes you compare on the causal variable must differ only with respect to the causal variable. Other variables must be controlled or randomized.

According to the National Safety Council, deaths per million boat passenger hours in 1973 were:

canoe (no motor)	1.66
canoe (motor)	0.14
sailboat (no auxiliary)	0.52
sailboat (auxiliary)	0.44

The death rates are higher in canoes and sailboats not equipped with motors than in canoes and sailboats equipped with motors. The conclusion seems inescapable: Motors provide a safety factor—and it is easy to think of reasons why this might be the case.

Despite its seeming inevitability, however, this conclusion does not follow. Before we can say that whether or not a boat has a motor is causally related to death rate, we must be sure that the class of boats with motors differs in no other way from the class of boats without motors. Because we have taken no such precautions and have no reason to believe that the National Safety Council has, we cannot justify this conclusion.

Indeed, it is quite likely that other causal factors are involved. For example, canoes with and without outboards are likely to be engaged in different activities. Canoes with outboards do not run white water, the most hazardous of canoeing activities. This difference could be a possible cause of the difference in death rate. Furthermore, a sailboat with an auxiliary is more likely to be a large sailboat than is a sailboat without an auxiliary. Since small sailboats are more likely to tip over and perhaps are also more likely to be owned by people new to sailing, this difference also could be a possible cause of the difference in death rate.

Let us put the lesson in more general terms. When there is a predictive relationship between A and B, there are always four possible causal patterns.

$A ===> B$	A is the cause.
$B ===> A$	B is the cause.
$A <==> B$	Both A and B are causes, in a feedback loop.
$C ===> A, B$	Neither A nor B, but some third variable, C, is the real cause.

An example of the third possibility, reciprocal causality, is falling in and out of love. A makes a move toward B, perhaps a lingering glance. This causes B to make a move toward A, fluttering eyelashes or a smile. This in turn causes A to make a further move, and "one thing leads to another."

The fourth possibility is the one that presents the greatest difficulty. The reason seems to be that, in this case, the real cause is neither of the variables mentioned in the statement of relationship. Thinking of possible "third variables," like thinking of acts, events, and goals, is a matter of creative thinking. In our example, possible "third variables" include the use to which the boat is put, the size of the boat, and the experience of the operator.

As another example, there happens to be a predictive relationship between ministers' income and profits in the liquor industry, such that ministers' income tends to be high in those years in which profits in the liquor industry are high and low in those years in which profits in the liquor industry

are low. The possible causal interpretations are that ministers' income is the cause (perhaps ministers support the
liquor industry through their purchases), that profits in the
liquor industry is the cause (perhaps ministers invest in the
liquor industry and derive part of their income from it), and,
most probably, that something having to do with the general
state of the economy is the cause. (In good times everybody's
income, including that of ministers and that of the liquor
industry, tends to be high, and in bad times everybody's income tends to be low.)

A way to ask yourself whether controlled comparison
has been satisfied is to ask yourself whether the presumed
cause has been *manipulated*. When you manipulate a variable
properly, you change that variable and only that variable; in
other words, you change it and control the others. Whereas
the concept of control emphasizes what is not changed, the
concept of manipulation emphasizes what is changed.

For example, let us say that you learn that in the Nether-
lands there is a positive relationship between the density of
storks and the human birth rate (those areas that have many
storks have many human births, and those areas that have
few storks have few human births) and that you want to test
your old suspicions about whether storks do, in fact, bring
babies. To find out whether the stork variable is the cause
you will have to manipulate, or change, this variable in some
way. Perhaps you can frighten storks away from some areas
and attract them to others and then see whether the areas
with fewer storks now have fewer babies and the areas with
more storks now have more babies.

Controlled comparison requires, among other things,
that the high-stork-density and low-stork-density areas initially differ in no way other than in terms of the density of
storks. If you have frightened the storks away from areas in
which there are many retired citizens and attracted them to
areas in which there are many newlyweds, any difference in
birth rate will not be clearly attributable to the difference in

density of storks. To rule out the possibility that it can be attributed to other differences, the other differences must be controlled.

There are two kinds of control: *control proper* and *randomization*. Both are satisfactory methods. In control proper, you would keep the numbers of newlyweds and retirees in the high-stork-density condition exactly the same as those in the low-stork-density condition, thus making it certain that any difference in birth rate could not be accounted for by differences in numbers of newlyweds and retirees. In randomization, on the other hand, you would assign areas randomly to the two conditions, thus making the numbers of newlyweds and retirees in the two conditions approximately the same and making it likely, but not certain, that any difference in birth rate could not be accounted for by differences in numbers of newlyweds and retirees. (For a discussion of how to assess this likelihood and a more thorough comparison of control proper and randomization in general, see Anderson (1971, chs. 4 and 7).) The point of this section is that, if neither control proper nor randomization has been carried out, controlled comparison has almost certainly not been satisfied.

There is a classic pattern of fallacious thinking that violates both the comparison and the controlled comparison rules. It is called *post hoc ergo propter hoc* (after this therefore because of this) thinking. It is the reasoning of the rooster who thought that, because the sun came up after he crowed, the sun came up because he crowed.

A state supreme court justice has inadvertently provided us with an example of *post hoc ergo propter hoc* thinking by publicly going through the following line of reasoning.

> Most of those who use hard drugs started out with marijuana. Therefore, in order to curb the use of hard drugs, we should have more severe penalties for using marijuana.

Can you spot the problems?

In the first place, the judge has failed to make a comparison. To see this, let us enter some data that would be quite consistent with what he has said in a cross-classification table.

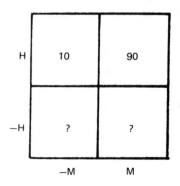

The judge said that most of those who use hard drugs started out with marijuana. The fictitious data in the table are quite consistent with this; 90% of those who use hard drugs started out with marijuana. However, if 90% of those who do not use hard drugs had also started out with marijuana, there would be no relationship, at all. The first 90% is not sufficient to tell us whether there is or is not a relationship. Actually, the judge is not on very dangerous ground here, for it is probably the case that, while most of those who use hard drugs started out with marijuana, far fewer of those who do not use hard drugs have ever used marijuana. Let us be generous then, and count this error as just a technicality.

The judge's second error, however, is far more serious. In order to be able to say that the use of marijuana is causally related to the use of hard drugs, we must be certain that those who do not use marijuana and those who do use marijuana differ in no other way that could possibly be a cause of a difference in the use of hard drugs. Because we have no reason at all to believe that all variables other than the use of marijuana that could possibly affect the use of hard drugs have been either controlled or randomized, we are not justified in making any causal inferences. The judge has failed to make a controlled comparison.

The judge believed that the relationship is causal, not simply predictive, for he hoped to control the use of hard drugs by controlling the use of marijuana, not simply to predict who would eventually use hard drugs from a knowledge of who was using marijuana. When you talk about control, you are talking about causality.

Referring back to our checklist, there are four possible causal interpretations. One is the judge's interpretation, that marijuana is the cause. Two others are that hard drugs is the cause or that both marijuana and hard drugs are causal in a reciprocal manner; however, both of these possibilities can be ruled out by the fact that the use of marijuana preceded the use of hard drugs. A more serious possibility is that some third factor, or factors, is the real cause. Personality factors and social factors are likely candidates. Perhaps people who are not "turned on" by life tend to seek mechanical turn-ons, like drugs; and perhaps people who have such people for close friends tend to follow their example.

If factors such as these are the real causes, then increasing the penalties for using marijuana could actually increase the use of hard drugs. Because increasing the penalties for using marijuana would do nothing about the real causes, people would be as inclined as ever to use drugs. The only question would be which drugs to use. One reason for using marijuana is that the penalties are not severe. Increasing the penalties for using marijuana would remove this reason for not using hard drugs. Because he failed to get his facts straight, the judge was inclined towards a course of action that could have accomplished the opposite of what he desired. (We are not saying that it would have this effect, but simply that it could. All that we are saying is that the data the judge cites do not rule out this possibility.) The step to causal interpretations is an important one and one that should be taken with caution.

It might be helpful to summarize this section on inductive reasoning in terms of the concept of *differences*. Operational definition and comparison require certain differences. Operational definition says in part that, if you are going to regard words as referring to different things, there should be differences in their operational definitions. And comparison says that, if you are going to make any statement about differences, you must first observe differences. Operational definition, sampling, and controlled comparison call attention to "dangerous differences." Operational definition says in part that there should be no important differences between the way you use a word in one context (for example, one in which you have obtained data) and the way you use it in another context (for example, one in which you are making a decision). Sampling says that there should be no important differences between the sample on which you have based a statement of fact and the sample to which you are generalizing that statement. And controlled comparison says that, before you can attribute a given difference to a particular cause, you must be sure that there are no important differences between the situations being compared other than the difference on the variable presumed to be the cause. When people say, "other things being equal," what they usually mean is, " 'dangerous differences' not being present."

DEDUCTIVE REASONING

Whereas inductive reasoning moves from observations to statements, deductive reasoning moves from statements to other statements. Deductive reasoning is a matter of "putting two and two together." Once inductive reasoning has gotten us some facts, some statements about the world that we think are quite likely to be true, it is usually well worth our while to think deductively about these statements. We think deductively about statements (a) to make sure that they are consistent with one another and (b) to infer new statements from them.

We are performing a consistency check when we note the inconsistency between (a) the fact that the zoo director recommended termination of the assistant zoo director on the grounds that he is not outstanding in the area of public relations and (b) the fact that the established policy is that a candidate assistant zoo director is to be retained if, during the trial period, he proves to be satisfactory in both internal management and public relations and outstanding in at least one. This inconsistency might lead us to look for hidden motives on the part of the zoo director.

We are inferring other facts from those that come immediately to mind when we reason from the observation that there are cobwebs across the trail to the conclusion that no one is likely to have come this way earlier today. And we are carrying this process one step further when we reason from the fact that no one is likely to have come this way earlier today to the conclusion that the members of our party who went on ahead of us didn't come this way, either—and that either they or we are lost. We might then go on to reason from the memory that earlier we passed some people on the trail who said that they had just come from our destination (and to reason from the fact of the cobwebs) that it is we who are lost and that we had better turn around and head back to find out where we went wrong.

Deductive reasoning can be of great value. It can extend our knowledge far beyond the narrow confines of memory. When we think deductively, however, we must be careful, for deductive reasoning can easily go awry. (See, for example, Wason and Johnson-Laird, 1972.) Consider Andrew Marvell's poem, "To His Coy Mistress," which has been excerpted below.

Had we but world enough, and time,
This coyness, Lady, were no crime. . . .

But at my back I always hear
Time's winged chariot hurrying near. . . .

Now therefore, while the youthful hue
Sits on thy skin like morning dew,
And while thy willing soul transpires
At every pore with instant fires,
Now let us sport us while we may. . . .

The argument of the poem may be summarized as follows.

If we had time, coyness would be appropriate.

We do not have time.

Therefore, coyness is not appropriate.

Though the conclusion is admirable, the logic, as we shall see, is faulty.

This is to be contrasted with the correct and helpful reasoning in the following example of looking for some keys we have misplaced.

If the house was locked, I would have to have taken the keys out of the car in order to have gotten into the house.

The house was locked.

Therefore, I must have taken the keys out of the car.

So you decide not to look in the car for the keys. If you had not gone through this reasoning, you might have spent a good deal of wasted time searching around in the car. The Greeks have a saying: He who doesn't have brains has feet!

To continue with the coffee shop example, let us say that you have learned, inductively, that all successful coffee shops have at least some contemporary foods and music. And let us say, further, that you had already planned, before you learned this, to include some of these features in your coffee shop. (This makes the node an event node, rather than an act node, and thus we can attach probabilities to its branches.) You could then reason that your coffee shop is likely to be successful.

Did you follow this line of reasoning? If so, you went astray, for the reasoning is unsound. It goes as follows.

> If a coffee shop is successful, then it has at least some contemporary foods and music.
> My coffee shop will have at least some contemporary foods and music.
> Therefore, my coffee shop will be successful.

The error is of the same kind as that in Marvell's poem.

How do we evaluate deductive reasoning to determine whether it is correct or not? The general answer is by decomposition. We break the problem down into steps that are so small that we cannot help but reason correctly about them, and then we assemble the judgments about the parts into a judgment about the whole. There are a number of schemes that have been conventionally employed for doing this, such as Euler diagrams, Venn diagrams, and the propositional calculus. The figure below shows how the statement "All ten-speeds have handbrakes" would be represented by Euler diagrams and Venn diagrams and how the statement "If X is a ten-speed, then X has handbrakes" (which need not be treated differently from "All ten-speeds have handbrakes") would be represented by the propositional calculus and tree diagrams:

Euler diagram

Venn diagram

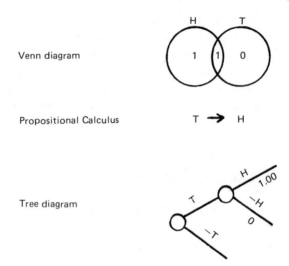

Propositional Calculus   T ➔ H

Tree diagram

We shall break with convention and employ decision trees for two very good reasons. One, decision trees make it clearer how to apply deductive reasoning to decision making. Two, decision trees can be made to deal with both deterministic and probabilistic statements.

In decision tree terms, Andrew Marvell's major premise, that, if we had time, coyness would be appropriate, can be represented as follows.

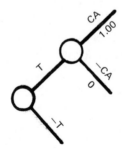

This is a conditional probability. The "if we had time" takes us out the "T" branch, and the "coyness would be appropriate" tells us that the p of coyness being appropriate under these conditions is 1.00 (otherwise he would have said, "Coyness might appropriate," or something of the kind.) The next thing he says is that we do not have time, which takes us out the "$-T$" branch. Since there is no information about whether coyness is or is not appropriate on this branch, there is nothing we can conclude, yet he goes right on to conclude, erroneously, that coyness is not appropriate under these conditions. If Marvell had known how to draw a decision tree, he might well have avoided this error.

The two most common errors in interpreting "if . . . then" statements seem to be to conclude from "If A then B" (a) "If B then A" and (b) "If not A then not B." The first of these is called illicit conversion. The second is the error Marvell made.

Let us look at the correct reasoning about the keys. The major premise that, if the house was locked, I would have taken the keys out of the car, can be represented as follows.

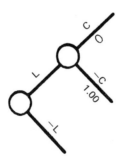

Again, we have a conditional probability. The "if the house was locked" takes us out the "L" branch, and the "I would have taken the keys out of the car" tells us that the p of the keys being in the car ("C") is 0 and that the complementary probability $1 - p$ of the keys not being in the car ("$-C$") is 1.00. The next statement is that the house was locked, which takes us out the "L" branch. This forces us to continue on out the "$-C$" branch, because its p is 1.00, and to conclude that the keys are not in the car. So the conclusion is correct.

So far, the only p's we have dealt with have been 0 or 1.00. We have dealt only with deterministic statements. This seems a little unrealistic, since not much in this world is all that certain. We shall want to extend our reasoning to include intermediate p's.

Let us say that, if there is wind tomorrow, you plan to ask Ann to go sailing. You figure that there is a 75% chance of wind tomorrow, and Ann says yes two out of every three times that you ask her to go sailing. So more likely than not it'll work out. But wait! People are not very good at making intuitive judgments about probabilities that depend on other probabilities (see Slovic, Fischhoff, and Lichtenstein, 1977; Wyer, 1974), so let's work this out. The following tree will do the job.

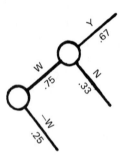

When you were estimating the probability that "things would work out," you were thinking of going out the wind branch ("W") and out the yes branch ("Y"). The p of going out the "W" branch is .75, and the conditional p of going out the "Y" branch is .67. To get the p of going out both branches, we multiply:

$$.75 \times .67 = .50$$

There's not a better than even chance that things will work out, after all. It's a tossup. In general, we tend to overestimate the p that two or more uncertain events will both occur (Bar-Hillel, 1973.) The way to correct this error is to employ decomposition, to estimate the separate p's and then to combine them by means of the appropriate mathematics.

Let us consider a somewhat more complicated case. Let us say that we have the following items of information about coffee shops.

> 40% of coffee shops are successful.
>
> 95% of successful coffee shops have at least some contemporary foods and music.
>
> 90% of unsuccessful coffee shops have at least some contemporary foods and music.

What we would like to know is the probability that a coffee shop that has at least some contemporary foods and music will be successful. Many people would say, in the present case, that this p is somewhere around .95. However, they are neglecting to take two things into account: the base rate of 40% and the fact that the relationship between having at least some contemporary foods and music and success is not very high (the p of success is .90 without contemporary foods and music and .95 with, a very small difference). The correct p is much closer to the base rate of .40 than it is to .95!

Because the probability we need is not given to us directly, we shall have to arrive at it by a process of reasoning. Let us begin by representing what information we have in terms of a decision tree.

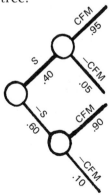

To find out what proportion of coffee shops with contemporary foods and music are successful, we must divide the number of coffee shops that have contemporary foods and music and are successful by the total number of coffee shops that have contemporary foods and music. This is equivalent to dividing the proportion of cases that sort to the end of the S/CFM path by the proportion of cases that sort to either the end of the S/CFM path or the end of the −S/CFM path.

But before we can do this we must get the proportions at the ends of the paths. The process is not all that difficult: To obtain the probability of arriving at the end of a path, as we have seen, you multiply the probabilities of branching onto that path at each node along the way. Thus, the probabilities at the ends of the four paths in our tree are:

$$
\begin{array}{llll}
\text{S/CFM} & .40 \times .95 = & .38 \\
\text{S/−CFM} & .40 \times .05 = & .02 \\
\text{−S/CFM} & .60 \times .90 = & .54 \\
\text{−S/−CFM} & .60 \times .10 = & \underline{.06} \\
& & & 1.00
\end{array}
$$

These probabilities must, of course, sum to 1.00, since they exhaust all the possibilities. (At the first step, we cut the "pie" into two pieces, and, at the second step, we cut each of these pieces into two more pieces. No matter how many times we do this, all the pieces still have to add up to the whole "pie.")

Notice how these calculations take account of the .40/.60 base rate. Notice also how they take account of the degree of relationship between the predictor (having at least some contemporary foods and music) and the criterion (success.) This is the precise way of accomplishing the intuitive adjustment we talked about earlier: adjusting the base rate in the direction of the probability you would estimate on the basis of the case data, adjusting it farther the more trustworthy your case data are.

All this can be done in terms of a cross-classification table, if you prefer. The information you begin with would be represented as follows.

	$-S$	S
CFM	.54	.38
$-$CFM	.06	.02
	.60	.40

The statement that 40% of coffee shops are successful is represented in the marginal p's of .40 and .60. The statement that 95% of successful coffee shops have at least some contemporary foods and music is not represented directly; there is no p of .95 in the table. Instead, .95 is multiplied by .40 to yield the p, .38, of a coffee shop both having contemporary food and music and being successful. And .05 is multiplied by .40 to yield the p, .02, of a coffee shop both not having contemporary food and music and being successful. The statement that 90% of unsuccessful coffee shops have at least some contemporary foods and music is handled in a similar manner, yielding the p's of .54 and .06. Next, the p's in the cells are added up the other way to yield the marginal p, .92, that a coffee shop has contemporary foods and music and the marginal p, .08, that a coffee shop does not have contemporary food and music.

Whether we arrive at this point by means of a tree or a cross-classification table, the proportion of coffee shops with contemporary foods and music that are successful is thus: $.38/(.38 + .54) = .41$. Similarly, the proportion of coffee shops without contemporary foods and music that are successful is: $.02/(.02 + .06) = .25$. Assuming that we can satisfy the assumptions of a causal relationship, we can enter these figures into a decision tree that incorporates an act node.

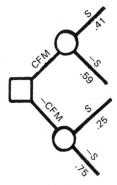

Later we shall see how we could use such information in making a decision.

In arriving at these probabilities, we followed two rules for combining probabilities. These should be made more explicit. (See Table 3-2.)

1. *Multiplication Rule.* The multiplication rule applies to probabilities along the same path in a tree. It yields the probability of going down a particular branch at the first node AND a particular branch at the second node (AND a particular branch at the third node, etc).

   The multiplication rule applies to independent events. Events are said to be independent when the occurrence of one is not related to the occurrence of the other. An example of two independent events is the occurrence of heads on each of two coins.

   The multiplication rule states that, given two independent events, A and B, the p that both A and B will occur is the product of their separate p's. The p that one coin AND another will both come up heads is $.5 \times .5 = .25$. The p that a coffee shop offers contemporary foods and music AND is successful is $.40 \times .95 = .38$.

   The multiplication rule can be extended to any number of independent events. For three such events, you would multiply three p's; for four, you would multiply four p's; and so forth. The multiplication rule enables us to determine the probability of following any branch of a decision tree all the way to its end.

2. *Addition Rule.* The addition rule applies to probabilities on alternative paths in a tree. It yields the probability of going down one path OR another (OR another, etc).

   The addition rule applies to mutually exclusive events. Events are said to be mutually exclusive if the occurrence of one precludes the occurrence of the other. An example of two mutually exclusive events is the occurrence of heads and the occurrence of tails on the same coin.

   The addition rule states that, given two mutually exclusive events, A and B, the p that either A or B will occur is the sum of their separate p's. The p that a coin will come up heads OR tails is $.5 + .5 = 1.00$. The p that a coffee shop offers

TABLE 3-2.
Rules for Deductive Reasoning

1. Multiplication Rule
   To obtain the probability of both of two independent events occurring, multiply their separate probabilities.
2. Addition Rule
   To obtain the probability of either of two mutually exclusive events occurring, add their separate probabilities.

contemporary foods and music and is successful OR offers contemporary foods and music and is not successful is .38 + .54 = .92. This is how we obtained the denominators for the p's that we entered in the final decision tree.

The addition rule can be extended to any number of mutually exclusive events. For three such events, you would add three p's; for four, you would add four p's; and so forth. The addition rule enables us to determine the probability of following one OR another branch of a decision tree.

Note that, given two independent events, A and B, the p of A and/or B occurring is neither the product nor the sum of their separate p's. In tossing two coins, the p of getting heads on one or the other or both is neither .5 × .5 = .25 nor .5 + .5 = 1.00. The best way to see what the correct p is, is to work the possibilities out in terms of a tree diagram, as follows.

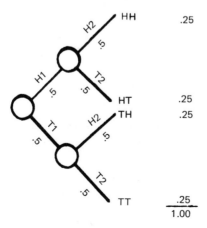

HH	.25
HT	.25
TH	.25
TT	.25
	1.00

111

Because there are three paths, each having a p of .25, leading to one or more heads, the p of getting heads on one or the other or both of two coins is $.25 + .25 + .25 = .75$.

If you would like to play with a related problem that could win you some money, try this one.

> A couple has two children. One is a boy. What is the probability that the other is a girl? (The answer is not .50, even though we assume, for the sake of this problem, that half the births are boys and half are girls.)
>
> *Hint:* Note that we said that one child is a boy, not that the first-born child is a boy. We have a tree with two event nodes, one for the first-born child and one for the second-born child, yielding four equally probable paths: BB, BG, GB, and GG. Because one of the children is a boy, we rule out the GG path. You should be able to take it from there.

Now that we have the multiplication and addition rules in hand, let us return to the keys problem and state it more precisely. Recall that the first statement was that, if the house was locked, the keys would not be in the car. This is a conditional probability, and we represented it as follows.

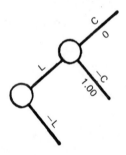

The second statement was that the house was locked. Since this is a certainty, we can place a p of 1.00 on the "L" branch and a complementary p of 0 on the "−L" branch. Furthermore, we can use the multiplication rule to compute p's of reaching the ends of the various paths.

$$1.00 \times 0 = 0$$

$$1.00 \times 1.00 = 1.00$$

$$0 = 0$$

Reaching the second end point is a certainty; that is, it is certain that the house was locked and that the keys are not in the car. Reaching either of the other end points is an impossibility.

Now, let us see how we can handle a word like "some," and let us look at a slightly more complicated form of argument.

> All flowering plants reproduce sexually.
> Some of the parson's plants are flowering plants.
> Therefore, some of the parson's plants reproduce sexually.

Unlike any of the arguments we have considered so far, this one involves two conditional p's. Let us see how it can be represented in a decision tree. The first premise, "All flowering plants reproduce sexually," would be represented as follows.

The second premise, "Some of the parson's plants are flowering plants," would be represented as follows.

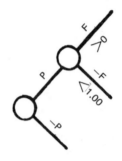

We are told only that some of the parson's plants are flowering plants. This is a vague statement. All it really tells us is
that it is not the case that none of the parson's plants are
flowering plants. This is saying simply that the probability is
greater than 0 (>0) and the complementary probability (1 −
p) is less than 1.00 (< 1.00).

Now, we have to assemble these two trees into a single
tree, for, if you cannot get different statements into the same
tree, you cannot draw any conclusion that involves combining their meanings. It is easy to assemble the above two trees
into a single tree, because the "F/−F" node is common to
both. Because the statement applies to all flowering plants, it
certainly applies to the parson's.

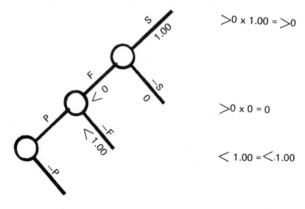

>0 x 1.00 = >0

>0 x 0 = 0

$< 1.00 = <1.00$

Because we are talking about just the parson's plants, we go out the "P" branch and use the multiplication rule to find the p's at its various endpoints. Each endpoint represents a valid conclusion. Starting at the top and reading down, these are:

Some ($p > 0$) of the parson's plants are flowering and reproduce sexually.

None ($p = 0$) of the parson's plants are flowering and do not reproduce sexually.

Not all ($p < 1.00$) of the parson's plants are nonflowering.

The first is the conclusion that we are interested in.

So far, we have not talked about "flipping" trees. To see what this means, consider the statement, "Where there's smoke, there's fire," which can be treed as follows:

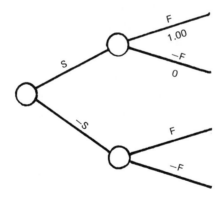

Let's say that someone wonders whether this statement means the same thing as, "Where there's fire, there's smoke"—or, "Where there's no fire, there's no smoke." The problem is that, while the original statement begins with a smoke/-smoke distinction, these statements begin with a fire/-fire distinction. To see whether these statements can be represented by the same tree as, "Where there's smoke, there's fire," we must "flip" this tree over. If we flip the tree without worrying about the probabilities, it will look like this:

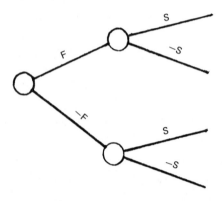

When you have simple if-then statements, with probabilities of 0 and 1.00, adding the probabilities to the flipped tree is easy. The basic rule is to begin with the 0 probabilities. The 0 probability in the original tree says that there is no way of getting from the Smoke path to the -Fire path. This means, in the flipped tree, that there is no way of getting from the -Fire path to the Smoke path; if you go out the -Fire path, the probability of going out the Smoke path will be 0. This probability has been added to the end of the −F/S path in the tree below:

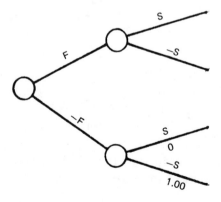

Thus, while, "Where there's no fire, there's no smoke," does mean the same thing as the original statement, "Where there's fire, there's smoke," does not.

It is also possible to flip a tree with more probabilities and with probabilities other than 0 and 1.00. To see how this is done, we shall need a different example. Assume that an architectural firm has been successful on about 50% of its competitive bids and that the senior partner has predicted 70% of these, though he has also predicted success for 50% of the failures. This information can be treed as follows:

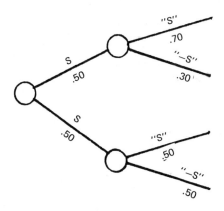

Let us say that you wish to know what the probability is that a given competitive bid will be successful, given that the senior partner has predicted that it will be successful. To answer this question will require flipping the tree, because, while the original tree begins with the success/-success distinction, the question begins with the "success"/"-success" distinction. (The words with quotes indicate predicted outcomes and the words without quotes indicate actual outcomes.)

In flipping a tree of this complexity, it helps to go by way of a cross-classification table:

S	.15	.35	.50
−S	.25	.25	.50
	"−S"	"S"	

This table was obtained in the same way as the one on page 109, so this much is not new.

What we do now is add the cells vertically to obtain the column totals of .60 and .40. These are the probabilities we attach to the initial branches on the flipped tree. Next, we place the probabilities that are in the four cells at the four end points of the tree.

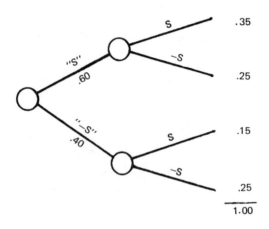

And, finally, we employ the multiplication rule to obtain the intermediate probability that we are after, the probability that the competitive bid will be successful, given that the senior partner has predicted success:

$$.60X = .35$$
$$X = .35/.60$$
$$X = .58$$

Any other intermediate probability can, of course, be obtained in the same fashion.

We might close this section on deductive reasoning by just mentioning a very important kind of deductive reasoning that we use all the time: *ordinary arithmetic*. It is ordinary arithmetic that we use to figure out such things as the total amount of money we will be paying for interest on a house loan, or the cost per ounce of differently packaged foods, or the total amount of money a 40-mile-per-gallon car will save us over a 20-mile-per-gallon car in a five-year period. You already know the rules of arithmetic. What needs to be said here is that we should use them more often than we do.

As one example, a recent report on running shoes gave a separate rating for wear, and yet it would seem more meaningful to divide cost by mileage to get a cost/mile index. After all, what is the advantage of long wear, other than a savings in money? As long as two shoes have the same cost/mile index, there is little basis for choosing between a long-wearing shoe and a short-wearing one. Indeed, one might even prefer the short-wearing shoe, so he could change shoes more frequently and thus keep up better with improvements in design.

Arithmetic is often essential as a corrective to intuitive judgments. The tissue paper problem provides a dramatic illustration.

> Imagine doubling a piece of tissue paper twice, by folding it in half and then folding it in half again, so that it is now four layers thick. And imagine that this procedure were continued until the paper has been doubled 50 times in all. (Assume that this is possible.) How thick will the folded paper be if a single sheet is .001 inch thick?

Most people guess about a foot or two. The mathematics goes as follows. After one doubling, it is 2(.001) inch thick; after two doublings, it is $2 \times 2(.001)$ inch thick, or 2^2 (.001) inch thick; and after 50 doublings, it is $2^{50}(.001)$ inch thick. This works out to be around 17,770,000 miles, over one-fourth the distance from the Earth to Venus! Sometimes our intuitive judgments are badly in need of correction.

A very practical illustration of this same principle is the growth of populations. Consider one family with 4 children. If all of these children follow their parents' example and this is continued for 10 generations, the tenth-generation descendents of these parents would number 1,048,576 individuals, the population of a rather large city! We cannot trust common sense in making judgments about such matters.

A related problem is the growth of investments. Let us say that you hear of a friend who has invested $100 per year at a 7% annual rate of return and accumulated $4100 in 20 years. You would like to start an investment program yourself, but you would like to make more money than this. Would it be better to try to invest it at double the rate of interest, at 14%, or to start your investment program early enough so that you can accumulate money over double the length of time, 40 years? (Assume that both the 7% and the 14% investments have the same level of risk associated with them.) The answer may surprise you. At double the rate of interest, 14% for 20 years, you will accumulate $9103; while at double the length of time, 7% for 40 years, you will accumulate $19,964! Once the appropriate arithmetic reasoning has been gone through, the moral is self-evident: Start investing early!

Reasoning can take us well beyond what we are able to see or remember directly. Creative thinking can take us even farther, though with considerably less certainty. While reasoning gets us to what is certain or at least probable, creative thinking takes us on to what is merely possible. As we shall see, the means by which it does this is a loose, associative process that often contrasts sharply with the tightly meshed rules of reasoning.

RECOMMENDED READING

ANDERSON, B. F., *The Psychology Experiment: An Introduction to the Scientific Method* (2d. ed.). Monterey, Calif.: Brooks/Cole, 1971.

BARKER, S. F., *The Elements of Logic* (2d ed.). New York: McGraw-Hill, 1974.

4

Creative Thinking

It's a poor sort of memory that works only backwards," said the Queen in *Through the Looking Glass*. A memory that works backwards, one that establishes, comprehends, and retains facts about what is or has been, is largely what we have been talking about in the last two chapters. Though facts are essential in constraining thought to what is workable, they nevertheless leave open a vast array of possibilities, and it is out of these possibilities that we must fashion the future. Because possibilities are just that and not actualities, they do not present themselves to us—rather, we must seek them out, construct them, invent them. It is time to see how we can get our memories to "work forwards," to invent the possible. Such invention is what we call creative thinking.

Creative thinking is involved at every step in the growing of decision trees. At act nodes we have to invent possible courses of action. At event nodes we have to imagine possible states of the world. And, at the end points of the paths, we must, as we shall see in a later chapter, think of bases for evaluating where we have gotten.

Creative thinking, it is widely agreed, is the generation of ideas (a) that are unusual, or original, and (b) that satisfy some standards of value. To say that half of 8 is 100, though original, satisfies no standards and is not creative. To say that half of 8 is 4 satisfies the standards of sound reasoning but is not original; hence, it also is not creative. However, to say that half of 8 is 0 (when cut horizontally!) or 3 (when cut vertically!) is in some measure both original and creative.

The standards of value by which creativity is judged may be practical: An invention must work. Or they may be social: A work of art must communicate. Originality is usually defined with respect to the culture; for an idea to be called creative, it must ordinarily be new to the culture. Inventing the hot air balloon now would not be considered creative, for it has already been invented. However, for an idea to be creative psychologically, it need only be new to the person who thought it up. If you invented a hot air balloon without knowing that such a thing had been invented before, that would be a psychologically creative act. From this point of view, we all invent things from time to time that are creative—if not a hot air balloon, at least a new way of tying luggage on the car or a new method for shaping cookie dough. The fact that many of these ideas may have been thought of before does not keep their invention from being creative acts. If we recognize this, we may be better able to identify and encourage small acts of creativity in ourselves. Although small acts of creativity may have no effect on our culture, they can make our own lives and the lives of those around us a good deal more pleasant. Creativity is not the exclusive property of geniuses; it comes in both large and small sizes. It is something that we all have—and something that we all can develop.

The ability to think creatively, like the ability to think critically, seems to be based in part on attitudes and in part on techniques, so to become more creative we would do well to learn something about both the attitudes and the techniques that characterize exceptionally creative persons.

THE CREATIVE ATTITUDE

As we noted in the last chapter, attitudes seem to be important for both critical and creative thinking; intelligence and method are not all there is to either. But the creative attitude seems to be quite different from the critical attitude. The creative attitude seems to be based more on a love of adventure than a desire for certainty, disposed more to build than to destroy, inclined more to go ahead than to hold back—in short, more positive than negative. If we look at exceptionally creative persons to see how the creative attitude is expressed in their personalities, we find that they can be characterized as (a) possessing inner strength, (b) being open to experience, and (c) being highly motivated. Seeing how these characteristics are expressed in creative people should give us a more concrete understanding of what the creative attitude is really about.

Inner strength. We all need structure to guide us as we thread our way, decision by decision, through life, but that structure can come either predominately from within or predominately from without. Creative people seem to take their guidance from within. They have what Carl Rogers calls an "internal locus of evaluation." They are more in touch with their own feelings and thoughts. They seek to shape their environment, rather than allow themselves to be shaped by it. They form their opinions independently and are not inclined simply to go along with the judgment of a group or of society. (See Barron, 1965; Cattell and Drevdahl, 1955; MacKinnon, 1962.) The independence of judgment that characterizes creative people seems to be well described in the opening lines of Rudyard Kipling's "If":

> If you can keep your head when all about you
> Are losing theirs and blaming it on you;
> If you can trust yourself when all men doubt you,
> Yet make allowance for their doubting too.

Openness to experience. The "make allowance for their doubting" suggests an openness to experience. Creative persons, perhaps because they have such high internal structure, are also comfortable with less external structure and more open to experience. They are comfortable with ambiguity, being more accepting of, and even preferring, the complex and the incomplete. For example, they prefer the drawings on the left to those on the right in the figure on page 126.

And they are also more open to inner experience; metaphors and the search for analogies appeal to them more than straightforward reasoning (Barron, 1965). They are more interested in the possibilities inherent in a situation than in practical facts (MacKinnon, 1962; Carlyn, 1977). Their sense of adventure, their preference for the activity of discovering to the state of knowing, is well captured in these lines from Tennyson's "Ulysses":

> Yet all experience is an arch where–thro'
> Gleams that untravell'd world, whose margin fades
> Forever and forever when I move.

The openness of creative people to effortless associative and metaphoric processes—to what Rollo May has called the "daimonic"—may relate to the fact that creative people fre-

These drawings were preferred
by creative individuals

These drawings were preferred by
randomly chosen individuals

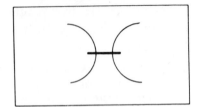

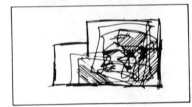

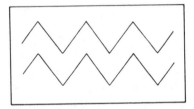

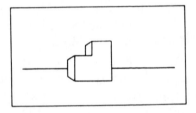

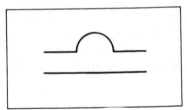

quently talk of the process of creation as a dialogue between themselves (effortful processes) and their product (represented by the effortless processes of perception and associative memory) and even insist that they themselves (that is, their effortful processes) are not in control of the creative process. Whereas the critical attitude resists automatic processes, the creative attitude is receptive to them and makes use of them.

High motivation.   In addition to an internal locus of evaluation and a preference for the complex and the incomplete, creative persons possess a willingness to work very hard at the problems they are interested in (Roe, 1953, ch. 5; MacKinnon, 1960, 1961). They develop a "healthy obsession" with their problem. Much as love draws a lover, their problem tends to draw them into total involvement. They may work months or years on a problem that another person would give up on after only a few minutes. As Edison said, "Genius is 1% inspiration and 99% perspiration."

There may be several reasons why creative people are willing to work so hard. One might have to do with their inner strength. It might be that creatives are willing to work hard because they are confident that they will eventually succeed. Most of us give up before we have given ourselves a real chance to solve the problem we are working on. As a consequence we fail again and in doing so reinforce the self-defeating attitudes that caused us to give up in the first place. It has been found that, when these self-defeating attitudes are countered by asking people to continue working on a problem beyond the point at which they have come up with what they believe to be their best effort, they often come up with ideas that are even more creative than their previous "best" effort (Hyman, 1964).

Another reason why creative people are willing to work so hard might have to do with their openness to experience. It might be that they are willing to continue working because they are not so uncomfortable about the masses of conflicting facts that present themselves, the fact that for a time things may seem to get more complicated rather than less, and the fact that the question as to whether they will be able to solve the problem they are working on remains unresolved. Thus, inner strength, openness to experience, and high motivation may all be but different facets of the same splendid jewel.

Research (Stein, 1974, pp. 65–66) suggests that simply imagining yourself to be creative can increase the number of creative ideas you are able to come up with. Presumably, role-playing a creative person strengthens our creative traits. The reason for including a description of the creative personality in this chapter is that it should be possible to adopt the creative role more effectively the more knowledge you have about what such persons are really like.

The popular suggestion to defer judgment (Osborn, 1963) is a suggestion to leave your creative hat on, and to set your critical hat aside, while generating ideas. It is, apparently, not so much a suggestion to defer evaluation, which seems to be important in getting ideas as well as in getting rid of them (Manske and Davis, 1968; Hyman, 1964), as it is a suggestion to defer the critical attitude (Parnes, 1963, 1967). When you defer the critical attitude and adopt the creative one, you evaluate in a growth-stimulating manner, trying to think of what is good about an idea, instead of evaluating in a growth-inhibiting manner, trying to think of what is wrong with an idea. Osborn tries to encourage positive evaluation in his "brainstorming" sessions by calling first on "hitchhikers," those who have ideas that build on the ideas of others in the group. (A person indicates that he has a hitchhike by snapping his fingers, rather than simply raising his hand.) Perhaps because our schooling places so much stress on the critical attitude, or perhaps because aspects of the creative attitude are associated so much with childishness and immaturity, it requires thought, effort, and practice to reawaken and develop it.

Let us turn now from the attitudes of the creative person to the things he or she does when thinking creatively. There are a number of specific techniques which creative people say they use to help them get ideas and which, in many cases, have been tried out by ordinary people and found to work for them, too.

TECHNIQUES FOR STIMULATING CREATIVITY

We shall look at quite a number of techniques for stimulating creativity, but before we look at the techniques themselves, there are some things that should be said about them.

1. The techniques will not do your thinking for you. They are not ways of making your work easier so much as ways of enabling you to work harder and more effectively.

2. Many of the techniques will seem too simple to be of any help in generating truly creative ideas. Indeed, creativity by its very nature may seem to be beyond the range of any techniques—more a matter of waiting for the happy thought to present itself than of actively seeking it out. Two things should be said in response to this. One, there is evidence (Maier, 1931) that at least one of the mechanisms on which the techniques are based works for both those who are aware of the source of their ideas and those who believe their ideas to come "out of the blue." And, two, the basic operations of a computer are also simple, but when put together, they are capable of achievements that can surprise even the programmer.

3. The techniques will usually not give you a finished idea but a direction that you can use to get to an idea. This point is especially important to keep in mind. Consider the case of a person who was trying to devise a method of mounting a compass on a small boat. One technique produced the idea of a fishnet. Though a fishnet would not make a very good device for mounting a compass, he was able to use the idea of a fishnet to get to the idea of the device that attaches a rod to a reel, and this could be adapted for mounting a compass. Later, the same technique produced the idea of an axe. Again, one would be hard pressed to figure out a way to mount a compass with an axe, but the idea of an axe suggested a mounting something like a knife switch. This "steppingstone"

approach is typical. Often a good idea is not one, but two steps away, and you have to step over a bad idea to get to the good one. As the poet Schiller said, "Regarded in isolation, an idea may be quite insignificant and venturesome in the extreme; but it may acquire importance from an idea which follows it." You will usually have to force the techniques to work (Gordon, 1961, 1971) by taking that extra step. The techniques will be far more useful to you if you maintain the creative person's attitude toward the incomplete. When a technique gives you an idea, look beyond whatever ridiculous qualities it may have, seek out its promising qualities, and see what you can do with these. Truly creative ideas virtually always come in the guise of fools.

4. There seems to be no point in using the techniques if you are already coming up with ideas. It's when you've run out of ideas and are staring at a blank piece of paper or when your ideas have been going around and around over the same ground that you have a real need for the techniques.

5. If the list of techniques seems a bit bewildering in its complexity, it would probably be wise to start with just one or two techniques and practice these until you feel comfortable with them before attempting to add any others to your repertoire. It is certainly not necessary to use all the techniques in order to think creatively. It seems likely that any of a number of techniques could get you to the solution of most problems, and it seems quite likely (though this question does not seem to have been researched) that different creative thinkers have different favorite techniques.

Anyhow, here's the list. (See Table 4.) Take a look at it, and see what suits your fancy.

The techniques for stimulating new ideas can be grouped broadly into two categories: stimulus variation and coding variation. The stimulus variation techniques take advantage of the fact that our thoughts tend to be tied to the stimuli about us, what we are currently looking at, listening to, or sensing in some other way. By changing stimuli, these techniques change our thoughts and give us a fresh perspective.

The coding variation techniques take advantage of the

TABLE 4.
Techniques for Creative Thinking

A. Vary the stimuli about you in order to vary your thoughts.
   1. Observe carefully.
   2. Use checklists.
   3. Rearrange the elements of the problem.
   4. Discuss the problem with someone else.
   5. Take a break.
B. Vary the way in which you represent the problem in order to vary your thoughts.
   1. Abstract Coding
      Represent the problem in terms of abstract codes, attempting to state it in verbal or mathematical symbols or analyzing it into attributes and recombining the attributes.
   2. Concrete Coding
      Represent the problem in terms of concrete codes, translating it into actions, pictures, or analogies.

fact that our brain is really a number of brains in one, each organized somewhat differently. The major distinction on which we have evidence, in addition to that between automatic and effortful processes (see pp. 8*f*), is between verbal and nonverbal processes. It seems that the left half of the brain, which controls the right side of the body, represents the world in an abstract, analytic, verbal manner; while the right half of the brain, which controls the left side of the body, represents the world in a concrete, global, spatial manner. Perhaps this is what has led poets to speak of the "right hand of reason" and the "left hand of intuition" (Bruner, 1964). (For a very small percentage of right-handers and about half of left-handers, it is the right side that is verbal and the left side that is nonverbal.)

Words are processed more rapidly when presented to the right ear or the right side of the visual field, both of which go directly to the left hemisphere. Nonverbal sounds, such as melodies, are processed more rapidly when presented to the left ear, and pictures are processed more rapidly when presented to the left visual field, both of which go directly to the right hemisphere (Milner, 1971). Not only does the material processed in the two hemispheres differ, but the mode of processing also appears to be different. The verbal hemisphere tends to process information serially, and the nonverbal hemisphere, in parallel (Cohen, 1973); verbal images seem to be specialized for handling order information, and nonverbal images, spatial information (Paivio, 1971).

We encountered the distinction between verbal and imaginal processes earlier in discussing techniques for binding items together in memory. Here, in discussing coding variation techniques for stimulating creative thought, we encounter it again. Indeed, the distinction must be relevant to every chapter in this book, since we use the same brain throughout. Yet on the basis of what is currently known, there is more to be said about the relevance of the distinction for memory and creative thinking, especially the latter.

The way in which the techniques of coding variation get us to look at our problem in new ways is by getting us to recode the problem from the language of one part of our brain into that of another. The techniques for coding variation can be subdivided into abstract coding techniques and concrete coding techniques. The former represent the problem in verbal, mathematical, or other analytic terms, while the latter represent the problem in muscular, graphic, or metaphoric terms.

It is important to point out that both the stimulus variation techniques and the coding variation techniques vary thought in ways that are relevant to the problem, not randomly. In this way, they maximize the chances that whatever new ideas are produced will actually be useful in solving the problem. We shall consider the techniques for creative thinking under three headings: stimulus variation, abstract coding, and concrete coding.

STIMULUS VARIATION

Observe carefully.   The first technique of stimulus variation is simply to observe the world about you carefully. As Nietzsche said, "Don't think. Look!" Observation frequently surprises thought. When you go to a place you have heard about, it seldom looks quite the way you thought it would; the first time you touched a horse or drove a car, the experience was almost surely different in subtle ways from what you had anticipated.

Thus, the artist looks at patterns in nature and at works by other artists to get ideas. The writer observes people and reads and, furthermore, attempts to write about subjects he has had personal experience with. The scientist pays close attention to data and is very often forced to new ideas by the data, themselves. A technique for getting management trainees to think creatively about management is to have them tour industries looking for problems. Getting the facts straight is a good way to get ideas for solving a problem, and, if you are stuck on a problem, a good thing to do is to go over the facts once again. *Careful observation and careful attempts to establish the facts, as unpretentious as they may sound, may very well be the best sources of ideas.*

Use checklists.   Using checklists is one of the easiest of the techniques for getting ideas. You can expose yourself to a large number of stimuli in a short period of time simply by looking through a list of items related to your problem. This is what we do when, in trying to recall a name, we consider each letter of the alphabet in turn and ask ourselves whether it could be the first letter of the name we are trying to remember. It is what the poet does in using a rhyming dictionary to bring to mind words with a particular rhyme pattern. It is what a chess player does when one of his pieces is attacked and he runs through the list: move the attacked piece,

133

capture the attacking piece, interpose a piece between the attacking piece and the attacked piece, attack a piece more valuable than the attacked piece.

The trick is to discover checklists that are relevant to your problem. For some tasks, it is helpful simply to look around the room and let various objects suggest ideas. For others, it is more helpful to look through the yellow pages of the phone book or through a mail-order catalogue or at neighboring books on the library shelf. For checklists more specific to a given problem you can look through an appropriate book, one on occupational categories (like the *Occupational Outlook Handbook*), or one on party ideas, or one on sailing hardware, or you can take a walk through an appropriate store. The following checklist (Osborn, 1963) is perhaps the best known of all checklists.

Osborn's Checklist

Put to Other Uses? New ways to use as is? Other uses if modified?

Adapt? What else is like this? What other idea does this suggest? Does past offer parallel? What could I copy? Whom could I emulate?

Modify? New twist? Change meaning, color, motion, odor, form, shape? Other changes?

Magnify? What to add? More time? Greater frequency? Stronger? Larger? Thicker? Extra value? Plus ingredient? Duplicate? Multiply? Exaggerate?

Minify? What to substitute? Smaller? Condensed? Miniature? Lower? Shorter? Lighter? Omit? Streamline? Split up? Understate?

Substitute? Who else instead? What else instead? Other ingredient? Other material? Other process? Other power? Other place? Other approach? Other tone of voice?

Rearrange? Interchange components? Other pattern? Other layout? Other sequence? Transpose cause and effect? Change pace? Change schedule?

Reverse? Transpose positive and negative? How about opposites? Turn it backward? Turn it upside down? Reverse roles? Change shoes? Turn tables? Turn other cheek?

Combine? How about a blend, an alloy, an assortment, an ensemble? Combine units? Combine purposes? Combine appeals? Combine ideas?

Even your own earlier ideas can serve usefully as a checklist, for earlier ideas are often seen to have a new significance in the context of later ones (Osborn, 1963).

We have already come across some important checklists in previous chapters. The decision tree is a checklist that reminds us to consider several alternative courses of action and various alternative futures. Both the decision tree and the cross-classification table are checklists that remind us of the information we need in order to be able to make a statement about a relationship. And the scheme, $A ===> B$, $B === > A$, $A < ==> B$, $C === > A, B$, is a checklist that reminds us of alternative causal possibilities. Finally, we are now proceeding through a checklist of techniques for generating ideas. Later, when you are trying to get ideas, it should be helpful to go back through this chapter to make sure that you have not overlooked a technique that could be of use.

Rearrange the elements of your problem. Rearranging the elements of your problem in space or in time can suggest alternative interpretations and lead to new ideas. A chess game looks almost like a different game when you view the board from your opponent's side, and new moves come quickly to mind from this perspective. It is more difficult to see a cork as useful in helping to solve a problem when it is in a bottle than when it is lying next to it (Duncker, 1945). And it is more difficult to figure out how to find the area of the triangle on the next page.

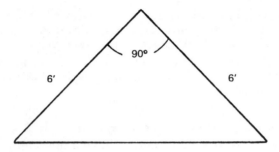

than if you rotate it until one of the six-foot sides is horizontal and the other vertical. In the new orientation, it is easier to see the triangle as half a square and the area as equal to $(6 \times 6)/2 = 18$ square feet.

Temporal order, as well as spatial order affects the way we perceive things. An orange tastes sweet if eaten before brushing our teeth, but sour if eaten afterwards. The sequence,

SKYSCRAPER, TEMPLE, CATHEDRAL, PRAYER,

suggests the category "buildings," and "prayer" seems not to belong; whereas the sequence,

PRAYER, TEMPLE, CATHEDRAL, SKYSCRAPER,

suggests the category "religious things," and "skyscraper" seems not to belong (Cofer, 1951).

So you should rearrange the parts of your problem and work on the parts in different orders. You should also vary the order in which you work your problem in with other activities. Supposedly, it was taking a bath while working on the problem of determining the gold content of a crown that led Archimedes to the principle of specific gravity. After you have been working on a paper for a while, stop writing and do some more background reading before resuming writing.

Having worked on the paper will get you to see the background reading in a different light, and doing more background reading will establish a new perspective from which to view your paper.

Discuss your problem with someone else.   Talking to experts can, of course, be an excellent way to get ideas, but even talking over your problem with someone who has no expertise in the area may lead to suggestions, or even just questions, that will stimulate you to solve the problem.

As an example of how this can work, a boat owner had been trying for over an hour to repair his diesel auxiliary, while a guest he had promised to take sailing waited in the cockpit, unable to help because of the small size of the engine compartment. Finally the guest said, "What exactly is the problem? Maybe I can figure it out." The sailor described the problem, and the guest immediately suggested a solution.

"That's it!" the owner said and, disappearing below, fixed the engine within minutes. As it turned out, the solution the guest had offered was not the correct one, because he had not understood the situation correctly. Nevertheless, it provided the stimulus that suggested a genuine solution to the owner.

Take a break.   This is the second (and, regrettably, the last) technique for the improvement of thinking that requires no effort at all. The first was distribution of practice, which, you will remember, seems to allow some automatic process to strengthen memory traces. The second is called "incubation" (Helmholtz, see Whiting, 1958). All that you do consciously to initiate incubation is to give up working on the problem. Later, if incubation is successful, the germ of the solution will flash effortlessly into consciousness, often in a dramatic "Eureka!" or "Aha!" experience. The period between the time you give up working on the problem and the time the solution appears is called the incubation period. A familiar experience that may constitute a "miniature" example of incubation is trying to recall a word, giving up for a while, and then having the word suddenly come to mind (Polya, 1957). Several explanations have been advanced for the incubation effect (see Anderson, 1975, pp. 277–290), but such theoretical matters need not concern us here. All that need concern us is that taking a break is probably an effective way to get ideas.

One point is worth stressing, however. Creative thinkers uniformly report incubation as being effective only after a long period of conscious work (Helmholtz, see Whiting, 1958; Poincare, 1913; Ghiselin, 1952), and what little laboratory research has been done on the topic (Silviera, 1971) agrees in suggesting that a certain period of conscious work is necessary if incubation is to take place. Popular accounts, on the other hand, tend to emphasize the effortlessness that accompanies the moment of inspiration. For example, it is said that Watt invented the steam engine while out for a Sunday walk. It is true that this is how he got his inspiration, but it is also true that he had been working on the problem for a long time before he took that Sunday walk.

Thus, there are really two things you have to do consciously to initiate incubation: First, work on the problem until you have become thoroughly immersed in it and are genuinely stuck, and then, and only then, set the problem aside for a while.

ABSTRACT CODING

The techniques of coding variation, both abstract and concrete, contrast with those of stimulus variation in that they involve mental manipulations, rather than physical manipulations. The techniques for abstract coding, to begin with these, get you to represent your problem in a symbolic, analytic fashion—in the language of the "left brain" (Sperry, 1964; Sperry and Gazzaniga, 1967).

Translate your problem into symbols. We think differently about the names of things than about the things themselves (Karwoski, Gramlich, and Arnott, 1944), so try expressing your problem in words. For example, try explaining it orally or in writing to someone. This may sound like the suggestion just given, to discuss your problem with someone else, yet it is different. There need not actually be anyone else present for this technique to work—you can write, as well as talk—and, even if there is someone else present, that person need not say a thing—you could just as well be giving a speech as carrying on a conversation. Whereas the purpose of the first technique was to expose yourself to stimuli related to your problem, the purpose of this technique is to get you to code the problem in different terms, specifically in verbal terms. Of course, engaging in conversation puts you in a position where both techniques can operate simultaneously, and this undoubtedly explains why talking with others is such a good way to get ideas.

As one example of the value of attempting to communicate your ideas to someone else, a medical researcher who had worked on and off for eight years trying to determine why injection of the enzyme papain causes wilting of the ears in rabbits finally found the answer while lecturing on the problem. In attempting to explain the problem to students, he had to consider more closely an unlikely hypothesis that he had rejected at the outset on the basis of assumptions that would have been clear to anyone working in the area, though not necessarily to the students. In demonstrating an experiment that he had never thought necessary, he found that the rejected hypothesis was in fact the correct one (Barber and Fox, 1958). How many countless times have teachers similarly discovered a flaw in their reasoning only when they started to explain it to a class!

Once you have represented your problem or some aspect of it in words, you can apply verbal manipulations to these words to generate ideas. One technique, called symbolic analogy (Gordon, 1961, 1971), involves combining (a) an analogous noun and (b) a conflicting adjective. Thus, a symbolic analogy for a ratchet might be "dependable intermitency" (Prince, 1970. "Intermittency" is a noun analogous to ratchet, and "dependable" is an adjective that seems to conflict with intermittency. Similarly, a symoblic analogy for typing might be "solitary conversation." This might suggest making typing less solitary and more conversational by composing into a dictaphone and then typing from your own dictation. By speaking aloud and listening to yourself, you might perceive your flow of ideas differently, and this might result in improved quality of thought and expression.

Another kind of verbal manipulation is reversal (Osborn, 1953). Reversal can be accomplished in two ways. For example, the description, "Policemen organizing traffic," can be reversed to "Traffic organizing policemen," or to "Policemen disorganizing traffic." The first might suggest traffic organizing itself or, at least, traffic density determining the placement of policemen. The second might suggest organizing traffic by means of some device more predictable than policemen, such as traffic lights (DeBono, 1973.). As another example, "taking cars to gas stations," could suggest, "taking gas stations to cars." A successful business has been built on servicing cars while they sit idle in company parking lots during the day.

Mathematics is simply another language, and coding your problem into mathematical terms, if you feel comfortable with mathematics, can be quite helpful. Mathematics forces you to be quite precise and to look at your problem in a highly analytic way. It also permits manipulations that can enable you to recombine elements with great facility. And, remember, in creative thinking neither your mathematics nor your logic need actually be correct for it to work. In getting ideas, anything is fair.

Consider the following problem:

> You are in the land of Truers and Liars. Truers always tell the truth, and Liars always lie. On your way to the harbor, you come to a fork in the road. You wish to ask a person there which road leads to the harbor, but you do not know whether he is a Truer or a Liar. What question can you ask that will elicit the correct answer in either case?

This problem can be represented mathematically (a) by using $+1$ for a true statement and -1 for a false statement and (b) by using multiplication to represent making a statement about a statement. Thus, if a Truer made a true statement about a true statement, this would be represented as $+1(+1) = +1$. Similarly, if a Liar made a false statement about a false statement, this would be represented as $-1(-1) = +1$, also a true statement. Just as there are two ways to get a positive product, there are two ways to get a correct statement about which road leads to the harbor: Ask a Truer to tell the truth about a true statement he would have made, or ask a Liar to lie about a false statement he would have made. Thus, the question we are looking for might go something like this: "If someone had come along this way earlier and asked you which road leads to the harbor, what would you have told him?" (There is at least one other solution to this problem, suggested by this same mathematical representation. Can you see it?)

Analyze the elements of your problem into attributes. The idea here is to analyze the elements of the problem, either the materials out of which the solution is to be constructed or the goal, into attributes and to think about the attributes separately. We think differently about objects once we have analyzed them into their attributes (Glucksburg and Danks,

1968). According to Crawford (1964, p. 14), creativity generally proceeds through the selection of an attribute from one thing and applying it to something else. Whereas the idea of houses plus the idea of automobiles leads nowhere, the idea of renting houses plus the idea of automobiles suggests the idea of renting automobiles.

Thinking in terms of attributes helps you to get above the trees and see the forest, different attributes enabling you to see the forest from different vantage points. Thinking in terms of attributes helps you to keep from focusing on a narrow subset of possibilities.

One technique for discovering attributes is first to list ideas, then to cluster them together into groups of similar ideas, and then, finally, to ask yourself in what ways (in terms of what attributes) the ideas within each group are similar to one another and different from ideas in other groups. This technique is claimed to be particularly helpful for writing papers and reports (Rico,1977). A related technique for discovering attributes for evaluating alternative courses of action is first to rank the alternatives from most desirable to least desirable and then to ask yourself why you ranked them that way.

What we are talking about is an idea tree whose early branches represent general possibilities and whose later branches represent more particular possibilities. For example, if you were trying to think of ways to improve a telephone, you could begin by listing its various attributes (Crawford, 1954): color, size, weight, etc. The early branches in your tree would then be color, size, weight, etc. Next, you would take each of these general branches in turn, beginning with, say, color, and list more particular ideas for it, such as making phones that would glow in the dark; making clear plastic covers that you could color yourself with paint, fabric, or wallpaper; and so forth. (See Covington, Crutchfield, Davies, and Olton, 1974.)

One way to analyze the elements of your problem into

attributes is to think about the attributes of the materials you have to work with (Duncker, 1945); another is to think about the attributes of the goal (Duncker, 1945). The scout problem is an example of a problem for which analysis of the materials is helpful.

> Devise a method by which a scout who has been sent to check an area upstream can send a message back to his troops, indicating whether they should follow him or not, and send the message in such a way that it will be very difficult to block.

A good rule is to pick out all the important objects and persons in the problem and to think separately about each (Covington, Crutchfield, Davies, and Olton, 1974). All that the scout has to work with is the fact that he is uphill from his troops and near a river. Thinking about the river, you may see that it has the property of moving in the direction in which the scout wants his message to go. You might then think about the various properties of the river that might be made use of. The solution, which makes use of the fact that water dissolves things, is to dye the river one color for "go" and another for "no go."

The other way to analyze the elements of your problem into attributes is to think about the attributes of the goal (Duncker, 1945). If your problem is to find a better way to toast foods, analyzing toasting into browning and dehydrating can increase the number of possibilities that come to mind (Parnes, 1967). The squares problem is an example of a problem for which analysis of the goal is helpful. The problem is to determine how many squares there are in the following drawing.

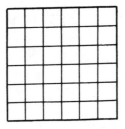

The first answer that usually comes to mind is 36. But analysis of the goal reveals that nothing is said about the size of the squares. There are, in addition to the 1-by-1 squares, 2-by-2, 3-by-3, 4-by-4, and 5-by-5 squares—and one 6-by-6 square.

Often, you find yourself in the middle of an idea tree like this and have to remind yourself to move up to a more general level. There are at least two occasions on which you should do this. One is when you have gotten into a loop, when you are going over the same ideas again and again. To get out of a loop, try to identify the common attributes of the ideas you have been generating so that you can avoid these (Wicklegren, 1974). For example, in trying to figure out a way to use radiation to destroy a tumor without harming the healthy surrounding tissue, some problem solvers spend all their time thinking of ideas like operating, sending the rays down the esophagus, and pushing the tumor closer to the surface. What these ideas have in common is the property of avoiding the healthy tissue. These problem solvers would be well advised to try to think of other kinds of ideas. Instead of avoiding the healthy tissue, how about immunizing it, or how about lowering the intensity of the rays on their way through it? The figure on page 144 shows an idea tree of possibilities for solving the tumor problem (Duncker, 1945). (The solu-

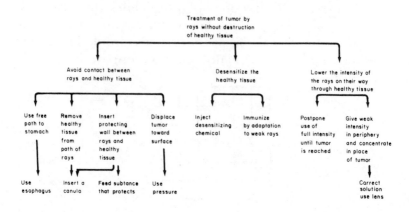

tion is to lower the intensity of the rays on their way through the healthy tissue and increase their intensity at the site of the tumor by sending rays in from different angles in such a way that they converge on the tumor.)

The nine-dot problem and the four-triangles problem provide further examples of problems where people tend to get into loops. The nine-dot problem presents the solver with a 3-by-3 grid of nine dots like the following.

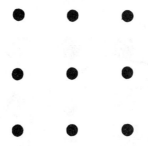

This problem requires that four straight lines be drawn, without lifting your pencil from the paper, so that they pass through all nine dots. The loop people tend to get into is confining their lines to the square defined by the outermost dots. The solution requires that they go outside this square. If a solver identifies this property common to his early solution attempts and tries to produce solutions of a different kind, he should be more likely to solve the problem. The solution is shown below.

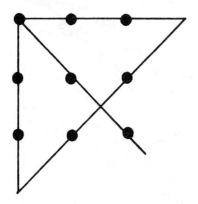

Actually, it is possible to solve this problem with three straight, connected lines. Can you see how? The solution is based on the fact that the dots, as drawn, are not points, but areas. The solution is shown below, with the dots enlarged to make it easier to show the solution.

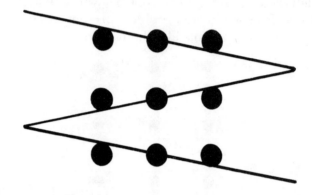

As if this were not enough, the problem can also be solved with a single straight line. This solution is based on the facts that the paper can be folded and that the line, as drawn, has width. This solution is accomplished by folding the outside columns of dots toward the center column and drawing a single line through them as follows.

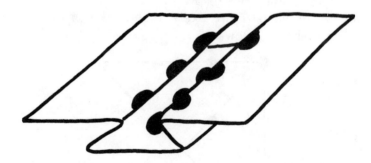

The four-triangles problem presents the solver with six kitchen matches and requires that four triangles be made from these matches without breaking any match.

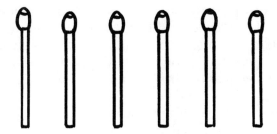

The loop that people tend to get into here is confining their constructions to the two dimensions of the table top. There appears to be only one solution to this problem, to construct a three-dimensional figure, a tetrahedron. This can be done by using three of the matches to form a triangle on the table top and then placing each of the other three matches so that it rises from one of the corners of this triangle to a common vertex above it.

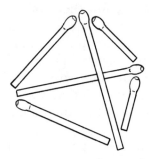

One time when you should move to a more general level is when you have gotten into a loop. Another is once you have achieved a solution. Once you have achieved a solution, you should attempt to generalize it so that it will be useful in as wide a range of future situations as possible. This is a matter of creative information storage, rather than creative information retrieval, and thus relates back to the chapter on memory, specifically, to the discussion of understanding.

Let us say that you are wondering why we say "salt and pepper" more often than "pepper and salt," "bread and but-

ter" more often than "butter and bread," and "men and women," but then, "ladies and gentlemen." To get ideas about
this problem, you might try to think of various attributes of
the words. Eventually, you might hit upon number of syllables and notice that the first member of each pair has fewer
syllables than the second.

Before you leave this problem and go on to other matters, however, you should attempt to generalize the solution.
It may seem a small step from the statement that, other
things being equal, words with few syllables tend to be produced before words with many syllables, to the statement
that, again other things being equal, simple items tend to be
produced before complex items. Yet the latter suggests many
more ideas. Perhaps, when you are planning your day, it
would be wise to clear away the little odds and ends first and
thus free your mind for the more difficult problems.
Perhaps, in presenting an argument, you should present the
simpler points first and follow these with the more complex
ones, for your listener's sake as well as your own. Perhaps it
would be better if our phone numbers were arranged so that
the four unrelated digits came first and the more complex
three-digit unit that is now the prefix came last (see Johnson,
1970). By generalizing your solution in this way, you can turn
the solution to one problem into the solution to a whole class
of problems.

Analysis into attributes is part of what we mean by understanding. It is worth stressing again that *trying to understand what you are working on, along with careful observation, may
very well be the most important source of ideas we have.*

Recombine attributes.   Recombining attributes is also part of
understanding: You can describe what you are trying to understand by specifying the combination of attributes that
characterizes it, thus placing it in a category. What is more to
the present point, however, is that by combining attributes in
novel ways, you can create descriptions of entirely new en-
tities (Zwicky, 1957).

As a practical example of this technique, a student was uncertain as to whether to major in psychology, English, or physical education. Her adviser asked her what attributes of each field most attracted her. She said that she liked the fact that psychology enabled her to understand people, but that she didn't want to help people with problems or to do research; that she liked writing, but not literature; and that she liked sports activities, but not the more scientific side of physical education. Putting the positive attributes "writing," "about people," and "in sports activities" together, her adviser asked whether she had considered sports writing. She lit up and said, "No, but that's a great idea!" and left to try the idea out by working as a sports writer on the school paper.

There are more systematic and thorough ways to combine attributes. One is our old friend cross-classification. By cross-classifying atomic number (number of protons) by atomic weight (number of protons plus number of neutrons)

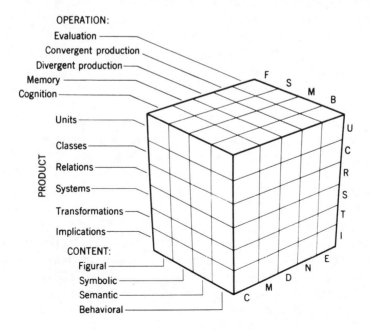

in what is known as the Periodic Table of Elements, Mendeleev conceived of many elements that had not yet been discovered. Similarly, J. P. Guilford cross-classified five cognitive operations, four contents, and six products and thus postulated 120 mental abilities, tests for many of which have since been developed (see figure on page 149).

Zwicky (1969, pp. 256–258), while director of the Aerojet Engineering Corporation, conceived of 576 possible types of jet engines by cross-classifying kinds of chemical reaction and kinds of media (vacuum, air, water, earth). Only three of these had been described in the technical literature. To these three, several dozen of the 576 have now been added, including the pulsejet, the aeropulse, and the hydropulse.

The other method for combining attributes is the sliding-columns method (Parnes 1977: personal communication), an incomplete cross-classification that is easy to carry out. Let us say that you want to write a story. A story generally has the following elements: characters, setting, goal, obstacle, means of overcoming obstacle, ending. Begin by thinking of some possible characters, say, a stage magician, a nymphomaniac, a wealthy leader of a religious cult. . . . Then think of some settings, such as a chartered yacht, a brain surgeon's mountain cabin, the English department at a small private college, and so forth, and some goals, such as to locate a lost will, to meet a lover, to obtain a political favor. Do this for obstacles, means of overcoming obstacles, and endings. Then list each set of attributes in a column, one for characters, one for settings, one for goals, etc. To get ideas for plots, slide the columns up and down and read across the rows.

How about a stage magician who has chartered a yacht to try to find a lost will. . . . The story almost carries you from there: The obstacle is that the skipper of the chartered yacht turns out to be the deceased's only living relative. He wants to get the will, so he can destroy it and keep the magician from getting a large share of the inheritance. As soon as he gets the sailing directions, he identifies himself and attempts to do away with the magician. The means for overcoming the obstacle is the magician's stage skill. . . .

CONCRETE CODING

The techniques for concrete coding get you to represent your problem in muscular, graphic, or metaphoric terms—in the language of the "right brain" (Sperry, 1964; Sperry and Gazzaniga, 1967). Concrete representations provide access to information in the memory that is not tapped by verbal representations (Anderson and Johnson, 1966). Gordon (1961, 1971) sees metaphors as important for "making the familiar strange" and thus freeing you from habitual ways of thinking. According to Prince (1970), the more strange and remote the metaphor, the better. For example, a mental block is a more remote metaphor for a closure than is a door.

Represent the problem in terms of your own actions. As the typist who is asked where the "Q" is on the typewriter suddenly realizes, the part of our brain that controls our action knows things that the parts of our brain that control imaginal and verbal processes do not—he has to move his finger and look at it before he can answer the question. If we can represent our problem in terms of this part of our brain, we may be able to think about it in a fresh way. There are at least two ways of doing this.

One is to manipulate the elements of your problem physically. It is a familiar experience to have solved a mechanical puzzle, even to have repeated the solution several times, before we are able to see how we solved it (Ruger, 1910). If the elements of the problem cannot be readily manipulated, then you can at least manipulate representations of them. If you are trying to solve an anagram, write the

letters on slips of paper, and move the slips of paper around
with your fingers. If you are trying to solve some problem
like the missionaries and cannibals problem (getting missionaries and cannibals across a river using only a small boat
and never allowing the cannibals to outnumber the missionaries), represent the missionaries and cannibals by pieces
of paper with M's and C's on them and move these back and
forth across a space on the table. Translating the elements of
your problem into manipulatable items actually has two
merits. In addition to enabling you to represent mental operations in terms of physical actions, it also provides you with
an external memory to keep track of where you are in your
work on the problem.

A second way to represent a problem in terms of your
own actions is to imagine that you are the critical object. This
is called personal analogy or role-playing. Creative people
immerse themselves in their work, identify with it, become it.
As an old Taoist quote puts it, "If you want to draw a bird,
you must become a bird." And Einstein (quoted in
Hadamard, 1945, pp. 142–143) wrote:

> The psychical entities which seem to serve as elements in
> thought are certain signs and more or less clear images which
> can be "voluntarily" reproduced and combined. . . . The
> above mentioned elements are, in my case of visual *and some of
> muscular* type." (Emphasis added.)

A technique that is used to get beginning writers to think
more creatively is to have them write in the first person present, that is, to write as though they themselves are carrying
out the action at that moment.

We can role-play people in working on interpersonal
problems, marketing problems, or the like, and we can role-
play objects in working on design problems of various sorts.
Role-playing people seems to be easier and more effective

(Myers, 1977), yet role-playing objects has also been reported to be quite effective. The following transcript from a Synectics session (Gordon, 1961, pp. 38–40) shows how objects can be role-played. The problem was to invent a new and practical constant-speed mechanism that would receive power from a shaft that could vary in speed anywhere from 400 to 4000 r.p.m. and yet deliver power through a shaft that would have a constant speed of 400 r.p.m. One after the other, each member of the group metaphorically attempted to effect with his own body the speed constancy required. Here are some excerpts from the recorded session. (Note, as you read, the willingness of creative people to play with quite "foolish" ideas.)

A: Okay, I'm in the damn box. I grab the in-shaft with one hand and grab the out-shaft with the other. I let the in-shaft slip when I think it's going too fast so that the out-shaft will stay constant.

B: But how do you know how fast the out-shaft is really going?

C: How do you feel in there?

A: Well, my hands are getting . . . too hot to hold I guess . . . at least one hand, that is . . . the one that's acting like a clutch . . . slipping.

C: B, how about you hopping into the box.

B: I see myself in there but I can't do anything because I don't have anything to measure r.p.m. or time. . . . I guess I'm in the same spot as A.

C: How about you D?

D: . . . I'm in the box and I am trying to be a governor . . . to be a feedback system . . . built in. . . . Let's see. If I grab the out-shaft with my hands . . . and let's say there's a plate on the in-shaft so that my feet can press against it. I put my feet way out on the periphery of the plate and . . . what I really would like is for my feet to get smaller as the speed of the in-shaft increases because then the friction would be reduced and I would hold onto the out-shaft for dear life and its speed might remain constant. . . . The faster the in-shaft went the smaller my feet would become so that the driving force would stay the same.

C: How could you get your feet smaller?

A: That's not the way to ask the question . . . better say, "How keep friction constant?"

E: If for some reason, some anti-Newtonian reason, your feet came closer together on the plate as the speed of the in-shaft increases then your leverage would be reduced. . . . I mean that you might keep the resultant force on the out-shaft constant.

C: I kind of go for that "anti-Newtonian" thing . . . we're fighting centrifugal force here.

E: How about a non-Newtonian liquid? . . . a liquid which draws near to the center of rotation instead of being flung out?

This thinking led to a mechanical version of the "anti-Newtonian liquid" that appeared to be efficient and economical.

As one final example, students of animal behavior frequently "anthropomorphize" (imagine what they would do or think if they were the animal) in order to get ideas for explaining animal behavior.

Represent the problem in terms of drawing or diagrams.   The effect of representing a problem in graphic terms can be quite powerful. "One good picture," the Chinese proverb tells us, "is worth a thousand words." A case in point is the substitution of Euler diagrams for symbolic logic notation. This innovation led to new advances in logic. Euler diagrams take statements like, "All men are mortals," "Some men are fools," and, "No men are perfect thinkers," and represent them as follows.

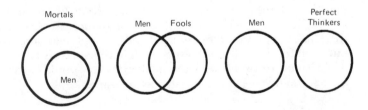

Consider also the following problem:

> A man climbs a mountain on Saturday, leaving at daybreak and arriving at the top near sundown. He spends the night at the top. The next day, Sunday, he leaves at daybreak and heads down the mountain, following the same path that he climbed the day before. The question is this: Will there be any time during the second day when he will be at exactly the same point on the mountain as he was at that time on the first day?

Analysis of the goal will tell you that the problem is, not to determine what the time will be, but simply to determine whether there will be such a time. It can help to represent this problem graphically, as below:

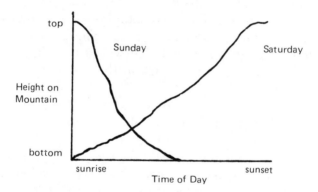

The ascent is represented by the line that begins at the lower left-hand corner of the graph and rises slowly to the top. The descent is represented by the line that begins at the upper-left-hand corner of the graph and goes rather quickly to the bottom. The point of crossing is a point at which time (on the horizontal axis) and place (on the vertical axis) are the same for both ascent and descent. So the answer is yes.

For a very valuable and entertaining discussion of the use of visualization to aid problem solving, see Robert McKim's *Experiences in Visual Thinking* (1972).

Represent your problem in terms of an analogy.   It can be helpful to ask yourself how your problem may have been solved by some mechanical or biological system. We often compare biological systems to mechanical ones, thinking of the heart as a pump or the brain as a computer. And a number of programs for enhancing creative thinking about engineering problems emphasize the value of comparing mechanical systems to biological ones (*Bionics,* 1968; Gordon, 1961, 1971; Halacy, 1965). The workings of the human ear suggested to Alexander Graham Bell part of the mechanism he used for transducing sound energy to electrical energy in the telephone (Gordon, 1961, p. 42). The hook closures on seeds suggested the principle on which Velcro nylon closure strips operate. The tube within which a shipworm works suggested to Brunel the use of caissons for underwater construction (Gordon, 1961, p. 42). The chromatophors that change color in chameleons and flounders by expansion and contraction suggested a design for a roof that would turn light in the summer to reflect heat and dark in the winter to absorb it (Gordon, 1961, p. 54).

Let us close this chapter on creative thinking with a protocol which demonstrates the use of several of the techniques by a person working on a rather ordinary problem. The problem was the one mentioned earlier of devising a method of mounting a compass in the cockpit of a small sailboat. The compass had to be mounted in such a way that it would be easy to detach when not needed and store safely away. The person had been working on this problem, on and off, for two months with no really satisfactory solution. The best solution he could come up with in that period of time was to mount a track on the centerboard cover (which comes up like a wall about a foot high in the center of the cockpit) and to fix a bar to the bottom of the compass that would slide into the track. The difficulty was that he could not find a suitable bar and track and it would be expensive to have such an arrangement made.

He then decided to try some of the techniques for creative thinking. He started with the checklist technique, looking through *The Last Whole Earth Catalogue.* A picture of a fishnet suggested the kind of mechanism for fastening a fishing reel to a rod. He rejected this idea as unsatisfactory, yet it was an idea that had not occurred to him before. Note that, as pointed out earlier, he used the stimulus of a fishnet in a loose way. He did not think of holding the compass in place with a fishnet, but used the idea of a fishnet to associate to related thoughts. Similarly, a picture of an axe suggested a fastening much like a knife switch, and a picture of a vise suggested adapting a ping pong net bracket. Both of these ideas he rejected.

He next tried verbalizing the critical mechanism: "clamp," "vise," "bolt," "holder," "gripper." The word "clamp" suggested something like a tie clip. The word "bolt" suggested a pin-and-slot arrangement.

Next, he tried analysis into attributes. He tried to classify the various ideas he had come up with so far in terms of their essential attributes: horizontal insertion, vertical insertion, screw, spring. He then attempted to generalize each of these. Right off, "spring" suggested the idea of a rubber spring, a hose, and this led to a solution he was satisfied with.

He purchased a four-inch-long piece of industrial hose for 80 cents and made a single lengthwise cut in it, so that it could be forced over the centerboard cover; he then fastened the compass to the hose by means of two stainless steel bolts. The device was inexpensive, was nonmagnetic, would not rust, acted as a shock absorber for the compass, and could be quickly attached anywhere along the centerboard cover, as well as in several other places in the cockpit. What he could not accomplish in two months without the techniques he accomplished in about fifteen minutes using some of them.

RECOMMENDED READING

Stein, M. I., *Stimulating Creativity: Individual Procedures,* vol. I. New York: Academic Press, 1974.

5

Heuristics
for Avoiding
Complexity

Up to this point we have been talking about getting ideas, about expanding the range of possibilities. We have seen how to get ideas from memory, how to add to these by reasoning, and how to add even further to these by means of creative restructuring. Up to this point the scope of possibilities has become increasingly wider.

But things can go too far in this direction; problems can become complex to the point where they are mind boggling. When problems become too complex, we tend to abandon serious efforts at problem solving, leaving the important decisions (whom to vote for, whether to undergo surgery, how to plan for retirement) to someone else or to chance and busying ourselves with less important but simpler decisions (what to wear today, where to go this summer). Indeed, a technique that demagogues and some hypnotists use to get their listeners to give up the responsibility for making decisions is to present as confusing a picture as they can of the current situation. When the freedom to choose leads to too much complexity, we are, in the words of Erich Fromm, all too inclined to "escape from freedom," leaving important decisions to others or to chance or fate.

Complexity can enter a problem at three points: at the act nodes, at the event nodes, and at the end points. There may be a multiplicity of possible courses of action to consider, a multiplicity of possible futures to take into account, or a multiplicity of bases against which to evaluate the end points of the paths—and the important problems of life usually involve complexity from all three!

The time has come to see what techniques are available for narrowing down the range of possibilities, for "unboggling" our minds and enabling them to operate rationally on our problems. While it is true that some narrowing is built into the memory, reasoning, and creative restructuring techniques for getting ideas, in that these techniques do not produce ideas randomly, but tend to produce only ideas that have some chance of being relevant to the problem under consideration, nevertheless, these are essentially techniques for getting ideas. We need techniques that deal more powerfully with the problem of getting rid of ideas.

In general, there are two kinds of techniques for reducing complexity, each applicable to acts, events, and values. These are algorithms and heuristics. An algorithm is a procedure that is sure to find a solution if there is one, while a heuristic is only an educated guess as to the direction in which the solution might lie. Algorithms are deterministic; heuristics, probabilistic. To make this clearer, let us see how algorithms and heuristics can be applied to a simple problem.

Consider an anagram problem. An anagram is a word whose letters have been scrambled up; the problem is to put the letters back in their proper order and discover what the word is. Consider a very simple anagram, the sequence EHT.

An algorithm that is applicable to anagram problems is to search systematically through all possible sequences of the letters: EHT, ETH, HET, HTE, TEH, and THE. If any of these sequences constitutes a word, this algorithm is sure to find it.

A heuristic that is applicable to anagram problems is to look for likely letter combinations. As soon as we find two or three letters that go together in a common sequence, like "TH," "ED," or "ING," we try leaving them that way. If we keep the "TH" together in the EHT anagram, we are left with only two possible sequences, E(TH) and (TH)E, one of which is the solution. The probability of discovering the solution on, for example, the first attempt has thus been raised from 1/6 to 1/2. Though the saving in this simple example is trivial, in real life it can be enormous.

Because heuristics are only educated guesses, however, they sometimes fail. If the anagram has been OHT, keeping the "TH" together would have led to O(TH) and (TH)O, neither of which is the solution. This is a very simple example of what we call a "tricky" problem, one for which trusted heuristics fail.

Because they are sure to find a solution if there is one, algorithms are generally to be preferred to heuristics. We shall be talking about algorithms in the two chapters after this. There are a great many situations, however, for which algorithms either would be prohibitively time-consuming or are not even available. This is especially likely to be the case for important practical problems in real life. In such cases, we have no real alternative but to employ heuristics. Heuristics will be the concern of this chapter.

The central theme that runs through all heuristics is constraint location: locating those aspects of the problem that are most likely to constrain further search. If you were looking up a paper by Miller and Isard, for example, looking under "Isard" would, obviously, constrain your search more than looking under "Miller." Similarly, in trying to find a time when several people can get together for a meeting, the best place to start is by considering the schedules of the busiest people; and, in thinking about redecorating a room, you will narrow your search down most rapidly if you decide on the carpet first, then the drapes, and lastly the paint. The idea is to simplify the problem by focusing, at least initially, on what seem to be the most important aspects. The "20–80 rule," as we noted earlier, states that 20% of the facts account for 80% of what is going on. These are the "vital few" among the "trivial many" (MacKenzie, 1972, pp. 51ff.), and it makes good sense to start with them.

We shall consider heuristics under three headings: knowing where to start, knowing how to break the problem up, and knowing where to head. Although we shall consider the various heuristics separately, you should keep in mind that they can be used together.

KNOWING WHERE TO START:
Working Forwards
and Working Backward

It's an all too familiar experience to be confronted by a problem that's so complicated we simply "don't know where to start." The best place to start in problem solving is usually at a point of high constraint, a point that narrows down our search as much as possible. Sometimes this point is at the "beginning" of the problem, and we will do best to "work forward"; at other times it is at the "end," and the best strategy is to "work backwards."

A story is told of a student who went to talk to his physics professor about why he never did well on examination questions. The conversation went something like this:

PROFESSOR: Why don't you try this question, and we'll try to see where you're going wrong: How could you use a barometer to determine the height of a building?

STUDENT: Well, I suppose you could measure the length of the barometer and then see how many times the length of the barometer will go into the height of the building and then multiply.

PROFESSOR: Uh, no . . . Maybe that's where you've gotten the wrong idea. You see, you have to make use of one of the physical principles you've learned in the course.

STUDENT: Oh! You could drop the barometer from the top of the building, see how long it takes it to fall, and then use the formula $S = \frac{1}{2}gt^2$!

PROFESSOR: No, no, no! You have to use a *different* physical principle. Can you think of another way?

STUDENT: Well, maybe you could strike the barometer against the top of the building, measure the number of seconds it takes the sound to reach the bottom, and multiply by 1100 feet per second.

PROFESSOR: (After a difficult period of silence.) Try an entirely different method.

STUDENT: Well, if none of those methods worked, I guess I'd go to the custodian and say, "If you tell me the height of this building, I'll give you a barometer."

This hopefully fictitious student generated a tree with a lot of useless ideas. The reason is that he did not constrain his search sufficiently. If he had been less exclusively focused on the goal of determining the height of the building and had thought more about the materials he had available, the barometer, he would have proceeded more directly to the solution. Analysis of the materials tells us that what a barometer does best is measure atmospheric pressure. This leads to the question, "How can I use differences in atmospheric pressure to measure height?" and the solution, which is, of course, to use the barometer as an altimeter.

(In the creative thinking chapter, we spoke well of thought processes not that much different from this student's, and we should not lose sight of the fact that, while heuristics usually confine our search in fruitful ways, they are only educated guesses, which can sometimes incline us

TABLE 5.
Techniques for Simplifying Complex Problems

1. Working Forward and Working Backward.
   Consider whether the materials or the goal constrain search more and proceed from the source of the greater constraint.
2. Planning.
   Rough out a plan for a solution in terms of just the important elements before attempting to work out a solution in detail.
3. Classification
   Think in terms of classes of elements rather than particular elements.
4. Hillclimbing.
   If you are unable to find a way to get all the way to the goal, look for a way to reduce the difference between your present position and the goal.

away from genuinely creative solutions. "An inventor," as Kettering said, "is a person who doesn't take his education too seriously." An artful balance is required here. The best thing to do is probably to generate some ideas using the heuristics, then, if these are not satisfactory, to generate others not using the heuristics or even violating them.)

Some problems are constrained more by the materials, the givens, and the most efficient way to solve these is to work forward from the givens to the goal. Practical problems, such as the problem of measuring the height of a building, usually conform to this pattern. Other problems are constrained more by the goal, and the most efficient way to solve them is to work backward from a consideration of the goal to the givens (Duncker, 1945; Polya, 1957). The structure of these two kinds of problems is diagrammed below:

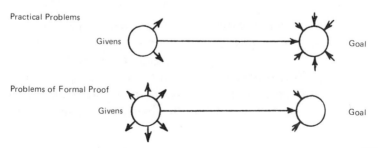

In practical problems, the difficulty usually lies in making do with what you have available. There are many ways to measure the height of a building, but few things you can do well with a barometer. Similarly, in the problem of discovering how a scout can send a message downriver to his troops, telling them whether to come ahead or not, and sending the message in such a way that it would be difficult to block, there are many ways to send a message, but few things you can do with a stream.

As one more example, consider the following problem:

> I still don't know whether it was fast thinking or whether Grandmother figured it out in advance. Anyway, she certainly did the right thing when our vicious ram suddenly lowered his horns and rushed at her.
>
> It happened in the sheep pasture, a big cutover field that was full of knee-high stumps. Here our ram ruled a flock of ewes and made war on anybody who ventured into his domain. That ram always terrified me, especially after I saw him hit a hired man hard enough to snap a bone in his leg. From then on, afraid to cross the pasture, I always walked around it.
>
> Not Grandmother! She just ignored the ram, and that's what she was doing this time I speak of. She had been picking wild plums on the other side of the pasture and was now carrying her filled pail back toward the house. She was halfway across the field when the ram spied her. He advanced a few slow steps—and then, while I watched fearfully from behind the fence, he put down his head and charged furiously.
>
> How did Grandmother trick the ram and get safely from the pasture?

There are many paths that lead to the goal of keeping a ram from butting you: closing a gate, climbing a fence, roping it, even shooting it. But there was no gate, or fence, or rope, or gun handy. The source of constraint in practical problems of this sort is generally in the givens, the materials available. All that we are told that Grandmother had were a pail of plums and the stumps in the field. It was one of the stumps that she made use of.

> Stepping behind the nearest tree stump, Grandmother faced the oncoming ram. She picked up her ankle-length skirt and apron and dropped them over the stump, concealing it completely. The ram crashed into the hidden stump with sickening force; then, badly dazed, he wobbled away . . . while Grandmother took up her pail and walked on. (Reprinted from *The Saturday Evening Post,* © 1949 The Curtis Publishing Company.)

Because practical problems are usually constrained more by the materials, it will usually be best, when you are applying the techniques of stimulus and coding variation for getting ideas for solutions to such problems, to apply them primarily to the materials.

In problems of formal proof, on the other hand, it is the final state, the goal, rather than the initial state, that most constrains the search. A geometry proof, once it is worked out, would begin with some theorems or axioms and end with the statement to be proved. The theorems and axioms provide little constraint, however, because they lead to large portions of geometry. It is only by thinking about the statement to be proved that we have any hope of usefully constraining our search.

As another example, trouble-shooting in inductive reasoning problems is usually best carried out by thinking about the conclusion, rather than the various rules for inductive reasoning. Whether a particular rule applies depends on the conclusion. For example, controlled comparison is not necessary for a statement of predictive relationship. Whether a particular study is adequate or inadequate depends on what conclusions you want to draw.

A number of other kinds of problems as well would seem to be solved more easily by working backward from the goal. In the writing of traditional poetry, for example, the most constrained place to begin writing a line is with the final word, for it must rhyme. Similarly, in writing many kinds of jokes, the most constrained place to begin is with the punch line. The following joke seems to be a very good example of this kind of joke (though it is not a very good example of a joke):

> One day, the zoo attendant noticed that the porpoises were engaged in lovemaking. Afraid that this might embarrass some people, he went to get some seagulls to feed them. On his way back with the gulls, he encountered a lion sleeping in his path. As he was stepping gingerly over the lion, a policeman arrested him. The question is: What was the charge?

The answer: Carrying gulls across a staid lion for immoral porpoises!

A good strategy for solving algebra word problems and, indeed, for comprehending many kinds of materials, is first to read quickly over the problem, noting what terms are used repeatedly and are thus likely to be the most important, then to read the problem a second time, carefully, beginning with the question at the end and, hence, working backward from this point.

Other problems where working backward would seem to be a better strategy than working forward are planning an end game in chess, planning a climbing route up a mountain, and planning how to prepare yourself for applying to graduate school. Near the end of a chess game, there are often fewer ways of achieving checkmate than ways of proceeding from your present position. A mountain has many places to start up it, but only one top. And, while there are many courses you can take, people you can meet, and activities you can engage in, there are many fewer ends states that will be acceptable to an admissions committee. Because such problems are usually constrained more by the goal, it will usually be best, when you apply the techniques of stimulus and coding variation to getting ideas for solving them, to apply these techniques to the goal.

Nadler (1963, p. 37) seems to be talking about working backward when he says, "A better system and method design is achieved by actually using an ideal system design as a model from which the recommended design makes a minimum departure than by using the present system analysis model from which the 'bad' activities are removed." This is what Gordon (1961) calls "fantasy analogy."

Nim games, in which each player takes away tokens subject to certain restrictions and tries to be the last, or not the last, to take a token, provide excellent examples of the usefulness of working backward (Wicklegren, 1974, p. 142). Consider the following such problem.

> Fifteen pennies are placed on a table in front of two players. Each player is allowed to remove at least 1 penny but not more than 5 pennies at his turn. The players alternate turns, each removing from 1 to 5 pennies, until one player takes the last penny on the table, and wins all 15 pennies. Is there a method of play that will guarantee victory? If so, what is it?

If you work forward on this problem, there are 5 opening moves you could make, 5 moves your opponent could make in response to each of these, and 5 moves you could make in response to each of his moves. Already, there are $5 \times 5 \times 5 = 125$ different possibilities.

If you work backward at the end you must be left with 5 or fewer pennies. To ensure that this will be the case, you must leave your opponent exactly 6 pennies on the turn before. If you leave him with fewer than 6, he could take them all; if you leave him with more than 6, he could leave you with 6. Working backward, then, you have already established an important constraint on your search. From here, it is easy to see that, if on your first move you leave your opponent with 12 pennies, then no matter how many he takes, you will be able to leave him with 6.

There are other problems where both the givens and the goal provide a great deal of constraint, and a good strategy for such problems would be to work from both ends in toward the middle. Laddergrams (Surrick and Conant, 1927), puzzles that require you to change one word into another, changing only one letter at a time and always producing words as intermediate steps, are examples of this type of problem. For example:

Change WHITE to BROWN in 10 steps.

(The solution to this laddergram is: WHITE, WRITE, TRITE, TRICE, TRACE, TRACT, TRAIT, TRAIN, BRAIN, BRAWN, BROWN.) For many problems, it will be difficult to tell in advance whether the givens, the goal, or both provide constraint, and, in such cases, you may just have to try working forward for a while and then working backward for a while.

KNOWING HOW TO BREAK THE PROBLEM UP: Planning and Classification

The idea here is to analyze the problem into subproblems, to "divide and conquer." To get some idea of the power of this heuristic, consider a simple problem in architecture. Let us say that you are designing a house and that you are considering, among other things, four floor plans (A, B, C, and D) and four styles (1, 2, 3, and 4). The tree would look like this:

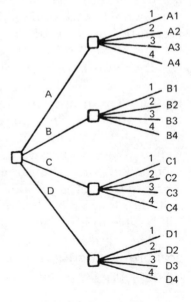

Altogether, there are 4 × 4 = 16 possibilities, a complicated tree even for such a simple problem. Suppose, however, that you treat selecting a floor plan as one subproblem and selecting a style as another, on the assumption that whatever floor plan and style you happen to decide upon can be made to go together. This will break the one complex problem into two much simpler problems, as follows:

Here there are only 4 + 4 = 8 possibilities, a considerable simplification. In real life, the simplification achieved is usually much greater (see Newell, Shaw, and Simon, 1962).

The trick, of course, is to discover subproblems that are relatively independent, to "carve the problem at its joints," as Aristotle so nicely put it. Doing this usually requires an intimate knowledge of the problem area. Each of the general heuristic methods, as we shall see, requires some specific knowledge of the problem area in order to be applied.

Analysis into subproblems is not quite the same as decomposition. The problem to which decomposition addresses itself is the limited capacity of effortful processing; because most problems involve more considerations than we can think about at once, we think about them in smaller pieces and then put the results of our thinking together. The problem to which analysis into subproblems addresses itself is the complexity of the world. Some problems are so complex that no conceivable intelligence could handle them without heuristics. For example, it has been estimated that in the simpler-than-life game of chess there are more possible moves than there are molecules in the known universe! No intelligence could consider all these. It should be no surprise, then, that even master players explore only a few branches to any depth (de Groot, 1965, e.g., 267). Most branches are "pruned" at an early stage by means of heuristics. Thus, while decomposition is an algorithm that helps us to deal with necessary complexity, analysis into subproblems is a heuristic that helps us to avoid having to deal with unnecessary complexity.

Two forms of analysis into subproblems deserve special comment. These are planning and classification. Planning selects important objects or actions for initial consideration, and classification selects important attributes for initial consideration. Let's begin with *planning*. To apply the planning heuristic, you simplify the problem by thinking about just the most important objects or actions in the problem situation. The steps in the solution to the simplified problem then become subgoals which divide the original problem into subproblems. There is experimental evidence (Reed, in Castellan and Pisoni, 1977) that establishing subgoals facilitates problem solution. To plan a summer trip initially think only of major points of interest and leave questions about particular rates and motels and restaurants until later. The decisions about the major points of interest would provide subgoals for further problem solving.

Consider the disk transfer problem. The problem is to move a pile of graduated disks from one of three posts to another (see figure below).

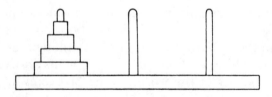

The two restrictions are that you should move only one disk at a time and that you should never place a larger disk on a smaller one.

To apply the planning heuristic to the disk transfer problem, consider just the largest disk. It would seem to be the most important, because it seems the most difficult to move. If you could move just this disk without bothering about the others, you would simply move it from the initial post to the target post and be done. This solution to the simplified problem now establishes a subgoal for working on the original problem: to get all the smaller disks onto the third post, so the largest disk can be freely moved to the target post. In working on this subprogram, you can again apply the planning heuristic, establishing the subgoal of getting the second largest disk onto the third post. Repeating the pattern of establishing lower subgoals on the way to higher subgoals in this way will quickly lead to the solution to this problem.

The idea in the planning heuristic is to decide on strategy before tactics. "First, I'm going to decide whether to go to Disneyland or the mountains," or "First, I'm going to try to get the largest disk onto the target post," or, "On Saturday, I'm going to participate in a political fund raising run; on Sunday, I'm going to test sail an International 470; and, sometime during the weekend, I'm going to have to put in some time on my book." By taking a small number of large steps instead of a large number of small steps, you go through the problem with seven-league boots. The essential point of the planning heuristic is to simplify problems by starting with what is important and leaving the details for later, confining at least our initial efforts at roughing out a solution to those "vital few" we mentioned earlier. This is why it is usually helpful to think in terms of such representations as outlines, rough sketches, models, maps—and decision trees—which retain only the most important aspects of the problem situation. Developing such a representation is what we mean by the phrase "getting on top of a problem." The idea is to make as many decisions as you can at this level, to stay on top of the problem as long as you can, before descending into the morass of details.

The second important way in which you can analyze a problem and break it down into subproblems is *classification,* selecting important attributes for initial consideration. In the architecture problem, we thought about the attributes of houses: floor plan and style. In deciding on a place to go for a summer vacation, you would think of characteristics of places rather than particular places. Would you like the place not to be too hot? Stay north. And historically interesting? Stay north and east. And near water? Stay on the New England seaboard. To apply the classification heuristic to the problem of selecting a stereo, decide whether you want a console, a compact, or components before getting any further into the maze of available possibilities. To apply it to the problem of finding out why the car won't start, check the cranking system by noting whether the engine turns over, the ignition system by seeing whether there is a spark at the plugs, and the fuel system by seeing whether there is gas at the carburetors, before getting further into details.

Consider the game of Twenty Questions. In Twenty Questions someone thinks of an object or event, and you have to find out what it is by asking twenty or fewer questions that can be answered by a simple yes or no. If you ask questions like, "Is it Sharon's pin?" or, "Is it the dog?" you are thinking in terms of items, rather than attributes. By thinking in terms of items, you are attempting to solve the entire problem at one stroke. For, if the answer to a question of this kind is "yes," you will have solved the entire problem; and, if it is "no," you will have made very little progress towards the solution. Instead, however, you could ask questions like, "Is it living or nonliving?" or, "Is it in this half of the room or that?" By thinking in terms of attributes, you divide the problem into subproblems, for no matter what the answer to a question of this kind is, you will not have solved the entire problem. On the other hand, no matter what the answer is, you will have learned something about the solution. Questions about attributes are generally far more efficient than questions about unanalyzed objects. (See Bruner, Olver, Greenfield, et al., 1966, pp. 86–89.)

As another example of the classification heuristic, consider the problem of finding a way of removing three matches from the following figure in such a way as to leave 4 squares.

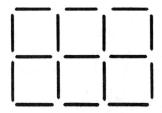

It is not difficult to see that the following patterns are all equivalent with respect to this problem:

In order to leave an "L" of 4 squares, regardless of its orientation, you would have to remove 4 matches instead of the 3 required. So an "L" is not the pattern you want to leave. Because all patterns that differ only with regard to orientation are equivalent so far as this problem is concerned, we can be sure that, if one such pattern will not solve the problem, the others will not either. Neither forward "L"s nor backward "L"s, neither rightside-up "L"s nor upside-down "L"s will work. And, what is important, we don't have to generate the other patterns to know this.

In this case, it is fairly easy to decide on what basis to classify acts, but in other cases it can be more difficult. Usually, it requires some measure of experience in the problem area to know what attributes are vital and what are trivial.

Once again, general methods must be coupled with specific experience to be effective.

It might help if we summarized the chapter to this point with a single example of the major heuristics. Because of its richness, chess will serve this purpose well. Working forward is appropriate in the opening game, since the initial positions are fixed. Later on in the game, where it is possible to think of actual checkmate positions, working backwards is more appropriate. Planning should ordinarily concern the "heavy" pieces, particularly those involved in any current action, with consideration of outlying pieces and pawns deferred until later. Classification can be helpful in the elimination of alternatives. For example, if one of your pieces is being attacked by a knight, you can eliminate from consideration the entire class of actions involving interposing a piece between the knight and the attacked piece, since knights can jump over other pieces. Finally, as we shall see in the next section, hillclimbing is also of great importance in chess.

KNOWING WHERE TO HEAD:
Hillclimbing

However you have analyzed your problem into subproblems, you must have some kind of test you can perform to establish that you have solved one subproblem and are ready to go on to the next. It is convenient to think in terms of two kinds of such tests, one deterministic and the other probabilistic. In the disk transfer problem very elementary reasoning processes can tell us for certain whether a disk is free to be moved to its target post, and in Twenty Questions we trust the other player to give us certain information as to whether we are correct about a particular attribute. Similarly, in cracking a combination lock, the experienced safe cracker can get reliable information from the clicks in the mechanism after each subproblem is solved. And, in the childhood game Button, Button, Where's the Button? (where one person hides a button, another looks for it, and the first person says "warmer" when the second person is moving in the direction of the button and "colder" when he is moving away from it), we trust the other player to tell us correctly whether we are, in fact, "warmer" or "colder."

But things are not always so easy. In chess, for example, there is no test that will indicate with anything like certainty whether you have played a good opening or a good middle game, much less made a good move. The only deterministic test is at the end of the game, when you win or lose. The best you can do in such cases is to consider where you are and where you would like to be and then ask yourself which of the acts you are considering moves you closest to where you would like to be. This is the essence of hillclimbing. The test that tells you whether you are "warmer" or "colder" is based on similarity or distance.

The name "hillclimbing" comes from the analogy of a person climbing a hill in a fog. Since he cannot see the peak, he looks up the hill a short way, walks to that point, looks up again, walks to that point, and so forth, gradually reducing the difference in elevation between his current position and the peak.

In anagram solving, for example, we can analyze the problem into subproblems by beginning with the consonants and then hillclimb by rearranging these until we achieve a high-frequency sequence, something that is closer to being a word than what we started with. We would then proceed to the next subproblem and plug in vowels in an attempt to complete the solution. In chess the cues that tell us that we are getting "warmer" are such things as the number of our pieces that are defended, the number of enemy pieces that are attacked, the number of squares that are attacked, and the number of center squares that are attacked.

The missionaries and cannibals problem provides another good illustration of hillclimbing—and one that contains a false peak. The problem goes as follows.

> On one side of a river there are three missionaries and three cannibals. They have a boat on their side that is capable of carrying two people at a time across the river. The goal is to transport all six people across to the other side of the river. At no point can the cannibals on either side of the river outnumber the missionaries on that side of the river (or the cannibals would eat the outnumbered missionaries.) This constraint holds only when there is at least one missionary on the side of the river where there are more cannibals. That is, it is all right to have one, two, or three cannibals on the same side of the river with zero missionaries, because they they would have no missionaries to eat.

The basis of similarity between your current position and the goal on which to hillclimb is, obviously, the number of people who have gotten across the river. At the act node for the first move, there are three branches: M, C, and MC. That is, one missionary could go across, one cannibal could go across, or one missionary and one cannibal could go across. The first possibility is ruled out by the fact that it would leave the remaining missionaries outnumbered by the cannibals, but the other two alternatives are genuine possibilities. If we hillclimb so as to increase the number of people who have gotten across the river, we will choose MC in preference to C.

The entire solution to the problem is diagrammed below.

| Step 1 | .... | Step 4 | CCC[B] |
| | MMMCCC[B] | | .... MMM |

| Step 2 | MC[B] .... | Step 5 | CC .... |
| | MMCC | | MMMC[B] |

Step 3	C	Step 6	MMCC[B] ....
	MMMCC[B]		MC
			—detour—

Step 7	MC .... MMCC[B]	Step 10	MMMCC[B] C
Step 8	MMMC[B] CC	Step 11	MMMC .... CC[B]
Step 9	MMM .... CCC[B]	Step 12	MMMCCC[B] ....

Note the step marked "detour." It is necessary, at this step, to *decrease* the number of people who have gotten across the river in order to avoid winding up on a false peak. Reaching a false peak is a danger in hillclimbing. In the analogy of climbing a hill in a fog, simply following the rule "Always climb upward" will not guarantee that you will get to the top of the hill. Simply following the rule "Always rearrange letters so as to increase the letter-sequence frequency" will not, as we saw earlier, guarantee that you will turn an anagram into a word. And simply following the rule "Always capture a piece if you can" will not guarantee that you will win the chess game (your opponent may have laid a trap for you and sacrificed a piece in order to lure you onto a false peak). Wicklegren (1974) offers some remedies for the problem of false peaks. In the first place, you should try to be aware of when you are hillclimbing (for we often hillclimb without being conscious of the fact). And in the second place, you should remind yourself, when you are hillclimbing, that you could very well be headed for a false peak. If you are simply aware of the problem, you should be more likely to recognize the false peaks when you get to them and quicker to turn around and head in another direction.

It should also be noted that in many cases hillclimbing is as much involved in the generation of subgoals as in their evaluation (Wicklegren, 1974, p. 94). In chess, for example, you say to yourself, "How can I attack one of his pieces?" as often as, "Will this move attack any of his pieces?". Of course, once a subgoal has been generated in this manner, it is possible to work backward from the subgoal as well as forward from your current position.

A good way to close this chapter might be to leave you with some questions you can ask yourself that could help you to see how to apply the various heuristics to the simplification of real problems. The most general of these questions is:

What is really important here?

You should ask yourself this question frequently. It should help you to identify the "vital few" and thus to locate a good start and to locate important elements for planning or attributes for classification. More specific questions are:

How can I break this problem into subproblems?

and the closely related:

What subgoals can I work toward?

These should help you to identify important elements for planning or attributes for classification and perhaps also to identify a useful basis for hillclimbing. A somewhat different question is:

In what direction should I go to come up with a result that will be closer to the goal than where I am now?

This question should help you to become aware of important bases of similarity on which you can hillclimb. Together, these questions should help you to avoid getting bogged down in unnecessary complexity.

6

Decision Making with Multiple Futures

I'm going to ask you some questions you won't know the precise answers to but that you will be able to make some guesses about. For example, while you probably do not know the exact area of Mexico, you can be certain that it is more than one hundred square miles and less than one billion square miles. To play this game, you should state a range of possible values for each uncertain quantity, such that you believe the range to be as likely to include the true value as not, that is, such that you feel that the true value has a probability of .50 of falling within the range and a probability of .50 of falling outside the range. (See Alpert and Raiffa, 1969.)

1. the area of Mexico
2. the length of the Mississippi River

3. the number of King Solomon's wives
4. the weight of an adult brain
5. the height of the Great Pyramid of Cheops
6. the lifespan of a giant tortoise
7. the number of taste buds in the human mouth
8. the number of Spanish-speaking people in the world in 1973
9. the percentage of copper in sterling silver
10. the number of U. S. presidents who won with less than 50% of the popular vote
11. the number of vocabulary entries in *Webster's Third International Dictionary*
12. the number of man-made objects orbiting the earth in 1978

Now, for the answers. The area of Mexico is .76 million square miles. The length of the Mississippi River is 2348 miles. The number of King Solomon's wives was 700. The weight of an adult brain is 3.5 pounds. The height of the Great Pyramid of Cheops is 481 feet. The life span of a giant tortoise is 190 years. The number of taste buds in the human mouth is 3000. The number of Spanish-speaking people in the world in 1973 was 200 million. The percentage of copper in sterling silver is 7.5%. The number of U. S. presidents who won with less than 50% of the popular vote is 13. The number of vocabulary entries in *Webster's Third International Dictionary* is 450,000. And the number of man-made objects orbiting the earth in 1978 was 4007.

If you estimated your ranges properly, close to half of the true values should fall within these ranges, and close to half should fall outside. How well did you do?

If you are like most people, considerably more than half of the true values fell outside your ranges. What this shows is that we tend to take seriously too narrow a range of possible futures. Whether we are anticipating what the area of Mexico will turn out to be when we look it up or predicting how a marriage will work out, we tend to be overly confident of our predictions. Indeed, in making decisions, we often plan only for the single most probable future. This is like looking only one way when crossing the railroad tracks.

One reason for the tendency to think in terms of a single future may be simply a lack of awareness of other possible futures. This is a problem in creative thinking. One question that can help you become aware of the uncertainty of the future is:

Which branch at the act node represents more of a gamble?

Any branch that represents a gamble should probably have an event node. Another question that can help you become aware of uncertainty is:

What values in the outcome table (see chapter 7) am I least certain about?

Uncertain values should probably be replaced by event nodes.

Lack of awareness is one reason for the tendency to think in terms of a single future; the need to avoid overwhelming complexity is another. It can be difficult enough to plan in terms of a single future, without worrying about two or three. This chapter presents techniques that should enable you to deal more easily and adequately with the problem of multiple possible futures.

The methods presented in both this chapter and the next are algorithms. Granted certain assumptions, they are sure to find the best course of action out of those considered. The general nature of the algorithms used in both chapters is decomposition: breaking a complex problem down into simpler problems, solving the simpler problems, and then combining the results. In this chapter, we shall see how to deal with many futures one at a time; and, in the next, we shall see how to deal with many goals one at a time.

One general point should be made before getting into the details of the algorithms. The algorithm for dealing with multiple futures often leads us to choose a course of action that, in the future that actually comes to pass, turns out not to be the best of those considered. Similarly, the algorithm for dealing with multiple goals often leads us to choose a course of action that, in terms of some of the goals, is not the best of those considered. A more satisfactory resolution in both cases would be to come up with a creative alternative that would be the best in all the futures contemplated or that would be the best in terms of all the goals being taken into account.

In dealing with multiple futures, this is what we mean by "keeping your options open." If you major in pre-med and don't get into medical school, you will find yourself out in the cold. If you major in biology, you will have a degree whether or not you get into medical school. If you buy a diesel-powered car and diesel fuel becomes hard to get, you will be in trouble. If you buy a gasoline-powered car and gasoline becomes scarce, you can convert to propane. If you buy an oil or gas-heated home and oil or gas becomes scarce, you will be in trouble. If you buy an electrically heated house and one source of electric power becomes scarce, there are others. Thinking of this kind can bypass the need for all that we are going to talk about in this chapter. However, because such thinking will not always be successful the techniques of this chapter will often still be necessary.

EXPECTED VALUE

Let us take as an example of a problem involving uncertainty about the future a practical decision that most of us make at least once, purchasing a house. To keep things as simple as possible, since other complications will soon force themselves upon us, let us consider just two houses and the one value dimension of size. Let us say that you have a family of four

TABLE 6.
Techniques for Dealing with Multiple Futures

1. Events.
   Think of events that might have important effects on the consequences of the courses of action that you are considering.
2. Creative Alternative.
   Try to create an alternative course of action that will be equal to or better than the others in each of the futures that you are considering. If you are unable to do this, proceed to steps 3 through 6.
3. Values.
   For each course of action, evaluate the consequences in each possible future, taking into account the value (usually negative) of gambling.
4. Probabilities.
   Estimate the probability of each possible future.
5. Expected Values.
   Determine an average value for each course of action by weighting its value in each possible future by the probability of that future.
6. Sensitivity Analysis.
   Determine the sensitivity of the decision to the estimated probabilities and values to see whether it might be worth seeking further information.
7. Choice.
   Choose that alternative with the highest expected value.

and that you would ordinarily prefer a three-bedroom house to a larger one. A three-bedroom house is large enough to accommodate your family and yet small enough to be easily maintained and to fit comfortably into your budget. There is a chance that your parents are going to come to live with you, however; and, if that happens, you will have to have a four-bedroom house. So you can't be sure what you want! "It all depends. . . ." This is certainly a familiar state of affairs.

It helps to represent such a problem in terms of a decision tree. In the decision tree below, there is an act node with a branch for buying a three-bedroom house and a branch for buying a four-bedroom house. On each of these branches is an event node with a branch for parents coming and one for parents not coming.

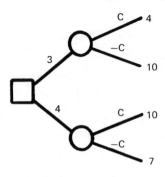

The numbers at the ends of the paths represent subjective value ratings. A three-bedroom house will be ideal (a
rating of 10) if your parents do not come, and a four-
bedroom house will be ideal (a rating of 10) if they do come.
Moreover, a four-bedroom house for a family of four, while
short of ideal (a rating of 7), is preferable to a three-bedroom
house for a family of six (a rating of 4.) We shall have more to
say about value ratings later.

But how do we go about actually making a choice? Let us
consider three cases: complete certainty, complete uncertainty, and any of the infinite number of possibilities in between. At one extreme, if you knew for certain that your
parents were coming, you would obviously choose a four-
bedroom house, with a rating of 10, in preference to a
three-bedroom house, with a rating of 4. And, if you knew
for certain that your parents were not coming, you would
choose a three-bedroom house, with a rating of 10, in preference to a four-bedroom house, with a rating of 7. This is
easy.

At the other extreme, if you didn't have the foggiest idea
whether your parents were coming or not, there are three
schools of thought as to what you should do: one pessimistic,
one optimistic, and one unbiased. (See, e.g., Miller and Starr,
1969, pp. 110–121, or Lee, 1971, pp. 38–39.) The pessimist's

approach maximizes minimum value. What he does is consider the worst thing that could possibly happen if he chooses one alternative (e.g., you buy a three-bedroom house and your parents come, for 4 points) and the worst thing that could possibly happen if he chooses the other alternative (e.g., you buy a four-bedroom house and your parents don't come, for 7 points). He then chooses the alternative (buying the four-bedroom house) that in these terms is the least unfavorable. He thus makes his decision entirely in terms of the worst possible futures and disregards other possible futures.

The optimist's approach, on the other hand, maximizes maximum value. What he does is consider the best thing that could possibly happen if he chooses one alternative (e.g., you buy a three-bedroom house and your parents don't come, for 10 points) and the best thing that could possibly happen if he chooses the other alternative. He then chooses the alternative that is the most favorable. (Here, this criterion points to no clear choice.) He thus makes his decision entirely in terms of the best possible futures and disregards other possible futures.

The third approach—called *maximizing expected value*—is generally considered to be the rational one, for it takes into account both good and bad futures. It does this by considering the average, or expected, value of each alternative over all futures and then choosing the alternative that maximizes this expected value. It is applicable to all degrees of certainty or uncertainty. We shall develop it for the case of an intermediate degree of uncertainty and later extend it to the case of complete certainty and the case of complete uncertainty.

Let us say that you estimate the probability that your parents will be coming to live with you to be .20 and the complementary probability that they will not be coming to live with you to be .80. And let us add these to the tree:

We now have the possibilities, the probabilities, and the values. The tree is complete, and we are now in a position to make our decision.

We could attempt to do this intuitively. You can see without any arithmetic that the value of buying a three-bedroom house is somewhere between 4 and 10. It would be 10 only if there were no possibility of your parents coming; because there is this possibility, the value is less than 10. Similarly, the value would be 4 only if there were no possibility of your parents not coming; because there is this possibility, the value is above 4. It seems reasonable to say that the value is closer to 10 than to 4, because the p of 10 is higher than the p of 4. Let us say that the value is 8. Similarly, you can see that the value of buying a four-bedroom house is somewhere between 10 and 7, but closer to 7. Again, this looks close to 8. If the difference were larger, as such differences often are, we might be able to handle this simple problem by taking the probabilities of the various futures into account in just this intuitive fashion. In close decisions or complex decisions, however, it is better to compute expected values, as we shall do now.

To see how to compute the expected value of each alternative course of action, let us say that you were to face this decision 10 times. Though you will not face this particular decision again, even once, you will surely face equivalent decisions many times in your life, and this is all the present logic requires. (This is not to imply that the principle of maximizing expected value cannot be defended in the case of a single decision. As an example of how it can, see Barclay, Brown, Kelly, Peterson, Phillips, and Selridge, 1977, pp. 39–46.) On 2 of these 10 occasions, the event with a probability of .20 would occur, and the value of the first course of action would be 4. On 8 of these occasions, the event with a probability of .80 would occur, and the value of this course of action would be 10. The average value would be:

$$\frac{2(4) + 8(10)}{10} = 8.8$$

Notice that this is the same as:

$$.20(4) + .80(10) = 8.8.$$

The general equation for calculating average value is thus:

$$EV = p_1V_1 + p_2V_2 + \ldots + p_kV_k.$$

EV stands for *expected value.* The average value is the value that we should expect.

The procedure for making decisions in the face of uncertainty is to compute an expected value for each of the alternative courses of action and then to choose that course of action with the highest expected value. We have seen that the expected value for buying a three-bedroom house is:

$$.20(4) + .80(10) = 8.8.$$

Similarly, the expected value for buying a four-bedroom house is:

$$.20(10) + .80(7) = 7.6.$$

Because 8.8 is greater than 7.6, the best choice, according to this procedure, is to buy a three-bedroom house.

Note that, according to the principle of maximizing expected value, the best decision is not always to prepare for the most likely event, nor is it always to choose the course of action with the highest payoff. To do so would be to base your decision on just the probabilities or just the values. Though people sometimes do base their decisions on just probabilities or just values (Slovic and Lichenstein, 1968), it would seem better to take both of these factors into account simultaneously in making a decision.

Note also that good decisions do not necessarily lead to good outcomes. The best choice is to buy the three-bedroom house, despite the fact that there is a very good chance that this will lead to the very worst outcome. The best we can do in an uncertain world is still short of perfect.

Of course, you wouldn't go to all this trouble just to decide whether to take an umbrella to work. Such calculations are worthwhile only for more important decisions. According to one rule of thumb, which shouldn't be taken too seriously, 1% of the resources allocated should be invested in making the decision about how to allocate them (Howard, 1973, p. 81). Thus, if you pay yourself five dollars an hour, you should invest 100 hours in deciding on a $50,000 home. The 1% rule seems reasonable for decisions of this magnitude or greater, but it does not seem to apply well to decisions of lesser magnitude. In the case of a $500 stereo the 1% rule would recommend that you invest only one hour in making the decision. At least for lesser decisions, the 1% rule seems to undervalue the decision making process.

The principle of maximizing expected value can be generalized to cases in which there is complete certainty and to cases in which there is complete uncertainty. To maximize expected value in cases where there is complete certainty about what will occur, you simply assign a p of 1.00 to that branch of the event node that represents the future that is certain to occur and p's of 0 to all other branches. Indeed, you don't even need an event node in such cases.

The more interesting cases are those where there is complete uncertainty about what will occur. In such cases you can assign equal p's to each of the branches of the event node. Thus you would assign a p of ½ to each of the two branches of an event node for tossing a coin, a p of ⅙ to each of the six branches of an event node for rolling a die, and a p of 1/52 to each of the 52 branches of an event node for drawing a card from a complete deck.

For many situations this may be a good approach to take. However, there is a potential problem in assigning equal p's to events about which you are completely uncertain. Let us say that you are uncertain about how much money you will make on a certain venture. And let us say that you have set up the following event node:

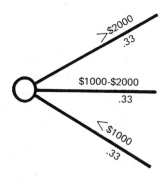

Because you have no idea whether your profits will be less than $1000, between $1000 and $2000, or greater than $2000, you assign each of these a p of ⅓. This sounds all very well and good, but let us say that you now decide to add another category:

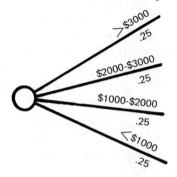

Again, because you have no idea into which category your profits will fall, you divide the p's evenly among the categories. This yields a p of ¼ for each category, including the category $1000-2000—which you earlier assign a p of ⅓! How can the same category have two different p's? Of course, it can't, and that's the problem.

The moral seems to be that, if you are unable to make a direct estimate of the p's for the branches of the event node, and if the appropriate way to divide the event node into categories is not clear (as it is for coins, dice, and cards), then you may have no alternative but to take the optimist's approach or the pessimist's approach. Fortunately it seems that we are usually able to make some estimate of the p's of various events that are important to us, and so we are usually able to maximize EV.

In estimating p's, you must take care to avoid the problems, discussed earlier, associated with inadequate sample size and sampling bias due to the selective nature of personal experience and memory. (See chapter 3.) Also if you have difficulty thinking of probabilities in the abstract, you may find it helpful to think in terms of concrete reference events with known probabilities. For example, instead of trying to figure the probability of striking water if you drill on your land, ask yourself whether it is more likely that you would strike water or that you would draw a white ball from an urn that contains

50 white balls and 50 black balls, thoroughly mixed. If you believe that striking water is more likely, change the reference event to drawing a white ball from an urn that contains 90 white balls and 10 black balls; in this way, gradually zero in on a reference event that you judge to have the same probability as the event you are interested in. (If the probability is very large or very small, you may have to think in terms of an urn with more than 100 balls.) Another kind of reference event is based on a probability wheel, the construction and use of which is described in the Appendix. Still another kind is various poker hands. Because there will virtually always be a large component of error in our estimates of p's, however, it is usually wise to perform a sensitivity analysis, as described below.

SENSITIVITY ANALYSIS

It is important always to check the results of your computations against intuition and never simply to follow blindly the dictates of the arithmetic. If the result of your computations seems intuitively reasonable, if you are inclined to say, "Sure, that's what I would have done anyway," then go ahead with the indicated course of action.

If, however, the result of your computations does not accord with intuition, then either the numbers are in error, or your intuition needs reeducating, or both. Usually, the way in which intuition needs reeducating is in being brought to an appreciation of the implications of various combinations of probabilities and values. Mathematics does for us what intuition cannot readily do, combine large amounts of information. If the calculations do not make sense immediately, you can usually come to see that they do by going over them and thinking about them.

Nevertheless, it may be that your numbers are in error, and they should be checked. You must check your arithmetic, of course, but the most likely place for error is in the numbers that you perform your arithmetic on: the probabilities and the values themselves. To see whether the trouble might lie here, we perform what is called a sensitivity analysis.

Let us illustrate sensitivity analysis by performing a sensitivity analysis on the probabilities in the house problem. The problem with which sensitivity analysis deals is the difficulty in assigning numbers to probabilities and values. There is usually an appreciable range of uncertainty when we assign numbers to such quantities. For example, you may be quite certain that the probability of your parents' coming is not larger than .50 nor less than .01, fairly certain that it is between .30 and .10, and not at all certain where it might lie within the range from .30 to .10. You said .20 earlier simply because you had to come up with a single number. The question that is asked in a sensitivity analysis is: Will changing the assigned numbers within the range of uncertainty lead to preference for a different course of action?

Let us consider the range from .10 to .30. Since a p of .20 was a low enough probability of your parents' coming to lead to a higher EV for the smaller house, a p of .10 would lead to an even greater difference in the same direction and would not alter the decision. We need not work out any exact values.

A p of .30, on the other hand, would shift the EV's in a direction that could possibly alter the decision. To see whether it would, we must perform the calculations. Substituting the p's of .30 and .70 in our original equations, we get:

EV(3-bedroom) $= .30(4) + .70(10) = 8.2$

EV(4-bedroom) $= .30(10) + .70(7) = 7.9$

The difference is still in the same direction, and so the decision would not be altered. There is a lesson here: Computation of *EV*'s can lead to a decision we can be confident in, even though we cannot be absolutely precise in our assignment of numbers to quantities.

A sensitivity analysis can also be performed on the values. To do so, you would substitute the values at those ends of your ranges of uncertainty that would be least favorable to the decision you have tentatively arrived at. If these substitutions do not change your decision, you can be confident in your decision. If they do, you will have to seek more information in order to achieve the necessary precision in your estimates.

Let us perform a sensitivity analysis on just one value figure, the 4 for the outcome where you have purchased a three-bedroom house and your parents come to stay. This value is difficult to estimate because what you would have to do in this case is buy a new house and just how costly that would be in time and money is difficult to foresee. Let us say that the range of uncertainty for this value is from 3 to 5. The end of this range that would be least favorable to the decision that you have tentatively arrived at is the 3. Substituting this in our equations, along with the probability from the least favorable end of that range of uncertainty, yields:

$$EV\text{(3-bedroom)} = .30(3) + .70(10) = 7.90$$
$$EV\text{(4-bedroom)} = .30(10) + .70(7) = 7.90$$

While the most probable figures point toward the purchase of a three-bedroom house, the least favorable figures indicate no clear decision. What do you do now?

One thing you could do is get more information, information that would enable you to be more precise about your values or information that would enable you to be more precise about your probabilities. In order to be more precise about your values, in this particular case, you would have to know, among other things, more about what is going to happen to the housing market in the next few years. This sounds like fairly costly information to obtain. In order to be able to be more precise about your probabilities, however, you would simply have to know more about what your parents are going to do in the next few years. This sounds like easy information to obtain. You could just ask them to be a bit more definite about their plans.

The decision to seek further information is itself a decision. There are at least four general courses of action you can take in response to a lack of information:

1. *leap.* You can make the entire decision now, as best you can, with the information you have on hand.

2. *look before you leap.* You can actively seek more information before making the decision.

3. *cross the bridge when you get to it.* You can delay the decision and wait for further information to make itself available. And, while waiting, you can make contingency plans, deciding on a best course of action for each of the possible futures.

If you anticipate that it is going to be at all costly, in time or money or some other terms, to wait for information or to seek it, such a decision might justify the computation of *EV*'s. The procedure for doing this is described in the Appendix.

THE VALUE OF RISK

If you were given a choice between accepting $1000 or taking a .50-.50 chance on either getting $3000 or losing $1000, you would surely take the $1000. Yet the *EVs* are equal:

$$EV1 = \$1000$$
$$EV2 = .50(\$3000) + .50(-\$1000) = \$1000.$$

These figures suggest that we should be indifferent between these two alternatives. Yet we are not, so there must be something wrong with the figures.

There is one important factor that we have not yet dealt with. One of these alternatives involves a gamble, and the other does not. Gambling itself has value, and this value is worth taking into account, especially in decisions that involve high stakes—and, of course, these are the very decisions for which it is worth taking the trouble to compute EVs' in the first place.

In this example the value of gambling is negative for most persons. Most of us prefer to play the house odds in such cases. We would prefer to avoid gambles like this one and opt for the guaranteed $1000. It is the negative value of large gambles that inclines us to buy insurance we pay insurance companies to take our negatively valued gambles from us and that, in the words of Hamlet, inclines us "to choose to bear the evils we have rather than fly to others we know not of."

In cases where the risk is not so great, however, gambling may actually have positive value. Given a choice between keeping a dollar and spending it on a ticket that gives a vanishingly small chance of winning a trip to the Caribbean, many would prefer to buy the ticket. Though a bird in the hand may, in one sense, be worth two in the bush, there is no denying the positive value of the adventure of the hunt. A certain amount of risk is the spice of life.

The preferred level of gambling differs from person to person. What is seen by one person as an attractive level of risk is seen by another as unattractive. While Tennyson's Ulysses might wish to "sail beyond the baths of all the Western stars until I die," others of us are content simply to picnic at a nearby park. Some of us are risk-seekers, and others are risk-avoiders. The value of gambling is related, in large part, to the extent of one's resources; the greater your resources, the more risk you can reasonably tolerate. This is why it is rational for insurance companies to take the very gambles that it is just as rational for individuals of modest income to get rid of.

Resources can be counted in terms other than dollars, for example, time and energy. We tend to be less willing to gamble on a shortcut when we have very little time to get to an appointment. Older people, whose time is running out on a larger scale, are less willing than younger people to gamble on career changes. A cross-country runner who is tired and has little energy left is less willing than one who is fresh to gamble on a new route. On the other hand, creative persons, who have such a great reservoir of inner strength, are more willing than most to gamble on success or failure.

Another way to say that gambling has value is to say that gaining and losing are not symmetrical. When losing a given amount would make more of a difference than winning it, the value of gambling is negative. When winning a given amount would make more of a difference than losing it, the value of gambling is positive.

We can attempt to take the value of gambling into account intuitively by subtracting a little (or a lot) from those EV's that involve gambles near 50-50. In simple cases, such as where we would be subtracting from the alternative with the lowest EV anyway, this is quite adequate. In other cases, we may wish to construct a utility curve.

A utility curve relates objective value, measured in such units as dollars or minutes, to subjective value, measured on an arbitrary scale of utility. Consider again the problem we started out with, the choice between accepting $1000 or taking a .50-.50 chance on getting $3000 or losing $1000. A utility curve for this problem should give us numbers that we can put in place of the objective values of −$1000, $1000, and $3000, so that our computations will then reflect the preferability of the first alternative.

There are five steps in constructing a utility curve.

Step 1. Indicate on the horizontal axis the range of objective values involved in the problem.

Step 2. Indicate on the vertical axis a range of from 0 to 1.00 utility units, setting 0 equal to the lowest objective value and 1.00 equal to the highest objective value.

This has been done below:

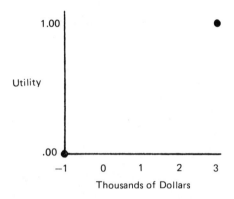

The two dots indicate that the final curve will terminate at these points.

The third step is to establish the objective value corresponding to a utility of .50.

Step 3. Establish the objective value that is subjectively equal to a .50–.50 gamble on the highest vs. the lowest objective value, and assign it a utility of .50.

Let us first do this and then see why we do it. In our case, we would ask what the objective value is of a .50-.50 gamble on either getting $3000 or losing $1000. This is equivalent to asking for a fair selling price for the gamble. We have already said that the selling price for this gamble would be less than $1000 for virtually everyone, but how much less? This will, of course, depend on the individual, but let us say that the objective value of this gamble to you is $750. This is to say, if you were given a choice between accepting $750 or taking a .50-.50 chance on getting $3000 or losing $1000, you would find it difficult to choose. (If you still find the first alternative preferable, then the $750 should be adjusted further downward; if, on the other hand, you find the second alternative now preferable, then the $750 should be adjusted upward.)

We then set this $750 equal to a utility of .50 and plot the new point on the graph.

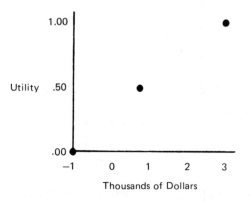

But why do we say that $750 corresponds to a utility of .50? Remember what utilities are supposed to do. When substituted for objective values, they should yield expected quantities (called expected utilities, or *EU*s, instead of expected values, or *EV*s) that correspond to our actual preferences, having taken risk into account. In terms of the old objective values, the results of step 3 would have been:

$EV1 = \$750$

$EV2 = .50(\$3000) + .50(-\$1000) = \$1000.$

Such calculations fail to reflect the fact that these alternatives are about equally attractive, because, as we have seen, they do not take into account the negative value of the gamble. In terms of utilities, the results of step 3 would be:

$$EU1 = .50$$
$$EU2 = .50(1.00) + .50(0) = .50.$$

Once we have established an objective value, such as our $750, that is subjectively equal to a .50-.50 gamble on the highest vs. the lowest objective value, the utility of that value will be equal to the EU of the gamble. Since the EU of a .50-.50 gamble on receiving either a utility of 0 or a utility of 1.00 is .50, the utility of the equally attractive alternative must also be .50.

Steps 4 and 5 in constructing a utility curve involve applying the operations of step 3 to finding the objective values corresponding to utilities of .25 and .75.

> *Step 4.* Establish the objective value that is subjectively equal to a .50-.50 gamble on the lowest objective value vs. the objective value corresponding to a utility of .50, and assign it a utility of .25.

A .50-.50 gamble on $750 or −$1000 is clearly worth less than $0. Someone would have to pay you to get you to commit yourself to such a gamble. The question is, How much? They would certainly have to pay you at least $125, because −$125 is the EV of this gamble. They would probably have to pay you a good deal more. Let us say that they would have to pay you $400. Then, by the above reasoning,

$$EU = .50(0) + .50(.50) = .25.$$

We can now add this point to the graph on page 200.

This leaves just one more point.

> *Step 5.* Establish the objective value that is subjectively equal to a .50-.50 gamble on the highest objective value vs. the objective value corresponding to a utility of .50, and assign it a utility of .75.

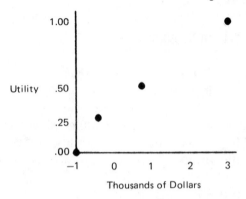

Here, the question you ask yourself is, what is a fair selling price for a .50-.50 gamble on getting either $750 or $3000? Again, we may wish to use the *EV* as a guide. This is $1875. If gambling with this much money has a negative value for you, you would prefer a certain $1875 to a gamble that has an *EV* of $1875, so the selling price would be below this figure. Let us say that you would be willing to either buy or sell this gamble for $1200. Then,

$$EU = .50(.50) + .50(1.00) = .75.$$

Adding this point completes the graph.

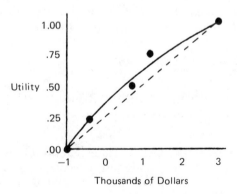

Note that this utility curve is bowed upward. The intermediate points tend to lie above the dashed straight line connecting the two extreme points. This indicates that the value of gambling is negative. If the curve were bowed downward, this would indicate that the value of gambling was positive; and, if it were a straight line, it would indicate that the value of gambling was zero. The curve might even be bowed downward in one portion and upward in another. This would indicate that the value of gambling was positive in the first portion and negative in the second.

Note that the points on this graph do not describe a perfectly smooth curve. Depending on how important the decision is, we may wish to go back and check our figures. One consistency check you can perform is to ask yourself whether you are indifferent about a choice between (a) getting the objective value associated with a utility of .50, which here is $750, or (b) getting a .50-.50 gamble on the objective value associated with a utility of .25, which here is −$400, vs. that associated with a utility of .75, which here is $1200.

Once you have constructed a utility curve that you feel satisfied with, you can read off the relevant values and enter them into your calculations of expected utility. Let us return to our original problem of the choice between accepting $1000 or taking a .50-.50 chance on either getting $3000 or losing $1000. You will recall that the EV's were equal:

$$EV1 = \$1000$$
$$EV2 = .50(\$3000) + .50(-\$1000) = \$1000.$$

Replacing objective values by utilities, we see that the EU's are far from equal:

$$EU1 = .70$$
$$EU2 = .50(1.00) + .50(0) = .50.$$

A sensitivity analysis can then be performed as a further check on the adequacy of the utility estimates. (Incidentally, you can also read the curve in the other direction, from utility units to dollars. Thus, what this gamble is really worth is .50 utility units or $750.)

Of course, this problem is so simple that in practice it might not be worthwhile to construct a utility curve. As the number of endpoints on the tree increases, however, the utility curve becomes an increasingly economical way to deal with the value of risk. It is an even greater economy when you consider the fact that the same utility curve can be used for any decision where the objective values fall within the range indicated on the horizontal axis. You can make up a utility curve and just "carry it around in your pocket" to use on future decisions.

RECOMMENDED READING

BARCLAY, S., R. V. BROWN, C. W. KELLY, III, C. R. PETERSON, L. D. PHILLIPS, and J. SELVIDGE, *Handbook for Decision Analysis*. McLean, Va.: Decisions & Designs, Inc., 1977.

BROWN, R. V., A. S. KAHR, and C. PETERSON, *Decision Analysis: An Overview*. New York: Holt, Rinehart & Winston, 1974.

7

Decision Making with Multiple Goals

Which of the following cars would you be most inclined to purchase? Put them all into a single rank ordering, with the one you like most at the top and the one you like least at the bottom. If you intend to play this game, don't read beyond the description of the last car until you have finished your ranking.

Car A is an intermediate-sized car that sells for $5270. It has good handling under both normal and emergency conditions. Its brakes are good in stopping power and very good in resistance to fading. Its front seat comfort is good, and its rear seat comfort is fair. Its ride is good with a light load, but only fair with a full load. It is quiet. It gets 16 miles per gallon. Its expected repairs are worse than average.

Car B is a compact that sells for $4998. Its predicted repairs are better than average. It gets 20 miles per gallon. Its brakes are good in stopping power and very good in resistance to fading. Its handling is good under normal conditions and fair under emergency conditions. Its ride is good with a light load and fair with a full load. It is noisy. Its comfort is fair, both front and rear.

Car C is a subcompact that sells for $5019. Its expected repairs are better than average. It gets 26 miles per gallon, and its brakes are good, both in stopping power and in resistance to fading. Its comfort is fair in the front seat and poor in the rear seat, and its handling is fair under normal conditions and poor under emergency conditions. Its ride is poor with both a light and a full load, and it is noisy.

Car D is a compact that sells for $5068. It is noisy. Its comfort is fair, both front and rear. Its ride is good with a light load and fair with a full load. Its handling is good under normal conditions and fair under emergency conditions. It gets 20 miles per gallon. Its brakes are very good in both stopping power and resistance to fading. Its predicted repairs are better than average.

Car E is a full-sized car that sells for $7286. Its comfort, both front and rear, is good. Its brakes are good in stopping power and very good in resistance to fading. Its predicted repairs are better than average. Its ride is good with a light load and fair with a full load. It is quiet. Its handling is good under normal conditions but poor under emergency conditions. It gets 12 miles per gallon.

Did you rank Car B above Car D? Most people do. Actually, these cars are identical in all respects but two: cost and the stopping power of their brakes. Car D costs $70 more than Car C, but the stopping power of its brakes is rated as very good, instead of just good. Isn't the difference between good and very good brakes, which could be a matter of life and death, worth $70? When asked this way, most people say yes, even though their overall ranking implied a no.

Problems involving multiple goals are very common in life. In evaluating job opportunities, we consider not only income, but also insurance and retirement benefits, opportunity for personal growth, effect on one's family, opportunity for making a contribution to society, etc. In deciding on a stereo, we consider not only sound quality, but also versatility, durability, appearance, and, of course, cost. Even investment options (stocks, bonds, real estate, life insurance, and the like), which you might think would differ in only one way—the amount of money you will make—turn out on closer examination to differ in a number of respects: rate of return, tax status, recoverability of principal, regularity of income, diversification, freedom from care, etc.

In large companies, manufacturing seeks to minimize unit costs of production and hence favors long, uninterrupted production runs, which result in large inventories composed of relatively few products; finance seeks to minimize the capital tied up in inventory and hence wishes low inventory levels; and sales seeks to give outstanding service to customers and hence wishes to maintain a large inventory of a wide variety of products. Top management must weigh these various goals against one another. In addition management must often also take into account environmental, political, and ethical considerations along with the more narrowly economic ones.

Not only are problems involving multiple goals common, but they are unduly difficult to resolve. A person might easily decide between a gift of $1000 and one of $1001, but the choice between $1000 and, say, a free vacation in Hawaii might prove more difficult, even though the difference in true worth in the second case is unlikely to be as small as $1 (Shepard, 1964, p. 275).

The general way to deal with decision problems involving multiple goals is our old friend decomposition. Break the problem down into its components, solve the simpler problems, and then put their solutions together to yield a solution to the overall problem. We shall consider four ways of doing this: (a) cut-off screening, (b) elimination of trade-offs, (c) the sum-of-the-features method, and (d) the sum-of-the-ratings method. Some of these are "quick and dirty." They

are appropriate for less important decisions or for preliminary screening. Others are more precise, but they also take
more time. They are appropriate for more important decisions.

But first a word about the goals themselves.

THE GOAL SET

The goal set should be complete, minimal, and nonredundant. It is complete if all important goals are included.
Generating many goals in order to ensure that the goal set is
complete is, of course, a matter of creative thinking, and the
creative thinking techniques of chapter 4 should help here.
In particular, the following checklist has been found useful.

> *Tangible and intangible consequences.* It is relatively easy to think
> of tangible consequences, such as monetary gains or losses,
> interest value of activities, and effects on health, but we are
> less likely to take into account such intangible consequences as
> self-approval or social approval based on morals or ideals.
>
> *Immediate and long-term consequences.* Our planning horizon
> tends to be short, and we have to remind ourselves to consider
> remote consequences of our activities.
>
> *Consequences for self and for others.* Here, the bias is towards
> thinking in terms of consequences for ourselves and to give
> insufficient thought to the consequences for family, friends,
> and society. Indeed, sometimes the word "others" should in-
> clude other peoples, other generations, and even other
> species.
>
> *Benefits and costs.* We tend to be more oriented towards bene-
> fits than costs. This may be, in part at least, because we are
> goal-seeking creatures and because problems are interrup-
> tions in goal-directed behavior. Whatever the reason, it has
> been found helpful (Janis and Mann, 1977) to have the deci-
> sion maker imagine that he has made the decision that he is
> presently inclined toward and that things have gone very
> badly, worse than he thought they would. Using the concrete
> coding technique of role-playing and thinking through the

scenario in vivid detail often brings to mind previously unanticipated costs.

In addition to being complete, the goal set should also be minimal and nonredundant. The goal set is minimal if no unimportant goals are included. Goals are unimportant (a) if they are unimportant in themselves or (b) if the alternatives do not differ substantially with respect to them. A classic example of the latter is what are called "sunk costs." Let's say that you're driving across town for something and that it occurs to you halfway there that it would have been wiser to have called ahead first. It also occurs to you that you could still stop and call at the next pay phone, but, because you have already gotten into your car and driven this far, you decide simply to go on and drive the rest of the way.

Note the reason for the decision: "because you have al-

TABLE 7.
Techniques for Dealing with Multiple Goals

---

1. Goal Set.
   Generate a goal set that is complete, minimal, and nonredundant.
2. Elimination by Aspects.
   Eliminate those courses of action that have unacceptable values on any goals.
3. Creative Alternative.
   Try to create an alternative course of action that will be equal to or better than any of the remaining ones with respect to each of the goals that you are considering. If you are unable to do this, proceed to steps 4 through 6.
4. Values.
   Evaluate each remaining course of action on each goal.
5. Composite Values.
   Obtain a composite value for each course of action.
6. Sensitivity Analysis.
   Determine the sensitivity of the decision to the values you have estimated to see whether it might be worth trying for more precise estimates.
7. Choice.
   Choose that alternative with the highest composite value.

---

ready gotten into your car and driven this far." These are sunk costs. While it's true that you might have avoided these costs if you had called ahead earlier, they are "water over the dam" now. Because these costs will have been incurred whether you go out the "phone" or the "don't phone" branch of the act node you are considering, they are irrelevant to the decision. It is easy for us to become irrationally committed to a course of action because we have already invested so much in it.

The goal set is nonredundant if no goal appears more than once. Redundancy can creep into a goal set in subtle ways. A common way is by including both cause and effect. For example, "increase in farm income" and "increase in livestock yield" may be redundant in that the only importance of the latter is in the effect it has on the former (McKean, 1958). Similarly, "salary" and "status" may be redundant to the extent that status is dependent on status symbols that the salary makes possible. Double-counting goals in this way gives them undue weight in the final decision.

Relevance trees are devices that can help to ensure completeness and nonredundancy in the generation of goals (Keeney and Raiffa, 1976, pp. 41ff). An example relevance tree is shown below.

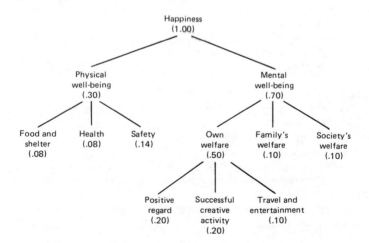

A relevance tree generally begins with some overall goal, such as "happiness" or "the good life." This is then divided into nonoverlapping subgoals, here "physical well-being" and "mental well-being," and total importance (1.00) is divided among them in a way that seems appropriate (here, .30 for physical well-being and .70 for mental well-being.)* These subgoals are divided in turn into lower subgoals, and the importance weights are further divided among these. Actually a relevance tree is just an idea tree with relevance weights to indicate the extent do which each subgoal contributes to achieving its superordinate goal. Moving up in such a tree answers the question "Why?" and moving down answers the question "How?". The process of growing the tree stops when the importance weights become so finely divided as to be negligible. The weights at the bottom of the tree can be used in connection with the sum-of-the-ratings method below.

Now that we have a set of goals clearly in mind, we must evaluate the various alternative courses of action against them. There are a number of ways to do this.

CUT-OFF SCREENING

In cut-off screening (Tversky, 1971), you consider one attribute at a time and eliminate alternatives that are unsatisfactory with respect to that attribute. Thus, in choosing among cars, you might begin by considering cost and eliminating all those cars that you cannot afford. If you have a family of four, you might also eliminate all those that seat only two persons; and, if you have a trailer, you might eliminate those that are not powerful enough to tow a trailer.

A television commercial that advertises a computer course nicely illustrates cut-off screening (Tversky, 1971).

*Weights are meaningful only in the context of a particular problem, to indicate the relative importance of a full change on each goal from the lowest to the highest value in that problem.

"There are more than two dozen companies in the San Francisco area which offer training in computer programming." (Announcer puts two dozen eggs and a walnut on the table.)

"Let us examine the facts. How many of these schools have on-line computer facilities for training?" (Removes several eggs.)

"How many of these schools have placement services that would help find you a job?" (Removes more eggs.)

"How many of these schools are approved for veterans' benefits?" (Removes more eggs.)

This continues until the walnut alone remains, at which point the announcer cracks the nutshell, which reveals the name of the company, and concludes:

"This is all you need to know, in a nutshell."

Cut-off screening is much like the classification heuristic for analysis into subproblems. A major difference is that, while the heuristic avoids generating the alternatives in the first place, the algorithm deals with alternatives that have already been generated.

If we distinguish between musts and wants (Kepner and Tregoe, 1965), those features you feel that you cannot do without and those that you could do without but would nevertheless like to have, cut-off screening applies to the musts, and the other methods apply to the wants. It is a perfectly satisfactory way of eliminating those alternatives that do not have features that you must have. An advantage is that it is easy; you have to consider only one attribute at a time. A disadvantage is that it does not take into account how much more satisfactory than the minimal acceptance value each alternative is. Among several different cars, all of which you can afford, some will be less expensive than others. While the car you buy must cost less than a certain amount, you want it to cost as little as possible. Except for relatively unimportant decisions, cut-off screening seems most appropriate as a preliminary screening method, to be followed up with one of the methods below. After applying cut-offs to musts, the next step is to establish trade-offs among wants.

ELIMINATION OF TRADE-OFFS

Elimination of trade-offs may, in some cases, be as precise as any of the methods we shall consider, yet it is very easy to apply. This method was described over two hundred years ago in a letter from Benjamin Franklin to Joseph Priestley, and we can do no better than to quote the letter.

> London, Sept. 19, 1772
>
> In the affair of so much importance to you, wherein you ask my advice, I cannot, for want of sufficient premises, advise you what to determine, but if you please I will tell you how. When these difficult cases occur, they are difficult, chiefly because while we have them under consideration, all the reasons pro and con are not present to the mind at the same time; but sometimes one set present themselves, and at other times another, the first being out of sight. Hence the various purposes or inclinations that alternately prevail, and the uncertainty that perplexes us. To get over this, my way is to divide half a sheet of paper by a line into two columns; writing over the one Pro, and over the other Con. Then, during three or four days consideration, I put down under the different heads short hints of the different motives, that at different times occur to me, for or against the measure. When I have thus got them all together in one view, I endeavor to estimate their respective weights; and where I find two, one on each side, that seem equal, I strike them both out. If I find a reason pro equal to some two reasons con, I strike out the three. If I judge some two reasons con, equal to some three reasons pro, I strike out the five; and thus proceeding I find at length where the balance lies; and if, after a day or two of further consideration, nothing new that is of importance occurs on either side, I come to a determination accordingly. And, though the weight of reasons cannot be taken with the precision of algebraic quantities, yet when each is thus considered, separately and comparatively, and the whole lies before me, I

think I can judge better, and am less liable to make a rash step, and in fact I have found great advantage from this kind of equation, in what may be called moral or prudential algebra.

Wishing sincerely that you may determine for the best, I am ever, my dear friend, yours most affectionately.

Benj. Franklin

The only problems with this method are that it may be difficult to find exact trade-offs to eliminate and that it does not yield values that can be entered into a decision tree. The sum-of-the-features and sum-of-the-ratings methods do not have these limitations.

SUM-OF-THE-FEATURES METHOD

Both the sum-of-the-features and the sum-of-the-ratings methods employ a cross-classification of (a) the course of action being rated, by (b) the basis of value on which each course of action is being rated. An example of such a cross-classification, or outcome, table would be one where the courses of action are various jobs and the bases of value are income, difficulty of the work, interest level of the work, and so forth.

Cross-classification forces us to make comparisons in applying facts to decision making. We must keep in mind, however, that these comparisons should be controlled comparisons. If information about one job, for example, is based on reading, another on talking to someone, and another on personal experience, some adjustments may have to be made for these differences, for we are interested only in differences that will result from taking one course of action or the other.

An outcome table organizes our information for us, but it does not make our decision. It is at this point that we apply either the features or the ratings method to obtain a composite value for each row that can then be entered into the decision tree at the appropriate end point. It is important to remember that where you are taking into account both multiple futures and multiple goals, the two analyses should be combined to yield a single result, a single indication as to which course of action you should take. The following figure shows diagrammatically how this can be done.

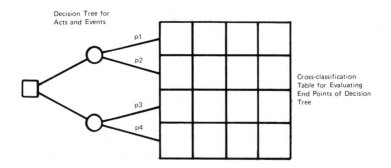

Decision Tree for
Acts and Events

p1

p2

p3

p4

Cross-classification
Table for Evaluating
End Points of Decision
Tree

All that the features method requires is the following. First, assign a (+) or a (−) to each response alternative on each dimension to indicate whether it seems to you to be especially good or just satisfactory on that dimension. (Presumably, alternatives that are less than satisfactory on any dimension will already have been eliminated in a cut-off screening stage.) Then add up the (+)s for each alternative and select the one with the greatest number of (+)s.

To illustrate this method, let us simplify the car problem. Assume that you are considering only three cars, Car A, Car B, and Car C, and assume that you are evaluating these cars on only three dimensions: cost, comfort, and predicted repairs. Let us say that you have assigned −++ to Car A, −++ to Car B, and +−− to Car C, on cost, comfort, and predicted repairs, respectively. (Since (+) always means good, a (+) on cost would mean that cost is low, not high.) Adding up the positive features yields a 2 for Car A, a 2 for Car B, and a 1 for Car C. Thus, the method indicates that you should prefer either A or B to C, but it does not indicate which you should prefer between A and B. Often the method will give you a clear first choice, though it does not do so in this example. If the decision is not too important, you might be quite satisfied with any alternative that ties for first place by this method. If the decision is important, you can take a step in the direction of the ratings method by distinguishing between features that merit double (+)s and those that merit just single (+)s. Or you can just go ahead and use the ratings method.

SUM-OF-THE-RATINGS METHOD

The sum-of-the-ratings method requires that you assign a rating, instead of a (+) or (−), to each response alternative on each dimension. There are two ways of doing this: (a) rating all dimensions in terms of a single common dimension and (b) rating each dimension separately.

If you rate all dimensions in terms of a *single common dimension,* the best dimension to use is usually money or what is called "willingness to pay." Money is a good dimension for this purpose simply because we are so used to putting prices on things. Whenever we pay for a vacation, we put a dollar value on travel; whenever we buy art, we put a dollar value on beauty; whenever we pay for medical care, we put a dollar value on health; and, whenever we fill out our income tax honestly, we put a dollar value on morality.

In pricing out dimensions, it's helpful to distinguish between objective and subjective dimensions, those that can be priced out simply by performing calculations and those that require a judgment of monetary worth. Examples of *objective dimensions* are the price of a car, which is already in dollars, and such factors as interest, gas mileage, and repairs, each of which can be transformed into dollars by means of the appropriate calculations. In our example, we have two objective dimensions, cost and predicted repairs. In the case of cars, it is probably most appropriate to think of benefits and costs in terms of dollars per month, so let's say that the costs of Cars A, B, and C are, respectively, $100, $90, and $60 per month. Such figures would be obtained by adding the purchase price to the total anticipated interest costs, subtracting the price you expect to get when you eventually sell the car, and dividing the result by the number of months you expect to own the car. And let's say that the anticipated monthly costs for repairs are $10, $8, and $15, for Cars A, B, and C, respectively.

Examples of *subjective dimensions* are style, safety, and comfort. To attach a dollar figure to a subjective dimension requires more than calculations; it requires judgment. In our example, we have just the one subjective dimension of comfort. Perhaps the simplest way to begin attaching dollar figures to subjective dimensions in this case is to imagine a reference alternative that has the lowest value of any alternative on each dimension. (In other cases, the status quo makes a convenient reference alternative.) Here, this imaginary alternative would have the comfort and predicted repairs of Car C. Then ask yourself how much this alternative would be worth to you. Let's say you feel that the imaginary reference alternative is worth $100 a month.

Next, ask yourself how much more you would be willing to pay each month to go from the comfort of the reference alternative to that of the most comfortable car. Let's say that this car is Car A and that you would be willing to put out another $20 a month for this difference in comfort. Now, ask yourself how much more you would be willing to pay each month to go from the comfort of the reference alternative to that of Car B. Let's say that this is $15. Finally, check yourself by asking whether you would be willing to go from $115 a month to $120 a month to increase the comfort from that of Car B to that of Car A.

To obtain a *composite value* for each alternative, you simply add the benefits and subtract the costs. In our example, this would yield the following composite values:

	Cost	Repairs	Comfort		Composite
Car A	−$100	−$10	+$120	=	$10
Car B	−$90	−$8	+$115	=	$17
Car C	−$60	−$15	+$100	=	$25

The second method for assigning a rating to each response alternative on each dimension is to rate *each dimension on its own terms,* instead of in terms of a single common scale. The usual way to do this is to use a 10-point scale where 1 represents the least desirable value and 10 represents the most desirable value. You can either let 10 represent the most desirable value possible, the most desirable value that you are likely to encounter, or the most desirable value that characterizes any of the alternatives under consideration. Correspondingly, 1 would then represent the least desirable value possible, the least desirable value that you are likely to encounter, or the least desirable value that characterizes any of the alternatives. Whatever you decide, be consistent throughout.

When you rate each dimension on its own terms, you can't simply add up the ratings, because a unit change on one dimension doesn't necessarily mean the same thing as a unit change on another dimension. It would be like adding inches to feet. If you added inches to feet you could get strange things happening, such as 1 foot plus 10 inches and 10 feet plus 1 inch yielding the same nonsensical total of 11!

What you have to do when you have rated each dimension on its own terms is to adjust the units on each dimension so that a unit change on any one dimension will have the same importance to you as a unit change on any other dimension. (This would be like multiplying inches by a weight of 12 and feet by a weight of 1.) To do this, you (a) assign an *importance weight* to each dimension, (b) multiply all the ratings on each dimension by its importance weight to get them into common units, and then (c) add up the weighted ratings. Thus, the composite rating for each alternative will be a weighted sum.

Let's run through an example on this. Assume that you have rated Car A 4-6-8, Car B 4-7-6, and Car C 7-2-1, on cost, comfort, and predicted repairs, respectively. This would yield an unweighted sum of 18 for Car A, 17 for Car B, and 10 for Car C, and an unweighted average of 6.0 for Car A, 5.7 for Car B, and 3.3 for Car C. Either way, Car A comes out on top.

But an unweighted sum or average assumes that the various bases of value are equally important to you, that the units are the same. This is seldom the case. Let us say that, in the car example, cost is actually the most important thing to you and that comfort and predicted repairs are of lesser and about equal importance. To express this in numbers, let us say that your weights for cost, comfort, and repairs are, respectively, .7, .2, and .1. What these weights represent are the values to you of moving the full distance from 1 to 10 on each scale. What they say, for example, is that the worth to you of moving the full distance on the comfort scale is less than one-third that of moving the full distance in dollars on the cost scale.

In assigning weights you must be careful to maintain your original definition of 1 and 10 as the most extreme values possible, the most extreme values that you are likely to encounter, or the most extreme values that characterize any of the alternatives. If you have chosen the last definition, for example, it will be possible to assign a very low weight to a very important factor. This can happen if the alternatives do not differ greatly on that factor. For example, safety is an important factor, since it can be a matter of life and death, but, if the cars you are considering don't differ much on safety, then the difference between 1 and 10 on that scale won't be important to you.

Importance weights are generally made to add to 1.00.

Whether or not they do will have no effect on the relative differences among the weighted sums of the alternatives, yet importance weights that add to 1.00 may be easier to think about and estimate accurately. You can always make importance weights add to 1.00 by dividing each by their sum. For example, 1, 2, and 5 add up to 8, not 1.00. But dividing each by 8 yields: .125, .250, and .625, which do add up to 1.00.

Combining ratings and weights, we obtain the following weighted sums:

Car A $.7(4) + .2(6) + .1(8) = 4.8$
Car B $.7(4) + .2(7) + .1(6) = 4.8$
Car C $.7(7) + .2(2) + .1(1) = 5.4$

Thus, Car C comes out on top, completely reversing the ranking on the basis of the unweighted ratings and agreeing closely with the ranking obtained by pricing out each factor. Weights can make a difference.

Some people object that these numerical methods are "too mechanical" and don't trust them. However, research suggests that the intuitive judgments that such people are comfortable with are based on just such a sum of separate judgments. The difference between the present techniques and intuitive judgments is that, whereas intuitive judgments, because of the limited capacity of effortful processes, can take only two or three factors into account (Slovic, 1966; Hoffman, Slovic, and Rorer, 1968), the present techniques can take all important factors into account.

For example, success in predicting future grade point average and future length of hospitalization has been found to be greater when information from different cues is combined mechanically than when it is combined intuitively, even by trained specialists (Meehl, 1954.) More surprising, even when adding is not the appropriate arithmetic operation, adding the ratings can yield better estimates than global intuitive estimates (Yntema and Torgerson, 1961; Pollack, 1962).

A point should be made about costs and benefits. Both the features and the ratings methods subtract costs from benefits to yield a measure of *profit*. This seems, and usually is, perfectly reasonable. There is one case, however, where it makes better sense to divide costs into benefits to obtain a *benefit-cost ratio*. (See Gardiner and Edwards, 1975, p. 19.) This is where you are choosing, not a single alternative, but as many as you can fit into a limited budget. Consider the following example, where "B" represents benefits and "C" represents costs.

	B	C	B − C	B/C
Alternative A	$6	$4	$2	1.5
Alternative B	2	1	1	2.0
Alternative C	2	1	1	2.0
Alternative D	2	1	1	2.0
Alternative E	2	1	1	2.0

If you have $4 to spend and can elect only one of the choices (as when you choose one mate, one vocation, one home to live in), then you take that choice with the highest benefit-cost difference that you can afford. Here that is Choice A, which will gain you $2. If you have $4 to spend and can elect any number of choices (as when you invest time or money in various activities), then you start with that choice with the highest benefit-cost ratio and work down until you run out of resources. Here, you would take Choices B, C, D, and E, which will gain you $4, instead of $2.

Quantitatively the ratings method is to be preferred to the features method, since the ratings make use of at least a 10-point scale and the features employ only a 2-point scale (plus and minus). Because the features method can tell you nothing that the ratings method cannot, there should never be any need to do both. Though this may be true from a strictly quantitative point of view, it is not necessarily true psychologically. The important psychological fact is that the two methods are different, and different statements of the same problem can lead us to think about it in different ways. This is a matter of coding variation. In general, where it is possible and where the importance of the problem warrants it, you would do well to use more than one method to think about the problem and then check the results against one another to locate any discrepancies. This technique is called "triangulation." It is often helpful to begin by counting positive features and then, after you have gotten a feel for the problem, to turn to ratings. It should also be helpful, of course, both to rate the dimensions separately and to rate them in terms of a common dimension, such as dollars.

This chapter has assumed that trade-offs are inevitable, that you have to give up something on one basis of value in order to get something on another basis of value. However, this may not be the case. While the above methods will enable you to choose the best from among a fixed set of alternatives, the best course of action may not even be in the set. There may be a course of action that enables you to get more on some bases of value without giving up anything on the others. Conceiving of alternative courses of action is, of course, a matter of creative thinking.

For example the sodium nitrate that is used as a food preservative prevents botulism, a deadly form of food poisoning, but also produces cancer. To treat this as a trade-off problem would mean asking ourselves what mix of botulism and cancer we find least abhorrent. To treat it as a problem in creative thinking would mean searching for a way of avoiding both botulism and cancer. The latter would seem preferable.

A good piece of advice for dealing with multiple goals, then, is not to turn to the techniques of this chapter until you have made an effort to come up with a course of action that is equal to or better than the others on all important bases of value. (The coding variation technique of combining the attributes of the goal can often help here.) If you can come up with such a course of action, the techniques in this chapter will be unnecessary—and you will have achieved a more satisfactory solution to your problem. The most creative way to deal with the problem of multiple goals is, when possible, to invent an alternative that satisfies them all.

Thus, we are often led, at what seemed to be the end of a critical thinking phase, back to creative thinking—" back to the drawing board." And that's the way problem solving often goes. Progress in problem solving seems to be at least as much cyclical as linear (Patrick, 1935; Janis and Mann, 1977, p. 196–197.) Creative and critical thinking are inextricably interlaced. So we might close this chapter with a final piece of advice: Though you may set your creative cap aside for a while, never put it in the closet! In working on problems, you often have to reiterate, that is, go back and do things over with a new insight in mind.

RECOMMENDED READING

Janis, I. L., and L. Mann, *Decision Making,* [ch. 14.] New York: Free Press, 1977.

Barclay, S., R. V. Brown, C. W. Kelly, III, C. R. Peterson, L. D. Phillips, and J. Selvidge, *Handbook for Decision Analysis.* McLean, Va.: Decisions & Designs, Inc., 1977.

Appendices

Memory Problems

Names. Develop a mnemonic for associating each of the sales representatives' names below with the names of their companies, so when you hear the representative's name you will remember the name of the company, and vice versa. Tell what techniques you would use to learn these names at a business meeting.

Ted Hartman   Kingsley Products
Jane Higgenbottom Meriwhether Industrial Supply

Floyd Greene	Byrd Industries
Laura Scott	MacGregor Sales and Service
Dick Roberts	The Jones Corporation
Henry Beech	Graves Sales and Service

Numbers. Develop a mnemonic for the numbers below (or for two numbers of your own choosing).

| fire | 232-2111 |
| police | 760-6911 |

Factual Material. Read the article below and develop a scheme for remembering it.

Problems of Rapid Population Growth

The rapid increase of population in the less developed regions presents a far more serious problem than the population increase in 19th-century Europe for the following reasons: (1) the increase is far more rapid (2.5 to 3.5 percent instead of 1 percent); (2) it affects a far greater population; (3) it is not susceptible to any compensation in such migratory and economic outlets as Europe found in the New World and Australasia.

The increased speed in the spread of antimortality techniques has rapidly raised the question of how an ever greater number of human beings, multiplying without controls of any kind, are to be fed. Faced with this vast problem, observers separate into two camps: the pessimists, with their unfavourable and even tragic prognoses (such as general famine), and the optimists, confident that science and technology can overcome these difficulties. A second conflict of scholars, not far removed from the first, exists between the "economic developers" and the "birth controllers." The former group favours an absolute priority for economic and cultural development, which, they contend, cannot fail eventually to trigger a decrease in fertility. The latter group hopes to work for birth control at the family level to reduce national population burdens—burdens that they assume must be alleviated before economic development can successfully be undertaken.

A defensible conclusion with respect to the matter of economic priority, even from the strictly economic point of view is difficult to ascertain. The cost of contraceptives capable of preventing the birth of a child can be much lower than the cost of investments and consumer goods necessary for that child's economic life (housing, food, tools, etc.)—but only if the contraceptives are reasonably efficient. When their efficiency is virtually nil, as may be the case among indigent and ignorant populations, economic development yields greater profits.

The difficulties met by such populations in the use of contraceptives have led to the search for new methods, such as the more efficient oral contraceptive (the Pill) and intrauterine devices, but even these are not yet entirely satisfactory. What are needed, perhaps, are pills with longer term action and intrauterine devices less susceptible to expulsions and complications. Some countries have resorted to what are usually considered to be "radical" birth-control techniques including surgical sterilization (India and Puerto Rico) and abortion (Japan, Tunisia, and the Communist countries). What may yet prove to be a more efficient means of encouraging birth control, however, may involve instilling in adults a love and appreciation of children and persuading them that they can extend better care to a smaller number of children.

That birth control can succeed without new contraceptive practices is proved by the experience of some countries, particularly in the Far East, whose birthrates had declined even before the use of the Pill and intrauterine devices, and continue still to decline (see Table 1.)

TABLE 1:
Selected Countries—
Births per 1,000 Inhabitants

	1956	1970
Singapore	44.4	23.0
Hong Kong	37.0	20.1
Taiwan (Formosa)	44.8	28.1
Mauritius	43.3	27.3

The alternative to a direct program of birth control—that is, a program giving priority to economic development—also involves frustrations. Even in a very sparsely populated country richly endowed with natural resources (Brazil, for example, or Zaire), overrapid growth of the population brings in its train an excessive need for demographic investments—that is, investments just to keep pace with the extra mouths to feed and bodies to clothe and shelter. Such quantitative investments reduce the availability of qualitative investments intended to raise the standard of living. Although it is always difficult to measure optimum growth, that point in most of the less developed countries seems to have already been passed (the figure of 2 percent per year might well be taken as an upper limit).

International discussion of population growth has been marked by wavering opinions on the necessity for measures on birth control. In February 1947, at the first meeting of the United Nations Population Commission in New York, the representative of the Soviet Union strongly opposed any restriction on the birthrate, thus opposing the U. S. The representatives of Roman Catholic countries similarly opposed those of the Protestant countries. At this time and for many years to come, the less developed countries—with their age-old traditions regarding fertility and with their new thirst for power and prestige—also generally opposed family planning. By 1962, however, after some 15 years of debates, the position had changed radically. A vote in the UN General Assembly in that year somewhat surprisingly split the nations into roughly three equal groups—those for birth control, those against it, and the remainder abstaining from opinion. In favour of a restriction of births were many African and Asian countries (particularly the Arab States), a new persuasion that prompted a cautious abstention from the Soviet Union. Since 1962 the tide of nations favouring the limitation of births has steadily swelled, particularly in Asia.

The continuing diversity in votes and opinions reflects, in part obviously, the great diversity among countries with respect to deathrates, birthrates, and levels of economic development or potential. Purely global studies of population have therefore become almost pointless; future studies must bear increasingly on regions and even on individual countries. India, for instance, faces almost terrifying population pressures as related to area, intense poverty, and density of population (436 inhabitants per square mile). In 1965 a threatened famine, following on two poor harvests, was narrowly avoided. Birth control has thus become a matter of national public welfare. In sub-Saharan Africa, on the other hand, the problem of the immediate future is far less urgent although malnutrition is at times dramatic enough. In Latin America the demographic and economic characteristics vary widely from country to country—with a relatively fine show of achievement in a country like Mexico, as contrasted with increasing poverty of ever-larger numbers in a country like Haiti. Everywhere in Latin America, however, the growth of the population is very rapid and tends to aggravate the problems of political stability. Generally speaking, whether or not predictions of the danger of a sudden general worldwide famine are accepted, serious local problems do remain unsolved, problems quite capable of provoking political complications.

(Reprinted with permission from "Population" in *Encyclopedia Britannica,* 15th edition, © 1974 by Encyclopedia Britannica, Inc.)

Reasoning Problems: Inductive Reasoning

For each of the problems, (a) indicate whether or not the information given is sufficient to justify the belief that the conclusion made is a statement about the world that is probably true, and (b), if it does not make such a statement, indicate which of the following rules for inductive reasoning it violates:

> operational definition
> comparison
> controlled comparison
> sampling

These rules are listed in decreasing order of importance. Operational definition is most important, because if it is violated you are not making any statement at all. Comparison and controlled comparison follow operational definition closely in that, so long as these three rules are satisfied, you can at least make a statement about the sample that has been observed. Sampling is last because it becomes important only when you take the final step of generalizing from the sample to a population. For each of the problems below, indicate the most important of these rules, if any, that has been violated.

1. Chain smokers have no will power. If they had, they wouldn't be chain smokers.

2. I won't put my seat belt on now because I've got to get to the store before it closes. I've driven years with a seat belt without an accident, so the chances are pretty slim that anything'll happen between here and the store.

3. Fifteen to thirty persons go through the Creative Engineering Program at General Electric each year. The participants are selected primarily through a combination of extensive interviews and tests. The program itself consists of eight stages: recognition, definition, search, evaluation, selection, preliminary design, demonstration, and follow-through. As evidence of the effectiveness of this program, graduates of the program produce patents at about three times the rate of nonparticipant engineers.

4. The Samsara Recycling Team recently presented the following income data on its patrons:

$0–$6000	16% of patrons
$6,000–$12,000	34% of patrons
$12,000–$20,000	44% of patrons
$20,000–$40,000	6% of patrons

It seems that lower and middle income people are more likely to recycle than higher income ($20,000 and above) people.

5. "You will make an important decision soon." (Chinese fortune cookie.)

6. The math department allows students to choose a lecture format or a tutorial format for the introductory statistics course. Year after year, the students electing the tutorial format do consistently better on a standardized national examination. It is concluded that the tutorial format is better than the lecture format for the population of students who enroll in introductory statistics in terms of producing high scores on the national exam.

7. In the early part of 1977, a large number of whales ran aground on the beaches of Florida and died. The question was, Why? Careful examination of the beached whales revealed that all had parasites in the inner ear, where the balance senses are located. Presumably, damage to the inner ear caused the whales to lose their sense of direction and run aground.

8. One hundred students sign up for a class in comparative anatomy. At the end of the term an evaluation form is filled out. Of the sixty completed forms, fifty say that they "would recommend the course to a friend." Satisfaction with the course, at least in terms of the number of students who say that they would recommend the course to a friend, seems to be high.

9. The questions asked by the students in class indicate a good understanding of the material being presented, so the class seems to be ready to go on to the next topic.

10. A person takes psychotherapy for two years, and both he and his friends notice a marked improvement in his capacity for work and pleasure and in both his relationships with others and in his ability to be comfortable when alone. He concludes that the therapy was effective.

11. A study of county extension agents' efforts in promoting artificial breeding of dairy cattle indicated that the rate

at which this breeding technique was adopted was almost directly related to the number of days a year that county extension agents spend on promoting the idea. Clearly, the extension agents have been effective in promoting this technique.

12. A follow-up study of a random sample of Volvos indicated that 9 out of 10 lasted 11 years. If I buy a new Volvo, the chances are 9 out of 10 that it will last 11 years.

13. A pollster who has spent a lifetime interviewing random samples of people says that in all his interviewing he has never met a truly educated person whom he didn't like.

14. In a study of a large random sample of medical patients with all kinds of illnesses, it is found that, in general, more optimistic patients (those who think it is likely that they will get better) recover more quickly. The conclusion is that it should be beneficial, in terms of recovery rate, to try to maintain an optimistic attitude in patients.

15. An instructor gives a political awareness test and an intelligence test to the students in his Modern Ideologies class and finds that they are above average on both measures. He concludes that, at least for the kind of people who take this class, the more intelligent a person is, the more politically aware he or she is, in terms of the tests he used.

Reasoning Problems: Deductive Reasoning

Read each problem, and answer the questions using trees.

1. If the only places in a town where you can buy mangoes are fruit shops, and all the fruit shops in that town are on Taylor Street, would it be true to say that the only places in that town where you can buy mangoes are on Taylor Street?

2. If (a) all mammals have warm blood, mamary glands, and hair and (b) all whales have warm blood, mammary glands, and hair, is it then necessarily true that all whales are mammals?

3. Assume that, "if the therapist is effective, then the patient is motivated." Is it then necessarily true that "the therapist is effective only if the patient is motivated"?

4. Assume that, "if the therapist is effective, then the patient is motivated." Is it then necessarily true that "the patient is motivated only if the therapist is effective"?

5. Assume that, "if the therapist is effective, then the patient is motivated." Is it then necessarily true that "the therapist cannot be effective if the patient is not motivated"?

6. Babies are illogical. Nobody is despised who can manage a crocodile. Illogical persons are despised. Therefore, babies cannot manage crocodiles. Does this conclusion, from Lewis Carroll, follow necessarily from the premises?

7. A couple is planning to take a plane to New York and then a boat to Greece. Three airlines fly from their home to New York, and five steamship lines go from New York to Greece. How many ways does this give them of getting from their home to Greece?

8. How many quantities can you make up from a nickel, a dime, and a quarter?

9. How many ways are there of seating three couples around a table if (a) men and women are to alternate, (b) no person is to sit next to his or her spouse, and (c) the host is to sit at the head of the table?

10. What is the probability that a die will come up 1? What is the probability that it will come up 1 on *both* of two successive rolls? What is the probability that it will come 1 on *either* one or the other or both of two successive rolls?

11. What is the probability that the numbers on two dice will add up to 7?

12. If a committee of 3 is randomly drawn from 8 men and 2 women, what is the probability that the committee will have no women on it?

13. If the probability of investment A making a profit is .60 and the probability of investment B making a profit is .70, what is the probability that one or the other or both will make a profit? (Assume that these probabilities are independent.)

14. In a certain school, 10% failed mathematics, and 12% failed English. Is the probability that a randomly selected student failed both math and English .10 times .12? Why?

15. If 70% of those with a particular diagnosis require surgery, 90% of those requiring surgery recover completely, and 20% of those not requiring surgery recover completely, what is the probability that a person with this diagnosis will recover completely?

16. Your engine clearly needs work. Of cars of this model and age that require work, 40% need reboring and crankshaft grinding. A mechanic friend tells you that, if an engine needs reboring and crankshaft grinding, the oil pressure, measured under certain conditions of engine speed and temperature, will be less than 30 psi 80% of the time; whereas, if it does not need this work, the oil pressure will be less than 30 psi only 30% of the time. If you have this test performed on your engine and the pressure is less than 30 psi, what is the probability that it needs reboring and crankshaft grinding?

Creative Thinking Problems

1. You are planning to move to another state. List all the things you should do in preparation for your move.

2. It is inevitable that the supply of oil will continue to diminish. List ways in which you could profit from this fact.

Drawing by Sidney Harris, reprinted from *The American Scientist*, © 1977, with permission of the artist.

3. Generate as many humorous titles as you can for the above cartoon.

Problems in Decision Making: Multiple Futures

For all of the following problems, assume that the value of risk is neutral.

1. Bob is going fishing. He could go up the Sandy, where the fish run about 5 pounds but where there are so many fisherman that the probability of landing a fish is only 1/10. Or he could go up the Clackamas, where the probability of landing a fish is 1/4 but where the fish are only about 2½ pounds. Where should he go?

2. Don is trying to decide which of two essay questions to answer on a take-home final. He is sure he understands the question to one, but he is also sure he doesn't know much about the answer. If he takes this question he is virtually certain of a B. He is only 60% certain that he understands the question to the other, but, if he does understand it correctly, he knows the answer very well. If he is right on that question, he can expect an A; if he is wrong, he will probably get a D. Which should he write on? (Assume that A = 4, B = 3, C = 2, D = 1, and F = 0.)

3. Roberta is thinking of taking Psy 299: The improvement of Thinking as a night course. It would cost her $100 to do so. She believes that it is more likely than not to do her some good, but still she is skeptical. She believes that there is a 10% chance that it will be effective. She estimates, as a very conservative minimum, that, if the course does her any good, it will be worth $100 a year to her, on the average, for the 40 years of her working life. Should she take the course or keep her $100? How much is the course worth to her?

4. Ashley has car trouble. She thinks the problem is in the voltage regulator. She brings the car into the garage and describes the problem to the mechanic. The mechanic agrees that the problem is most likely in the voltage regulator but says it should be checked out before being replaced. The charge for checking out the voltage regulator is $5.00. The cost of a rebuilt voltage regulator is $25.00. If Ashley believes that there is a 10% chance that the problem is not in the voltage regulator, should she have the mechanic check the old one first or simply install a rebuilt

one? How much is it worth to Ashley to have the mechanic check the voltage regulator?

5. Mr. Jones owns 20 acres of land very close to the route of a proposed freeway. He believes that there is a 40% chance that the freeway will be approved and a 60% chance that it will not. If it is approved, he believes that he can sell the land for $1,000,000. If it is not and an alternate route is selected, he would have to subdivide the land and sell one-acre building sites at $20,000 per lot. Costs associated with subdividing and selling amount to $2000 per lot. He has received an offer of $600,000 for the land from a large development company and must make a decision on their offer within 48 hours. Should he accept their offer?

6. Mr. Allen finds that the costs of a $100-deductible plan, a $50-deductible plan, and a no-deductible plan of insurance for his car are $100, $160, and $200, respectively. (The amount deductible is the amount paid by the car owner in the event of a loss, with the balance being paid by the insurance company.) Insurance statistics show that the average claim against collision policies is $600 and that the probability of an individual driver having an accident resulting in such a claim during any given year is .05. Which insurance plan should Mr. Allen choose?

7. A man is considering leaving his wife for another woman but decides to go to a marriage counselor first. The marriage counselor tries to get him to take a careful look at his decision. After telling the counselor how much more exciting the other woman is, the man begins to realize that he is not making a controlled comparison, that after he has known the other woman as long as he has known his wife he will probably not find her as exciting as he does now. It also occurs to him that there is a good chance that she will actually leave him. If he rates both women on a 10-point scale, his wife would get a 5, and the other woman would get a 10. But the other woman is more of a gamble. There is only a 5% chance that she will continue to be as exciting as

she is now (9 or 10), a 60% chance that she will turn out to be better than his wife (6, 7, or 8), and a fair chance (say, 35%) that she will leave him (0 on the scale). What should he do?

8. Sylvia is trying to decide whether to accept an offer of a date Saturday from Skip or Henri. If it doesn't rain, she and Skip would go sailing, which would be a big plus, but she and Henri would probably go for a walk, which would be neither especially good nor especially bad. If it does rain, they would have to find something to do indoors, which would be a big plus with Henri but an equally big minus with Skip. So she decides to call the weatherman before making up her mind. What is the critical probability of rain, above which she should date Henri and below which she should date Skip?

9. If a bird in the hand is worth two in the bush, what is the probability of catching a bird in the bush? (Work out the tree, assuming that the probability of catching any one bird in the bush is independent of that of catching any other bird in the bush.)

Problems in Decision Making: Multiple Goals

1. What is wrong with the following goal set for deciding whether to change schools?

> tuition already spent at present school
> future tuition costs
> quality of education

2. What is wrong with the following goal set for deciding on a job?

> income
> opportunity for personal growth
> responsibility
> social value of work
> standard of living (house, car, clothing, travel, etc.)

3. Assume that a person is planning to buy a car and has worked up the following table:

	R	B	EH	A	City mps	Hwy mps	Purchase Price	Selling Price
Car A	0	0	0	+	15	30	3000	2000
Car B	+	+	0	+	10	30	5000	3000
Car C	++	+	+	0	12	25	7000	4000
Car D	+	0	+	0	10	20	4000	2500

And assume that he has priced out the *annual* values of each of the subjective factors as follows:

R (repairs)
  0 = $0
  + = $750
  ++ = $1500
B (brakes)
  0 = $0
  + = $750
EH (emergency handling)
  0 = $0
  + = $500
A (aesthetics)
  0 = $0
  + = $300

Note that all the above factors are treated as benefits, so that a car that has a good repair record, for example, is regarded as being worth more money than one with a poor repair record. Finally, assume that this person drives 7000 city miles and 3000 highway miles per year and that the anticipated average fuel cost during the 5-year period over which he plans to keep the car is $1.00 per gallon. These factors are treated here as costs.

Which of these cars should he buy?

4. Phil Anthropist has been asked by three charitable organizations to serve as president. Because of limitations on his time, he will be able to say yes to only one of them. The most important factors affecting his decision are (a) the importance of the charitable cause, which he assigns a weight of .5; (b) the soundness of the management and fiscal policies of the organization, which he assigns a weight of .3; and (c) the extent to which the organization is not well known and widely supported, which he assigns a weight of .2. His ratings for organizations A, B, and C, respectively, are 10, 8, and 9 on the first factor; 6, 8, and 8 on the second factor; and 1, 9, and 5 on the third factor.

What is Phil's composite rating for each organization?

APPENDIX B: ANSWERS

Memory Problems

Because effective memory techniques turn out, in the final analysis, to be what works for *you*, it is not possible to give answers to any of the memory problems that are right for everybody. The best that can be done is to show some ways in which you *might* have applied the ABC ROAD techniques.

1. Ted Hartman can be associated with Kingsley Products by using the word-association technique for binding, e.g., "King of Hearts," or the image technique, e.g., the image of a Teddy bear with a heart on his sweater, hugging a king. Similarly, Meriwhether Industrial Supply can be associated with Jane Higgenbottom using the word-association technique, e.g., Ms. Higgenbottom (Meriwhether Industrial Supply = M. I. S. = Ms.), or by the image technique, e.g., the image of a boat named "Jane," hitting the bottom in merry weather. Similar techniques can be applied to the other representative-company pairs. If you have an opportunity to learn the pairs before the meeting, that would be preferable, because it would permit

greater overlearning. If you are not able to do this, at least be sure to repeat the pairs, along with their mnemonics, during the meeting. Of course, be sure in either case to cue each pair by associating it with some aspect of the person's appearance, once you know what the person looks like.

2. The number for fire can be coded, using the phonetic system, as "No MeN NeeD DeaTH." The number for police is a little more difficult, but the first seven consonant sounds in "CaTCH SuCH BaD Types" would do.

3. A variety of techniques can be brought to bear on organizing the population growth article so as to make it easier to remember. First, of course, such a long piece must be analyzed into components. One possible breakdown is: Problem, Proposed Solutions, and National Positions. The material in each of these sections can then be organized around a meaningful image. We shall suggest a graph for the first, a decision tree and goal table for the second, and a map for the third.

Problem. The problem addressed in the article is matching population to food supply. It has three aspects, which are presented in the following graph:

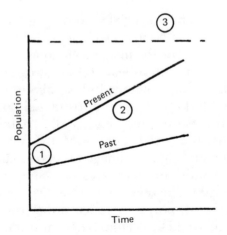

One aspect of the problem is that a greater population base is affected now than in the past; this is shown by the intersection of the "present" line with the vertical axis at a higher point. A second aspect of this problem is that there is a greater rate of growth now than in the past (as a consequence of improved antimortality techniques); this is shown by the steeper slope of the "present" line. The third aspect is that there are no longer any migratory or economic outlets; this is shown by the nearness of the "present" line to an absolute ceiling line.

Proposed solutions. The proposed solutions can be divided into birth control versus economic development, and the birth control solutions can be subdivided into the pill, the IUD, sterilization/abortion, and increased concern for the welfare of children. This analysis can assume an outline form, and it can be represented by the following decision tree:

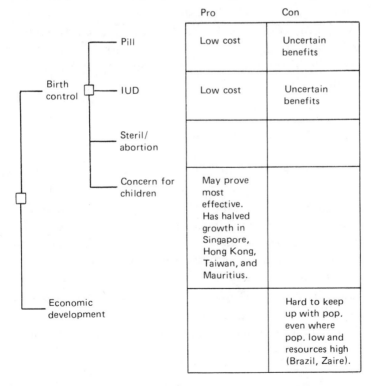

	Pro	Con
Pill	Low cost	Uncertain benefits
IUD	Low cost	Uncertain benefits
Steril/ abortion		
Concern for children	May prove most effective. Has halved growth in Singapore, Hong Kong, Taiwan, and Mauritius.	
Economic development		Hard to keep up with pop. even where pop. low and resources high (Brazil, Zaire).

The tree terminates in a goals table, which summarizes the arguments presented for and against various of the alternatives. (Note the empty cells. This is an example of cross-classification of attributes as a stimulus to creative thinking.)

National positions. The national positions are reported for three points in time: 1947, 1962, and since 1962. These can be represented in terms of the image of a map. The map for 1947 would show the U.S. and northern Europe (Protestant) pro, and South America and southern Europe (Catholic), Africa (the underdeveloped countries), and the USSR con. The map for 1962 would represent a movement south and east, picking up Africa, the Arabian peninsula, and Asia in the pro camp and causing the USSR to abstain. The division at this point is into equal numbers pro, con, and abstaining. The map for the period since 1962 would show a continued shift in the same direction, with pro increasing in Asia.

Of course, you would cue the material with questions, such as, "How has world opinion on population control changed over the last several decades?" and you would apply the ROAD techniques.

Reasoning Problems: Inductive Reasoning

1. Operational definition. "Chain smoker" is defined as lacking in will power, and the statement is thus circular.
2. Sampling. The statement is a statement of probability. The probability of having an accident when you are in too much of a hurry to put on a seat belt may well be different from the probability of having an accident when you have time to put on a seat belt.
3. Controlled comparison. The difference between the kind of people who pass the screening for the program and those who do not has not been controlled or randomized

(quite the reverse!) and could be the real cause of the difference in number of patents.

4. **Comparison.** Data are presented only for those who recycle; no comparison is made with data on those who do not recycle. Perhaps fewer than 6% of these are in the $20,000–40,000 range!

5. **Operational definition.** "Important" is not defined, and neither is "soon." Almost any event could fit the description. The statement is not testable.

6. **Controlled comparison.** The difference between the kind of students who elect the tutorial format and those who elect the lecture format is not controlled or randomized and could be the real cause of the difference in the scores on the national examination.

7. **Comparison.** Beached whales have not been compared with those still swimming about.

8. **Sampling.** This is a statement of probability. The probability that a randomly selected student will find the course worth recommending to a friend may be quite different from the probability that one of the 60% who do not drop the course find it this worthwhile.

9. **Sampling.** Those who ask questions in class do not constitute a random sample of those in the class.

10. **Controlled comparison.** Many changes may have occurred during the two years that could account for the improvement. These should be dealt with by randomization: assign people randomly to a therapy group and a no-therapy control group, then observe them at the end of two years.

11. **Controlled comparison.** There is no assurance, by way of control or randomization, that the areas in which extension agents spent many days a year promoting the technique and the areas in which they spent few days promoting the technique differed in only this one re-

spect. It is possible, for example, that they differed in the problems the cattlemen faced or in the receptivity of the cattlemen to new ideas and that such factors accounted for both the greater activity on the part of the agents and the greater number of adoptions. (Later research showed this in fact to have been the case.)

12. **Sampling.** Not everything we know about Volvos made earlier will necessarily be true of Volvos being made today.

13. **Operational definition.** "Truly educated" is not defined. If a defining characteristic of "truly educated" turns out to be being liked by this person, the statement is circular.

14. **Controlled comparison.** Since no variable was manipulated, the relationship is only predictive. One factor that has not been controlled or randomized that could be the real cause of both optimism and rapid recovery rate is the seriousness of the illness.

15. **Comparison.** To satisfy comparison, the instructor must look at people who are high and low on political awareness and people who are high and low on intelligence. However, he has looked only at people who are high on both measures.

Reasoning Problems: Deductive Reasoning

1. Yes. The tree looks like this:

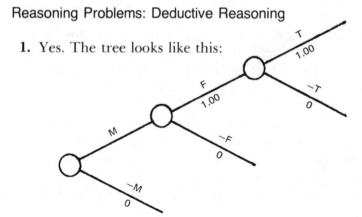

2. No. When you flip the first tree and attach it to the second, you find that the first tree tells you only about creatures *not* having warm blood, mammary glands, and hair.

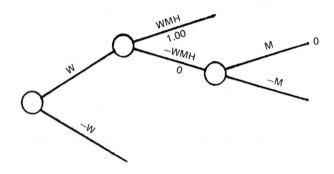

3. Yes. In the diagram below, the E branch is necessarily connected to the M branch.

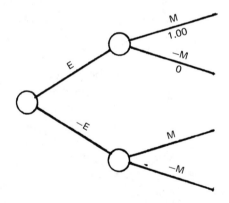

4. No. So far as we know, the probability of the M branch being associated with the −E branch may be greater than zero.

5. Yes. For this, we must flip the tree, as follows.

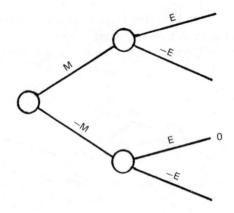

6. Yes. The three premises are represented by the three trees below.

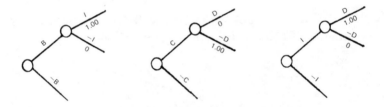

The first and third trees can be joined as below:

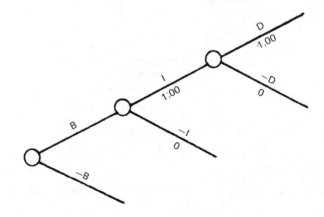

But we have to flip the second tree before we can hook it onto the first tree. Both of these steps have been taken below:

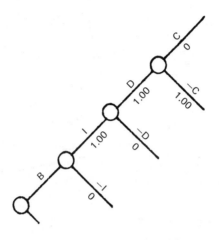

7. 15.

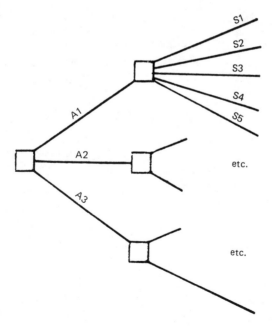

8. 7.

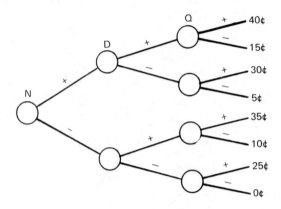

9. Two.

10. .17

$$.17 \times .17 = .03$$

$$.03 + .14 + .14 = .31$$

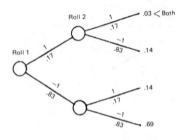

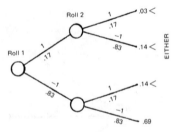

11. 1/6.

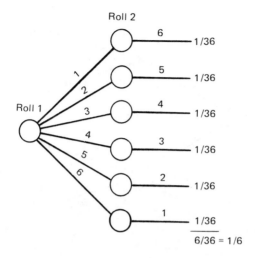

12. 8/10 × 7/9 × 6/8 = .47.

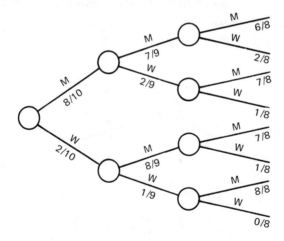

13. $.42 + .18 + .28 = .88.$

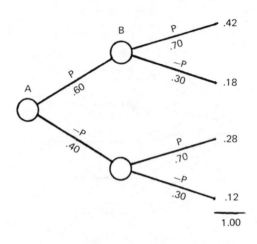

14. No. These are not independent probabilities. Those who fail math are more likely to fail English than those who do not fail math.

15. $.63 + .06 = .69.$

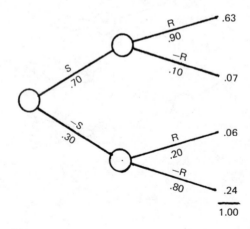

16. $.32/.50 = .64.$

<pre>
              .50   .50

    R   .08   .32   .40
   −R   .42   .18   .60

         ≥30 <30
</pre>

Creative Thinking Problems

1. A mover's checklist, obtainable from most moving companies, should be an immense help here. Classification can lead you to recognize the symmetry between moving out of one place and moving into another. For example, whatever utilities you have to shut down in the old place will probably have to be started up in the new place. It might also call your attention to the travel in between, which you might as well make as pleasant as possible. Role-playing should also help here, for example, imagining yourself first arriving in the new location and having to have a place to spend the night.

2. In generating ideas for ways to profit from the coming oil shortage, a checklist of petroleum products, which you could find in any encyclopedia, should be very helpful. It might remind you of petroleum products, such as plastics, synthetics, fertilizers, and insecticides, that you might not otherwise think of. Beginning at the other end of the problem, with a goals checklist, could suggest problems connected with such things as entertainment, recreation—and crime—that you might not otherwise readily associate with oil. Finally, analysis into attributes could get you out of all sorts of loops. It could suggest acquiring skills or knowledge, in addition to acquiring property, as possible courses of action. (You might want to take the coming oil shortage into account in planning your career, for example, by going into communication, which should become more important as transportation becomes less important.) It could suggest conservation of oil and oil products, recycling of oil and oil products, and substitution for oil and oil products. And it could also lead you to define "profit" broadly enough to include reducing losses that you might suffer as a consequence of the coming oil crunch, as well as increasing profits. For example, maybe you shouldn't buy that motor home, after all.

3. In generating titles for the cartoon, a purge might turn up possibilities like, "Whew! Those Martusians are certainly a sexually active lot!" or, "There must be an easier way to monitor the SALT agreement!" Analysis into attributes might get you out of the loop of commenting on what the man is seeing through the telescope and start looking around at the man himself and the room he is in, so stimulus variation could suggest titles like, "I wish I could get my nose unstuck!" or, "What a breakthrough! The canals are really railroad tracks!" Talking with someone else would be a helpful technique—just reading the ideas in this paragraph could have some of that effect.

Problems in Decision Making: Multiple Futures

1. $EV(\text{Sandy}) = .10(5) + .90(0) = .5$ pounds

   $EV(\text{Clack}) = .25(2.5) + .75(0) = .625$ pounds

   Go up the Clackamas.

2. $V(1) = 3$

   $EV(2) = .60(4) + .40(1) = 2.8$

   Answer the first question.

3. EV(take 299) $= .10(\$4000 - \$100) + .90(-\$100) = \$300$

EV(not take 299) $= 0$

Take the course.

4. She should just go ahead and install a rebuilt voltage regulator. It is worth only \$2.50 to her to have the mechanic check out her old voltage regulator.

5. V(take) $= \$600,000$

EV(not take) $= .40(\$1,000,000) + .60(\$360,000)$
           $= \$616,000$

Reject the offer.

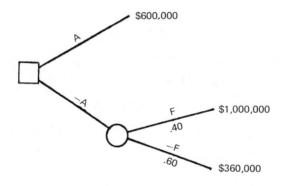

6. $EV(\$100\ D) = .05(-\$200) + .95(-\$100) = -\$105$

$EV(\$50\ D) = .05(-\$210) + .95(-\$160) = -\$162.5$

$EV(\$0\ D) = .05(-\$200) + .95(-\$200) = -\$200$

Choose the \$100-deductible plan.

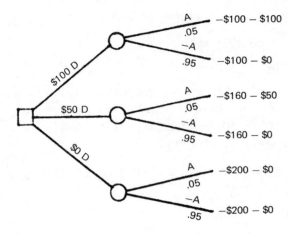

7. V(wife)   = 5

   EV(other) = .05(9.5) + .60(7) + .35(0) = 4.68

   Stay with his wife.

8. EV(Skip) = $X(-1) + (1 - X)(+1) = 1 - 2X$

   EV(Henri) = $X(+1) + (1 - X)(0) = X$

   The critical probability would be that probability at which

   EV(Skip = EV(Henri):

   $X = 1 - 2X$

   $3X = 1$

   $X = 1/3 = .33$

9. If these two alternatives (a bird in the hand and two birds in the bush) are equal in worth, then:

   $1 = X^2(2) + (X)(1 - X)(1) + (1 - X)(X)(1) + (1 - X)^2(0)$

   $1 = 2X^2 + X - X^2 + X - X^2$

   $1 = 2X$

   $X = \frac{1}{2} = .50$

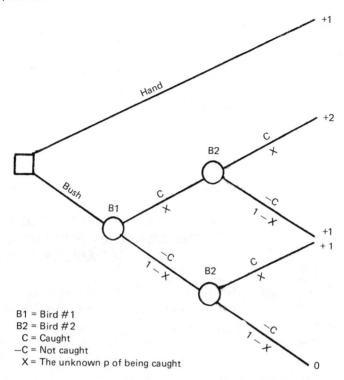

B1 = Bird #1
B2 = Bird #2
C = Caught
−C = Not caught
X = The unknown p of being caught

Problems in Decision Making: Multiple Goals

1. Tuition already spent at present school is a sunk cost and is irrelevant to the decision.

2. Since standard of living is to a large extent dependent on income, including both is double-counting.

3. He should buy Car C.

	R	B	EH	A	City	Hwy	Cost	
CAR A	0	0	0	300	−467	−100	−200	−467
CAR B	750	750	0	300	−700	−100	−400	+600
CAR C	1500	750	500	0	−583	−120	−600	+1447
CAR D	750	0	500	0	−700	−150	−300	+100

4. Organization B comes out on top.

	Imp .50	Mgmt .30	Unk .20	
A	10	6	1	7.0
B	8	8	9	8.2
C	9	8	5	7.9

APPENDIX C:
THE CONSTRUCTION AND USE
OF A PROBABILITY WHEEL

To construct a probability wheel (Spetzler and Stael von Holstein, 1975), (a) draw two equal circles on stiff paper, one on paper of one color and the other on paper of a contrasting color; (b) mark one of the circles into 10 equal segments and label the boundaries between the segments from .0 to .9; then (c) cut the marked circle on the .0 radius and the other on any radius and assemble them as shown.

To use the probability wheel, (a) turn the unnumbered side toward you, (b) rotate the circles with respect to one another until the proportion of the area of the circle that is unshaded (in this drawing) is equal to the probability of the event in question, then (c) turn the wheel over and read the probability off the scale on the back.

Matching the area of the unshaded portion of the circle to the probability of the event in question is, of course, the crucial step and the most difficult one. In doing this, it is helpful to think in terms of a choice between two imaginary bets: to bet on the event in question or to bet on the shaded portion of the wheel. If you choose to bet on the event in question, let us say a randomly selected coffee shop being successful, then you win a prize if the event occurs and win nothing if it does not occur.

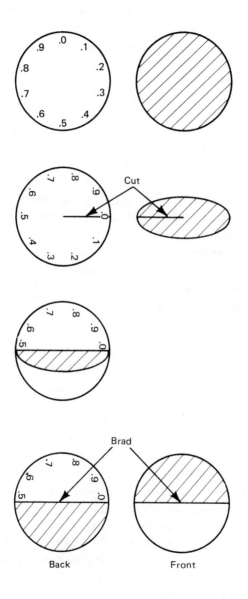

If you choose to bet on the shaded portion of the wheel, then we spin the wheel like a roulette wheel, and, if the pointer lands on the shaded portion, you win the prize; otherwise, you win nothing. Of course, the bets remain imaginary; we never actually spin the wheel, and we never wait to see whether the event in question will occur.

If you choose to bet on the shaded portion of the wheel, then the shaded portion is too large and should be made smaller. If you choose to bet on the event in question, then the shaded portion of the wheel is too small and should be made larger. If you find it difficult or impossible to choose, then your judgment of the probability that the shaded portion of the wheel will come up matches your judgment of the probability that the event will occur, and you can read this probability off the scale on the back.

This technique is appropriate for estimating probabilities for any of the four kinds of statements about the world: probabilities, conditional probabilities, predictive relationships, and causal relationships.

APPENDIX D: ADDITIONAL TECHNIQUES FOR PROBABILITY ESTIMATION

There are two additional techniques for probability estimation that are worth knowing: fractile estimation and probability estimation. We shall see how they can be used separately and in conjunction with one another.

Let us take a somewhat different look at the uncertainty about whether your parents are coming to live with you. Let us say that you know that they are coming but that you don't know when. You are sure that they will not come within six months but that they will come sometime before four years are up. You would like to divide the event node up into two or more branches and attach a reasonable p to each.

One technique for dealing with this case is fractile estimation. In fractile estimation, you begin by estimating that value above which about half of the cases would fall and below which about half of the cases would fall. This is the 50th percentile. Let us say that you believe that your parents are about as likely to come before two years as to come after that time. Then 2.0 years would be the 50th percentile. Next, considering only those cases that fall below the 50th percentile, estimate that value above and below which about half of them would fall. This is the 25th percentile. Let us say that, if your parents come before two years are up, they are about as likely to come before as after one and one-half years. Then 1.5 years would be the 25th percentile. Finally, considering only those cases that fall above the 50th percentile, estimate that value above and below which about half of them would fall. This is the 75th percentile. Let us say that this is 2.5 years. As a check, ask yourself whether you believe that about half of the cases would fall between the 25th and 75th percentiles—they should. In the example, you should believe that it is about as likely that your parents will come between 1.5 and 2.5 years as that they will come either before or after that period of time.

Another technique for dealing with this case is probability estimation. In fractile estimation, you begin with probabilities (the 25th, 50th, and 75th percentiles) and estimate the corresponding values on the variable of interest (here, time.) In probability estimation, you begin with values on the variable of interest (a year, a year and a half, two years) and estimate the corresponding probabilities. The first step in probability estimation is to divide the variable of interest into categories. Let us divide the time until your parents might come into the following categories: $< .6$, $.6–1.0$, $1.1–1.5$, $1.6–2.0$, $2.1–2.5$, $2.6–3.0$, $3.1–3.5$, and > 3.5 years. The next step is to estimate the proportion of cases that would fall in each category. Use of the probability wheel (Appendix C) should help here. If the estimated p's do not sum to 1.00, divide each p by the sum of the p's, and the sum of the resulting p's will then equal 1.00.

Let us say that this method yields the following p's for these categories: .00, .10, .15, .20, .25, .20, .20, .10, and .00.

You can use whichever of these techniques you find more comfortable; or, better yet, you can use both and check them against one another. The easiest way to check them against one another is to plot them on the same cumulative probability graph. In a cumulative probability graph, you plot cumulative p's on the vertical axis and values on the dimension of interest on the horizontal axis. The values on the vertical axis will always range from 0 to 1.00. Those on the horizontal axis will vary from problem to problem. In the example, they would be years until your parents arrive and would range from   .6 years to   3.5 years.

Cumulative p's are computed as follows. Using the results from the probability estimation method, the cumulative p's for each category are:

Category	Cumulative Probability
> 0.6	.00 = .00
0.6–1.0	.00 + .10 = .10
1.1–1.5	.00 + .10 + .15 = .25
1.6–2.0	.00 + .10 + .15 + .20 = .45
2.1–2.5	.00 + .10 + .15 + .20 + .25 = .70
2.6–3.0	.00 + .10 + .15 + .20 + .25 + .20 = .90
3.1–3.5	.00 + .10 + .15 + .20 + .25 + .20 + .10 = 1.00
> 3.5	.00 + .10 + .15 + .20 + .25 + .20 + .10 + .00 = 1.00

Since quartiles are cumulative p's, the results from the fractile estimation method do not need to be transformed in order to be plotted on a cumulative probability graph. The results of both methods are plotted on the following graph.

The results of the two methods agree well. The dimension of interest can now be divided into any convenient number of categories, to constitute branches of the event node, and the p for each category can be read off the graph, using the average of the two curves. This is done below for the categories: "before 2 years" and "after 2 or more years."

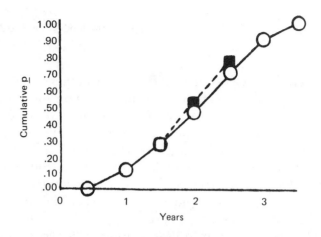

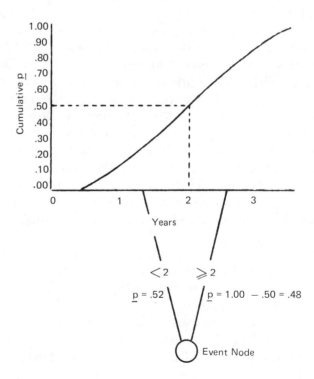

Let us return to the problem of deciding whether to buy a 3- or 4-bedroom house. Perhaps in order to obtain more precise information about the probability of your parents' coming you would have to pay for an expensive medical examination, or to pay for an analysis of their financial situation, or to incur the less tangible, but nonetheless real, cost of hurting their feelings. Or perhaps you would have to delay the decision to the point where you would miss an opportunity to make a good buy on a house or where you would have to pay for major repairs on your present house. The question then would be whether it is worth it. Might the cost of obtaining further information not be greater than the cost of making the less favorable choice on the original decision?

To answer this question, we must set up another decision tree, one which will include the original tree as a part. But, before we can do this, we will have to get some more probabilities. In particular, we will have to know (a) the p of getting each of the various possible answers to our question and (b) the conditional p of each of these answers being correct. These p's will enable us to take into account the amount of information we already have and the amount of additional information we are likely to get and thus to determine how much additional information we are likely to be getting for our money.

Let us say that you believe that, over the number of years involved, your folks will be about 90% accurate in their ability to predict whether they will be coming to live with you or not. More precisely, you believe that the p that they will say that they are coming, if they are coming, is .90; and you believe that the p that they will say that they are not coming, if they are not coming, is .90. This information is contained in the following table:

$$\begin{array}{ccc} & .74 & .26 \\ \text{C} & \boxed{.02 \quad .18} & .20 \\ -\text{C} & \boxed{.72 \quad .08} & .80 \\ & \text{``}-\text{C''} \quad \text{``C''} & \end{array}$$

This table requires explanation. To begin with, C means that your parents are coming; $-$C means that your parents are not coming; "C" means that your parents say that they are coming; and "$-$C" means that your parents say that they are not coming. You have already estimated the p of C to be .20 and the p of $-$C to be .80; these figures are the row marginals.

At this point we apply the multiplication rule for determining the p that both of two independent events will occur. If the p that your parents are coming is .20 and the conditional p that if they are coming they will say they are coming is .90, then the p that they are coming and they will say that they are coming is

.20 × .90 = .18.

This is the figure entered in the upper-left-hand cell, the one labeled C (for they are coming) and "C" (for they say they are coming). In a similar manner, we can compute the p's for each of the other cells:

.20 × .10 = .02,

.80 × .10 = .08, and

.80 × .90 = .72.

Finally, we apply the addition rule for determining the p that either of two mutually exclusive events will occur. If the p that your parents say they are coming and are coming is .18 and the p that they say they are coming and are not coming is .08, then the marginal p that they will say they are coming (whether or not they are coming) is:

.18 + .08 = .26.

Similarly, the marginal p that they will say they are not coming (whether or not they are coming) is:

.02 + .72 = .74.

Now we are ready to construct the decision tree. At first glance, this tree will seem very complicated. But remember that it is constructed and evaluated by simply reapplying the few basic rules we have already covered. Therefore, it will constitute a good review of these rules, as well as an extension of them.

This diagram requires a good deal of explanation. The "No Info" branch represents the case we began with, making the decision without getting any further information. We could attach the decision tree on page 186 to the end of this branch, but for simplicity we have represented it by the EV of the highest alternative, 8.8.

The "Info" branch represents the possibility of getting more information. The value of this course of action is uncertain because we do not know what the information will be and because we do not know whether or not it will be correct. If you ask your parents whether they are coming, they will say either that they are coming or that they are not. The probabilities of these events are .26 and .74, respectively, as obtained from the table we just worked up. Once you have this information, that is, once they have told you that they are coming or that they are not coming, you will revise your p's of their coming and not coming to those at the far right of the tree and, on the basis of these more accurate p's, decide to buy either a 3-bedroom house or a 4-bedroom house.

How do we evaluate the tree? We "fold it back," just as we do a simpler tree, by beginning at the right-hand side and working back to the major act node. Consider the act node following the "C" branch. The EV of buying a 3-bedroom house in this case is 5.86, and the EV of buying a 4-bedroom house is 9.07.

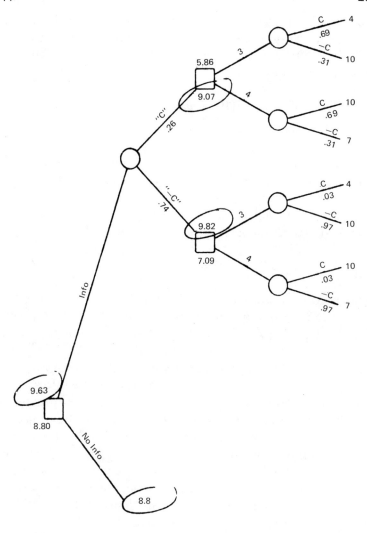

$EV^3 = .69(4) + .31(10) = 5.86$

$EV^4 = .69(10) + .31(7) = 9.07$

If your parents say that they are coming, you will maximize EV by buying a 4-bedroom house, so we can replace this entire sub-tree by the value 9.07. Now, consider the act node following the "$-C$" branch. The EV of buying a 3-bedroom house in this case is 9.82, and the EV of buying a 4-bedroom house is 7.90.

$$EV^3 = .03(4) + .97(10) = 9.82$$
$$EV^4 = .03(10) + .97(7) = 7.09$$

If your parents say that they are not coming, you will buy the 3-bedroom house, so we can replace this entire sub-tree by the value 9.82.

But we do not know for certain what your parents are going to say, so the EV of the ' "Info" branch is

$$EV = .26(9.07) + .74(9.82) = 9.63.$$

This is considerably higher than the EV of 8.8 for the "No Info" branch, so it appears that you should get the information, and perhaps you should. But we have not taken into account one thing: the cost of the information.

The simplest way to take account of the cost of information, at this point, would be think about what the information will cost you and ask yourself whether this cost is greater or less than the improvement from 8.8 to 9.63 on the subjective scale you have been using. Another way is to rate the cost of information on this same scale and subtract this figure from each of the value figures at the ends of the paths on the "Info" part of the tree, but not, of course, from any of the figures at the ends of the paths on the "No Info" part of the tree. Then you would compute EVs on this basis.

Seeking information often has a much higher EV than not seeking information. That is why businesses engage in research, governments engage in intelligence operations, and individuals seek both formal and informal education. And of course, that is why the considerations raised in the memory and reasoning chapters are so important.

BIBLIOGRAPHY

ABORN, M., "The Influence of Experimentally Induced Failure on the Retention of Material Acquired through Set and Incidental Learning," *Journal of Experimental Psychology,* 45 (1953), 225–231.

ADORNO, T. W., E. FRENKEL-BRUNSWIK, D. J. LEVINSON, and R. N. SANFORD, *The Authoritarian Personality.* New York: Harper, 1950.

ALLISON, G. T., *Essence of Decision: Explaining the Cuban Missile Crisis.* Boston: Little, Brown, 1971.

ALPERT, M., and H. RAIFFA. *A Progress Report on the Training of Probability Assessors.* Unpublished manuscript, 1969.

ANDERSON, B. F., *The Psychology Experiment: An Introduction to the Scientific Method* (2nd. ed.). Monterey, Calif.: Brooks/Cole, 1971.

ANDERSON, B. F., *Cognitive Psychology: The Study of Knowing, Learning, and Thinking.* New York: Academic Press, 1975.

ANDERSON, B. F., and W. L. JOHNSON, "Two Methods of Presenting Information and Their Effects on Problem Solving," *Perceptual & Motor Skills,* 23 (1966), 851–856.

ANDERSON, N. H., and S. HUBERT, "Effects of Concomitant Verbal Recall on Effects in Personality Impression Formation," *Journal of Verbal Learning & Verbal Behavior,* 2 (1963), 379–391.

ANDERSON, R. C., and J. L. HIDDLE, "Imagery and Sentence Learning," *Journal of Educational Psychology,* 62 (1971), 526–530.

ASCH, S. E., J. CERASO, and W. HEIMER, "Perceptual Conditions of Association," *Psychological Monographs,* 74, whole no. 490 (1960).

BARBER, B., and R. C. FOX, "The Case of the Floppy-Eared Rabbits: An Instance of Serendipity Gained and Serendipity Lost, *American Journal of Society,* 64 (1958), 128–136.

BARCLAY, S., R.V. BROWN, C.W. KELLY, III, C. R. PETERSON, L.D. PHILLIPS, and J. SELRIDGE, *Handbook for Decision Analysis.* McLean, Virginia: Decisions and Designs, Inc., 1977. CONR Technical Report TR-77-6-30.

BAR-HILLEL, M., *Compounding Subjective Probabilities.* Organizational Behavior & Human Performance, 1973.

BARKER, S. F., *The Elements of Logic* (2nd ed.). New York: McGraw-Hill, 1974.

BARRON, F., "The Psychology of Creativity," in *New Directions in Psychology, II* by F. Barron, W. C. Dement, W. Edwards, H. Lindman, C. D. Phillips, J. Olds, and M. Olds. New York: Holt, Rinehart & Winston, 1965.

BLOOM, B. S., and L. BRODER, *Problem-Solving Processes of College Students.* Chicago: University of Chicago Press, 1950.

BOUSFIELD, W. A., "The Occurrence of Clustering in the Recall of Randomly Arranged Associates," *Journal of General Psychology,* 49 (1953), 229–240.

BOWER, G. H., "Imagery as a Relational Organizer in Association Learning," *Journal of Verbal Learning & Verbal Behavior,* 9 (1970), 529–533.

BOWER, G. H., "Mental Imagery and Associative Learning," in *Cognition in Learning and Memory,* ed. L. W. Gregg. New York: John Wiley, 1972.

BROADBENT, D.E., "The Magic Number Seven After Fifteen Years," in *Studies in Long-term Memory,* eds. A. Kennedy and A. Wilkes, pp. 3–18. New York, John Wiley, 1975.

BROWN, R. V., A. S. KAHR, and C. PETERSON, *Decision Analysis: An Overview.* New York: Holt, Rinehart & Winston, 1974.

BROWN, R. V., A. S. KAHR, and C. PETERSON, *Decision Analysis for the Manager.* New York: Holt, Rinehart & Winston, 1974.

BRUNER, J. S. *On Knowing: Essays for the Left Hand.* Cambridge, Mass.: Belknap Press, 1964.

BRUNER, J. S., J. J. GOODNOW, and G. A. AUSTIN, *A Study of Thinking.* New York: Science Editions, 1962.

BRUNER, J. S., R. R. OLVER, P. M. GREENFIELD, J. R. HORNSBY, H. J. KENNEY, M. MACCOBY, N. MODIANO, F. A. MOSHER, D. R. OLSON, M. C. POTTER, L. C. REICH, A. McK. SONSTROEM. *Studies in Cognitive Growth.* New York: John Wiley, 1966.

CARLYN, M. "An Assessment of the Meyer-Briggs Type Indicator," *Journal of Personality Assessment,* 41, 1977, pp. 461–473.

CASTELLAN, N. J., JR., D. B. PISONI, and G. R. POTTS, eds., *Cognitive Theory,* vol. 2. Hillsdale, N. J.: Lawrence Erlbaum Assocs., 1977.

CATTELL, R. B., and J. E. DREVDAHL, "A Comparison of the Personality Profile (16 P. F.) of Eminent Researchers with That of Eminent Teachers and Administrators, and of the General Population," *British Journal of Psychology,* 46 (1955), 248–261.

COCHRANE, J. L., and M. ZELENY, eds., *Multiple Criteria Decision Making.* Columbia, S. C.: University of South Carolina Press, 1973.

COFER, C. N., "Verbal behavior in relation to reasoning and values," in *Groups, Leadership, and Men,* ed. H. Guetzkow. Pittsburgh: Carnegie Press, 1951.

COHEN, G., "Hemispheric Differences in Serial vs. Parallel Processing," *Journal of Experimental Psychology,* 97, 1973, pp. 349–356.

COVINGTON, M. V., R. S. CRUTCHFIELD, L. DAVIES, and R. M. OLTON, JR., *The Productive Thinking Program.* Columbus, Ohio: Chas. E. Merril, 1974.

CRANDALL, V. J., D. SOLOMON, and R. KELLAWAY, "Expectancy Statements and Decision Times as Functions of Objective Probabilities and Reinforcement Values," *Journal of Personality,* 24 1955, 192–203.

CRAWFORD, R. P., *Think for Yourself* Burlington, Vt.: Fraser, 1937.

CRAWFORD, R. P., *Techniques of Creative Thinking.* New York: Hawthorn, 1954.

CRAWFORD, R. P. *Direct Creativity with Attribute Listing.* Burlington, Vt.: Fraser, 1964.

DARWIN, C., *The Origin of the Species.* New York: P. F. Collier & Son, 1909.

DAWES, R. M., and B. CORRIGAN, "Linear Models in Decision Making," *Psychological Bulletin,* 81 (1974), 95–106.

DEGROOT, A. D., *Thought and Choice in Chess.* The Hague: Morton, 1965.

DEBONO, E. Lateral Thinking: Creativity Step by Step. New York: Harper and Row, 1973.

DUNCKER, K., "On problem-solving," *Psychological Monographs,* 58, whole no. 270 (1945).

EBBINGHAUS, H., *Memory: A Contribution to Experimental Psychology,* transl. by H. A. Ruger and C. E. Bussenius. New York: Teachers College, Columbia University, 1913.

EDWARDS, W., H. LINDMAN, and L. D. PHILLIPS, "Emerging Technologies for Making Decisions," in *New Directions in Psychology, II.* New York: Holt, Rinehart & Winston, 1965.

FEIGENBAUM, E. A., *An Information Processing Theory of Verbal Learning.* RAND Corp. Paper, P-1817, October 1959.

FISCHER, G. W., and W. EDWARDS, *Technological Aids for Inference, Evaluation, and Decision-Making: A Review of Research and Experience.* Technological report, Engineering Psychology Laboratory. Ann Arbor, Mich.: University of Michigan, 1973.

FIXX, J., *Games for the Super-Intelligent.* New York: Doubleday, 1972.

FIXX, J., *More Games for the Super-Intelligent.* New York: Doubleday, 1976.

FRANKLIN, B., "Letter to Jospeh Priestley," in *The Benjamin Franklin Sampler.* New York: Fawcett [Books Group-CBS Publications,] 1956.

FROMM, E., *Escape from Freedom.* New York: Holt, Rinehart & Winston, 1941.

FROMM, E., *The Sane Society.* Greenwich, Conn.: Fawcett, 1955.

GARDINER, P. C., and W. EDWARDS, "Public Values: Multiattribute-Utility Measurement for Social Decision Making," in *Human Judgment and Decision Processes,* eds. M. F. Kaplan and S. Schwartz, pp. 1–38. New York: Academic Press, 1975.

GARDNER, M., *Perplexing Puzzles and Tantalizing Teasers.* New York: Simon & Schuster, 1969.

GETZELS, J. W., and M. CSIKSZENTMIHALYI, *The Creative Vision: A Longitudinal Study of Problem Finding in Art.* New York: John Wiley, 1976.

GHISELIN, B., *The Creative Process.* Berkeley, Calif.: University of California Press, 1952.

GLUCKSBURG, S., and J. H. DANKS, "Effects of Discriminative Labels and of Nonsense Syllables upon Availability of Novel Function," *Journal of Verbal Learning & Verbal Behavior, 7,* 1968, 72–77.

GORDON, W. J. J., *Synectics: The Development of Creative Capacity.* New York: Harper & Row, 1961.

GORDON, W. J. J., *The Metaphorical Way.* Cambridge, Mass.: Porpoise Books, 1971.

GRUMMEL, W. C. *English Word Building from Latin and Greek.* Santa Clara, Calif.: Pacific Books, 1961.

GUILFORD, J. P., and R. HOEPFNER, *The Analysis of Intelligence.* New York: McGraw-Hill, 1971.

HADAMARD. J., *The Psychology of Invention in the Mathematical Field.* Princeton: Princeton University Press, 1945.

HALACY, D. S., JR., *Bionics: The Science of "Living" Machines.* New York: Holiday House, 1965.

HIGBEE, K. L., *Your Memory: How It Works and How to Improve It.* Englewood Cliffs, N. J.: Prentice-Hall, 1977.

HILGARD, E. R., and G. H. BOWER, *Theories of Learning* (4th ed.). Englewood Cliffs, N. J.: Prentice-Hall, 1975.

HOFFMAN, P. J. "The Paramorphic Representation of Clinical Judgment," *Psychological Bulletin, 57,* (1960), 116–131.

HOFFMAN, P. J., P. SLOVIC, and L. G. RORER, "An Analysis-of-Variance Model for the Assessment of Configural Cue Utilization in Clinical Judgment," *Psychological Bulletin,* 69 (1968), 338–349.

HOWARD, R. A. "Decision Analysis in Systems Engineering," in *Systems Concepts: Contemporary Approaches to Systems*, ed. R. F. Miles. New York: Wiley, 1973, 51–85.

HULSE, S. H., J. DEESE, and H. EGETH, *The Psychology of Learning* (4th ed.). New York: McGraw-Hill, 1975.

HYMAN, R., "Creativity and the Prepared Mind: The Role of Information and Induced Attitudes," in *Widening Horizons in Creativity,* ed. C. W. Taylor. New York: John Wiley, 1964.

IRWIN, F. W., "Stated Expectations as Functions of Probability and Desirability of Outcomes," *Journal of Personality,* 21 (1953), 329–335.

JANIS, I. L., *Victims of Groupthink.* Boston: Houghton Mifflin, 1972.

JANIS, I. L., and L. MANN, *Decision Making.* New York: Free Press, 1977.

JOHNSON, N. F. "Thinking and Organization in the Process of Recall," in *The Psychology of Learning and Motivation,* ed. G. H. Bauer, Vol. 4. New York: Academic Press, 1970.

KAHNEMAN, D. and A. TVERSKY. "On the Psychology of Prediction," *Psychological Review,* 80, 1973, pp. 237–351.

KARWOSKI, T. F., F. W. GRAMLICH, and P. ARNOTT, "An Experiment to Determine the Responses to Stimuli Representing Three Levels of Abstraction," *Journal of Social Psychology,* 20 (1944),233–247.

KATONA, G., *Organizing and Memorizing.* New York: Columbia University Press, 1940.

KEENEY, R. L., and H. RAIFFA. *Decisions with Multiple Objectives: Preferences and Value Tradeoffs.* New York: John Wiley, 1976.

KEPNER, C. H., and B. B. TREGOE. *The Rational Manager: A Systematic Approach to a Problem Solving and Decision Making.* New York: McGraw-Hill, 1965.

KINTSCH, W., "Models for Free Recall and Recognition," in *Models of Human Memory,* ed. D. A. Norman. New York: Academic Press, 1970.

KLEINSMITH, L. J. "Interaction of Arousal and Recall Interval in Nonsense Syllable Paired-Associate Learning," *Journal of Experimental Psychology,* 67, 1964, 124–126.

KLEINSMITH, L. J., and S. KAPLAN. "Paired-Associate Learning as a Function of Arousal and Interpolated Activity," *Journal of Experimental Psychology,* 65, 1963, 190–193.

KÖHLER, W., and H. VON RESTORFF. "Analyse von Vorgängen in Spurenfeld, II. Zur Theorie der Reproduktion," *Psychologie Forschung,* 21, 1935, 56–112.

LEE, W., *Decision Theory and Human Behavior.* New York: John Wiley, 1971.

LIBBY, R., and B. L. LEWIS, "Human Information Processing in Accounting: The State of the Art," *Accounting, Organizations, and Society,* 1 (1977), 60.1–60.24.

LOISETTE, A., *Assimilative Memory or How to Attend and Never Forget.* New York: Funk & Wagnalls, 1896.

LORAYNE, H., *How to Develop a Super-power Memory.* New York: Frederick Fell, 1957.

MACCRIMMON, K. R., "An Overview of Multiple Objective Decision Making," in *Multiple Criteria Decision Making,* eds. J. L. Cochrane & M. Zeleny. Columbia, S. C.: University of South Carolina Press, 1973.

MACKENZIE, R. A. *The Time Trap.* New York: AMACOM, 1972.

MACKINNON, D. W., "The Nature and Nurture of Creative Talent," *American Psychologist,* (17), 1962, 484–495.

MAHONEY, M. J., and C. E. THORESON, *Self-Control: Power to the Person.* Monterey, Calif.: Brooks/Cole, 1974.

MANDLER, G., "Organization and Memory," in *The Psychology of Learning and Motivation,* eds. K. W. Spence and J. R. Spence, vol. 1. New York: Academic Press, 1967.

MANDLER, G., "Memory Storage and Retrieval: Some Limits on the Reach of Attention and Consciousness." In *Attention and Performance, V,* eds. P. M. A. Rabbitt and S. Dornic. London: Academic Press, 1975.

MANSKE, M. E., and G. A. DAVIS, "Effects of Simple Instructional Biases upon Performance in the Unusual Uses Test." *Journal of General Psychology,* 78 (1968), 25–33.

MATLIN, M. and D. STANG. *The Polyanna Principle: Selectivity in Language, Memory, and Thought.* Cambridge, Mass.: Schenkman, 1978.

MAYER, R. E., and J. G. GREENO, "Structural Differences between Learning Outcomes Produced by Different Instructional Methods," *Journal of Educational Psychology,* 63 (1972), 165–173.

MCGAUGH, J. L., and M. J. HERZ, *Memory Consolidation.* San Francisco: Albion Publishing Co., 1972.

MCGUIRE, W. J., "A Syllogistic Analysis of Cognitive Relationships," in *Attitude Organization and Change,* eds., M. J. Rosenberg and C. U. Hovland. pp. 65–111. New Haven, Conn.: Yale University Press, 1960.

MCKEAN, R. N., *Efficiency in Government through Systems Analysis.* New York: John Wiley, 1958.

McKim, R. H., *Experiences in Visual Thinking*. Monterey, Calif.: Brooks/Cole, 1972.

Meehl, P. E., *Clinical versus Statistical Prediction*. Minneapolis: University of Minnesota Press, 1954.

Miller, D. W., and M. K. Starr, *Executive Decisions and Operations Research*. Englewood Cliffs, N. J.: Prentice-Hall, 1969.

Miller, G. A. "The Magical Number Seven, Plus or Minus Two: Some Limits on our Capacity for Processing Information," *Psychological Review*, 63, 1956, 81–97.

Miller, G. A., E. Galanter, and K. H. Pribram. Plans and the Structure of Behavior. New York: Holt, Rinehart, & Winston, 1960.

Milner, B. "Interhemispheric Differences and Psychological Processes," *British Medical Bulletin*, 27, 1971, 272–277.

Myers, S. *Role-Playing in Solving Object and Person Problems*. Unpublished research. Portland, Oregon: Portland State University, 1977.

Nadler, G., *Work Design*. Homewood, Ill.: Richard D. Irwin, 1963.

Neisser, U., and N. Kerr, "Spatial and Mnemonic Properties of Visual Images," *Cognitive Psychology*, 5 (1973), 138–150.

Newell, A., J. C. Shaw, and H. A. Simon, "The Process of Creative Thinking," in *Contemporary Approaches to Creative Thinking*, eds. H. E. Gruber, G. Terrell, and M. Wertheimer. New York: Atherton, 1962.

Newell, A., and H. A. Simon, *Human Problem Solving*. Englewood Cliffs, N. J.: Prentice-Hall, 1972.

Norman, D. A. *Memory and Attention: An Introduction to Human Information Processing* (2d ed.). New York: John Wiley, 1976.

Osborn, A. F., *Applied Imagination: Principles and Procedures of Creative Problem Solving* (3rd rev. ed.). New York: Scribner's, 1963.

Paivio, A. *Imagery and Verbal Processes*. New York: Holt, Rinehart, & Winston, 1971.

Parnes, S. J., *Creative Behavior Guidebook*. New York: Scribner's 1967.

Parnes, S. J. "The Deferment-of-Judgment Principle: A Clarification of the Literature," *Psychological Reports*, 12, 1963, 521–522.

Patrick, C. "Creative Thought in Poets," *Archives of Psychology*, 178, April 1935.

PETERSON, C. R., and L. R. BEACH, "Man as an Intuitive Statistician," *Psychological Bulletin,* 68, (1967), 29–46.

PIAGET, J., *The Origins of Intelligence in Children.* New York: International Universities Press, 1952.

POINCARE, H., "Mathematical Creation," in *The Foundations of Science,* trans. G. B. Halstead, New York: Science Press, 1913.

POLLACK, I., "Action Selection and the Yntema-Torgerson "Worth" Function." Paper read at the April 1962, meeting of the Eastern Psychological Association.

POLYA, G., *How to Solve It.* Garden City, N.Y.; Doubleday Anchor, 1957.

POSNER, M. I., *Cognition: An Introduction.* Glenview, Ill.: Scott, Foresman, 1973.

PRINCE, G., "The Operational Mechanisms of Synectics," *Journal of Creative Behavior,* 2 (1968) 1–13.

PRINCE, G. M., "Synectics: A Method of Creative Thought," *Journal of Engineering Education,* 58, (1968), 805–806.

PRINCE, G. M., *The Practice of Creativity.* New York: Harper, 1970.

RAIFFA, H., Chicago: Encyclopaedia Britannica Educational Corp., 1974.

REVLIN, R., and R. E. MAYER, eds., *Human Reasoning.* New York: Halsted Press, 1978.

RICO, G. L., "Metaphor, Cognition, and Clustering," in *The Eighth Western Symposium on Learning: Creative Thinking,* eds. S. L. Carmean and B. L. Grover, pp. 75–91. Bellingham, Wash., 1977.

RIPLEY, A., *Minute Mysteries.* New York: Pocket Books, 1949.

ROE, A. "A Psychological Study of Eminent Psychologists and Anthropologists, and a Comparison with Biological and Physical Scientists," *Psychological Monographs,* 67, no. 2 whole no. 352, (1953).

RUGER, H. A., "The Psychology of Efficiency: An Experimental Study of the Process Involved in the Solution of Mechanical Puzzles and in the Acquisition of Skill in Their Manipulation," *Archives of Psychology,* 2, no. 15, (1910).

SCHEIN, E. H., *Process Consultation: Its Role in Organization Development.* Reading, Mass.: Addison-Wesley, 1969.

SCRIVEN, M. *Reasoning*. New York: McGraw-Hill, 1976.

SHELLY, M. W., II, and G. L. BRYAN, eds., *Human Judgments and Optimality*. New York: John Wiley, 1964.

SHEPARD, R. N. "On Subjectively Optimum Selection among Multiattribute Alternatives," in *Human Judgments and Optimality*, eds. M. W. Shelly II and G. L. Bryan. pp. 257–281. New York: John Wiley, 1964.

SILVIERA, J. "Incubation: The Effect of Interruption Timing and Length on Problem Solution and Quality of Problem Processing." (unpublished doctoral dissertation, University of Oregon, 1971).

SLOVIC, P., "Cue-Consistency and Cue-Utilization in Judgment," *American Journal of Psychology*, 79 (1966), 427–434.

SLOVIC, P., B. FISCHHOFF, and S. LICHTENSTEIN. "Behavioral Decision Theory. *Annual Review of Psychology*, 28 (1977), 1–40.

SLOVIC, P., and S. LICHTENSTEIN. "Relative Importance of Probabilities and Payoffs in Risktaking," *Journal of Experimental Psychology, Monograph Supplement*, 78 (3, pt. 2), 1968, 1–18.

SPERRY, R. W., "The Great Cerebral Commissure," *Scientific American*, (January 1964).

SPERRY, R. W., and M. S. GAZZANIGA, "Language Following Surgical Disconnection of the Hemispheres," in F. L. Darley (Ed.), *Brain Mechanisms Underlying Speech and Language*. New York: Grune & Stratton, 1967.

SPETZLER, C. S., and C.-A. S. STAEL VON HOLSTEIN, "Probability Encoding in Decision Analysis," *Management Science*, 22 (1975), 340–358.

STEIN, M. I., *Stimulating Creativity: Individual Procedures*, vol. I: New York: Academic Press, 1974.

STEIN, M. I. *Stimulating Creativity: Group Procedures*, vol. II. New York: Academic Press, 1975.

STEVENS, S. S., "Mathematics, Measurement, and Psychophysics," in S. S. Stevens (Ed.), *Handbook of Experimental Psychology*. New York: John Wiley, 1951. pp. 1–49.

STRICKLAND, C. H., R. J. LEWICKS, and A. M. KATZ. "Temporal Orientation and Perceived Control as Determinants of Risk-Taking," *Journal of Experimental Social Psychology*, 2, 1966, 143–151.

SURRICK, J. E., and L. M. CONANT, *Laddergrams*. New York: J. H. Sears & Co., 1927.

TULVING, E. "Cue-Dependent Forgetting," *American Scientist*, 62, 1974, 74–82.

TVERSKY, A., "Elimination by Aspects: A Theory of Choice," *Psychological Review*, 79 (1972), 281–299.

TVERSKY, A., and D. KAHNEMAN, "The Belief in the Law of Small Numbers," *Psychological Bulletin*, 76 (1971), 105–110.

TVERSKY, A., and D. KAHNEMAN, "Availability: A Heuristic for Judging Frequency and Probability," *Cognitive Psychology*, 5 (1973), 207–232.

WALLACE, W. H., S. H. TURNER, and C. C. PERKINS, *Preliminary Studies of Human Information Storage*. Signal Corps Project No. 132C, Institute for Cooperative Research, University of Pennsylvania, December, 1957.

WALLAS, G., *The Art of Thought*. New York: Harcourt Brace Jovanovich, 1926.

WARD, W. C., and H. M. JENKINS, "The Display of Information and the Judgment of Contingency," *Canadian Journal of Psychology*, 19 (1965), 231–241.

WASON, P. C., and P. N. JOHNSON-LAIRD, *The Psychology of Reasoning*. Cambridge, Mass.: Harvard University Press, 1972.

WATSON, G., and E. M. GLASER, *Watson-Glaser Critical Thinking Appraisal Manual*. New York: Harcourt Brace & World, 1952.

WHIMBEY, A., with L. S. WHIMBEY, *Intelligence Can Be Taught*. New York: Dutton, 1975.

WHITING, C. S. *Creative Thinking*. New York: Reinhold, 1958.

WICKLEGREN, W. A., *How to Solve Problems*. San Francisco: W. H. Freeman & Company, 1974.

WILLIAMS, R. L., and J. D. LONG, *Toward a Self-Managed Life Style*. New York: Houghton Mifflin, 1975.

WYER, R. S., *Cognitive Organization and Change: An Information Processing Approach*. Potomac, Md: Lawrence Erlbaum Assocs., 1974.

YATES, F. A., *The Art of Memory*. London: Routledge & Kegan Paul, 1966.

YNTEMA, D. B., and W. S. TORGERSON, *Man-Computer Cooperation in Decisions Requiring Common Sense*. IRE Trans. Human Factors Electron., HFE-2, 20–26, 1961.

ZWICKY, F., *Morphological Astronomy*. Berlin: Springer-Verlag, 1957.

ZWICKY, F., *Discovery, Invention, Research*. New York: Macmillan, 1969.

Index